THEORY DEVELOPMENT IN THE INFORMATION SCIENCES

INFORMATION, A SERIES EDITED BY ANDREW DILLON

THEORY DEVELOPMENT IN
THE INFORMATION SCIENCES

EDITED BY DIANE H. SONNENWALD

UNIVERSITY OF TEXAS PRESS ⬥ *Austin*

Requests for permission to reproduce material from this work should be
sent to:
    Permissions
    University of Texas Press
    P.O. Box 7819
    Austin, TX 78713-7819
    http://utpress.utexas.edu/index.php/rp-form

⊗ The paper used in this book meets the minimum requirements of
ANSI/NISO Z39.48-1992 (R1997) (Permanence of Paper).

LIBRARY OF CONGRESS CATALOGING-IN-PUBLICATION DATA

Theory development in the information sciences / edited by Diane H.
Sonnenwald. — First edition.
       pages   cm — (Information)
    Includes bibliographical references and index.
    ISBN 978-1-4773-0824-0 (cloth : alk. paper) — ISBN 978-1-4773-0906-3
(pbk. : alk. paper) — ISBN 978-1-4773-0825-7 (library e-book) — ISBN 978-1-
4773-0826-4 (nonlibrary e-book)
    1. Information science.   2. Information theory.   I. Sonnenwald, Diane H.,
editor.
    Z665.T49636   2016
    020—dc23   2015024275

doi:10.7560/308240

CONTENTS

ACKNOWLEDGMENTS

THIS BOOK WOULD NOT HAVE BEEN POSSIBLE without the generosity of the authors who contributed chapters. I very much appreciate their willingness to share their experiences and insights. I would also like to thank Andrew Dillon, Fred C. Sonnenwald, Harry Bruce, and Tom Finholt for their helpful comments. It has been a pleasure to work with staff at the University of Texas Press; thank you. I continue to be grateful for the constant support of my husband, Fred Sonnenwald, in endeavors such as this one.

THEORY DEVELOPMENT IN THE INFORMATION SCIENCES

CHAPTER 1

EXPLORING THEORY DEVELOPMENT: LEARNING FROM DIVERSE MASTERS

DIANE H. SONNENWALD

AS KURT LEWIN (1951) ASSERTS, there is nothing more practical than good theory. Yet theory can be seen as threatening and coercive (Simon 1992), especially when presented as the only truth instead of one truth among many (Feyerabend 1993).

The goal of this book is to illuminate the theory development process in order to encourage, inspire, and assist individuals striving to understand theory, develop theory, or teach theory and theory development. Experienced researchers were asked to reflect on their experiences developing theory and to share their reflections, revealing the challenges, successes, failures, excitement, and satisfaction they experienced during the process. The result is fifteen chapters that discuss theory development from a variety of perspectives.

To facilitate exploration of the chapters, a brief introduction to the information sciences is provided. This is followed by discussions regarding types of theory and the theory development process, including stages of the process and resources that inspire and assist during the process and that, in turn, are impacted by new theory. Lastly, the format of the book is described.

THE INFORMATION SCIENCES

Emerging in the first half of the twentieth century as a discipline, the information sciences contribute to our understanding of how people, groups, organizations, and governments create, share, disseminate, manage, search, access, evaluate, use, and protect information, as well as how technologies can facilitate or constrain these activities. Broadly speaking, the information sciences focus on the interplay of people, information, technology, and social structures. The impacts of the information sciences have been numerous and diverse. US president Ronald Reagan, addressing the Association for Information Science and Technology (ASIS&T), put these impacts into perspective:

> By advancing the gathering, storage, and transfer of information, you've touched the lives of virtually every citizen and led the way to wider opportunity for all of us. That's because our scholarship, domestic prosperity, and competitive stance in the world marketplace depend as never before on our considerable information technologies and on how we use them. Your vital role in our increasingly efficient and wide diffusion of knowledge has been a tribute to you and a real blessing for our Nation. (Reagan 1978, p. 6)

Although the information sciences have had a far-ranging impact and are broad in scope, they are better known for borrowing theory from other disciplines than for introducing new theories. This may be a result of the applied focus in many of the information sciences, and the relatively young age of the field. However, there are notable exceptions, as the chapters in this book demonstrate.

TYPES OF THEORY

Throughout time and across disciplines, different perspectives regarding what constitutes theory have emerged. D'Andrade (1986) proposed that there are three major paradigms, or scientific worldviews, each of which incorporates different ways of seeing and knowing, and produces different types of theory: the physical sciences, the natural sciences, and the semiotic sciences. Theory in the physical sciences (e.g., physics, chemistry, astronomy, and engineering) is general, covering laws that explain and predict phenomena across time. Theory in the natural sciences (e.g., biology, geology, oceanography, economics, and some areas in anthropology and sociology) focuses on explanations and descriptions of complex mechanisms. Theory in the semiotic sciences (e.g., linguistics and some areas of psychology, anthropology, sociology, and communication) focuses on the discovery of imposed order based on meaning rather than natural or physical order.

This categorization helps explain why there are different perspectives on theory across disciplines. However, the information sciences span multiple scientific worldviews, and have historical theoretical foundations in each of these. Spanning and incorporating aspects from multiple worldviews is often valuable in addressing complex problems. However, questions regarding what constitutes theory and its purposes remain.

Gregor (2006) proposes five interrelated categories of theories, types 1 through 5, based on her analysis of research in information systems. Type 1 is theory for analyzing. These theories are descriptive and include taxonomies and classification schema that are complete or extendable. They aid in analysis, especially when little is known about a phenomenon. Type 2 is theory for explaining. These theories propose how, when, where, and why a phenomenon occurs. They should be plausible, credible, and consistent in explaining something new or not well understood. Type 3 is theory for predicting, that is, theory that describes what will be, but not why it will be that way. The predictions are typically based on a set of factors and are very useful when prediction has practical importance. They do not explain causal relationships. Type 4 is theory for explaining and predicting. Theories in this category describe a phenomenon, including how, why, when, and where it occurs, and what the outcomes should be when it occurs. These theories are typically referred to as *grand*, *strong*, or *meta-level* theories. Type 5 is theory for design and action. These theories describe how to do something, providing a road map of actions. They propose methodologies and processes.

Gregor's categories can be found across the information sciences and throughout this book, reflecting the broad and diverse nature of the field. Examples of type 1 theory development for information searching and browsing can be found in the chapters by Bates and Chang. Bawden, Buckland, and Crew discuss their approach to developing type 2 theories for understanding information, bibliometrics and information retrieval, and literary criticism, respectively. Development of type 3 theory, focusing on research publication systems, is discussed in the chapter by Meadows. Kuhlthau discusses how she developed a type 4 theory—her theory of the information search process. Olson and Olson, Dillon, Carroll, and Nardi discuss their efforts developing and using type 5 theories, focusing on remote scientific collaboration, reading, technology design, and activity theory. Thelwall demonstrates that all five types are found in webometrics.

However, Gregor's categorization may only be a starting point for the information sciences. For example, Järvelin suggests that theory regarding interactive information retrieval should be a combination of types 4 and 5, providing explanation, prediction, and technology development. Saracevic and McGann, by contrast, suggest that after years of effort, the quest for a theory of relevance and a theory of text and textualities still continues.

Thus, across the information sciences, we see multiple types of theories emerging, with some topic areas lacking theory. How do such theories emerge or fail to emerge?

THE THEORY DEVELOPMENT PROCESS

Two historic views regarding the theory development process are provided by Polanyi (1974) and Kuhn (1970). For Polanyi, theory development is achieved through objective and subjective means guided by an individual's scientific passion and vision of reality. Kuhn asserted that theories are grounded in shared paradigms and that the development of new theory begins with the awareness of an anomaly that violates the current paradigm. New theory only becomes accepted with difficulty; it must resolve a long-standing recognized problem and preserve a relatively large part of existing knowledge.

To complement these historic views and to provide a contemporary perspective, the authors in this book describe their personal experiences developing and using theory. Each chapter discusses various components of the theory development process. When considered collectively, these components can be conceptualized, or categorized, as stages that are influenced by, and help influence, various resources.

THEORY DEVELOPMENT STAGES

Stages in the theory development process are periods of time that involve specific types of activities. Activities described throughout the chapters can be categorized into three stages: elaborating a focus, conducting research, and making an impact (fig. 1.1). In the elaboration of a focus and the conducting of research, resources provide inspiration and assistance. As impacts are made, resources are transformed. The stages and resources provide a framework to synthesize and elucidate the collective wisdom interspersed throughout this book.

ELABORATING A FOCUS Elaborating a focus for theory development is a crucial step. A focus guides subsequent research and helps define the possible impact your theory can have. It allows you to more eas-

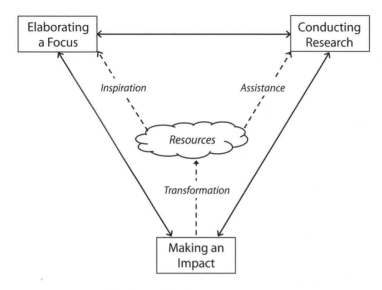

FIGURE 1.1. Stages of the theory development process

ily relate your work to other work, demonstrate how your work contributes new knowledge, and persuasively convince others regarding the importance of your work.

A focus can be expressed and explained in different ways. Hypotheses, questions, frameworks, models, analogies, and abstract, or high-level, scenarios are tools that can be used to present and explain the focus of your theory development efforts. Justifications for a focus can be expressed using statistical data, quotes from affected individuals, results from prior research, and government policies. Your intuition that a focus is important can be a good starting point, but further evidence is needed not only to procure resources, including the cooperation of study participants, but also to have results published in top-ranked forums. Identifying relevant and persuasive evidence can be challenging but, when done well, can subsequently make the focus appear obvious.

A focus can be iteratively refined and modified throughout the theory development process. Sometimes it is only near the end of the process when we can best express our focus so that it appears definitive, obvious, and important. A focus can also be iteratively extended throughout one's research career (e.g., see the chapters by Kuhlthau, McGann, Meadows, Saracevic, and Olson and Olson).

CONDUCTING RESEARCH   Conducting research typically involves designing a research plan, implementing that plan, and modifying the plan and its implementation when necessary. There are many books, articles, courses, and workshops discussing research designs and methods, and their suitability to different types of research foci. However, research designs and methods are often presented in a formulaic manner with little or no discussion of the next step, that is, theory development, in which interpretation, generalization, and implications of results are elucidated. In the present volume, the authors discuss this next step, moving beyond a discussion of research methods to illuminate the theory development process by providing personal insights.

Designing a research plan can be very challenging, especially when the focus is on phenomena not yet well defined in the literature (Chang, Kuhlthau). Placing meaningful boundary conditions on the phenomenon (Dillon) and developing a model mapping the domain (Järvelin) can help reduce complexity when one is designing a research plan. Other strategies include re-using data in unique ways (Buckland) and employing a cyclical approach, for example, alternating between reading literature, collecting and reading data, and analyzing data (Crew).

In the implementation of a research plan, tasks initially assumed to be straightforward can turn out to be more difficult than first imagined, and plans often require modification (Chang, McGann). For example, coding interview data based on topical content is often just a first step; further analysis is required to identify constructs, influences on constructs, and the meaning or importance of those constructs and influences (Chang). Using additional theoretical constructs, data visualization methods, and comparisons across contexts and time can be helpful when one is analyzing data in order to gain new insights (Crew, Buckland, Meadows).

We learn how to conduct research by conducting research, and, as McGann reminds us, learning by doing is learning by failure. Creating theory involves a careful, repetitive cycle of reading data, uncovering its meaning, and refining the representation of its meaning (Crew, Dillon).

In addition to these intellectual challenges, there can be political, social, and administrative challenges in the conducting of research (McGann). Researchers working in academia and other types of institutions have multiple demands on their time. Perspectives regarding required resources (including time) and expected outcomes can differ across segments of an institution. Researchers must navigate among these differences.

MAKING AN IMPACT   In this stage researchers focus on making an impact. Throughout the book, the authors discuss various types of impact their theoretical work has made. Just as important, authors discuss work they thought would have a significant impact, but did not. Traditionally the impact of theory is measured by citations to the publication(s) presenting the theory. Disagreements with our theory may emerge explicitly in publications presenting opposing views (Chang, Crew) or implicitly when the number of citations to our theory disappoints (Thelwall).

Other typical measures of publication impact include the reputation (according to national and international rankings) of the journals and conferences where the theory is published, and the reputation of the book publisher when a theory is published in a book. Praise and criticisms found in letters to the editor and book reviews are also common measures of impact.

For multiple reasons, scholars debate the validity of these impact measures. There is a limited amount of citation data collected for some disciplines, and also for publications in languages other than English (Chang). Furthermore, these measures do not capture impact outside academia.

New types of impact and ways to measure them continue to emerge. Examples of alternative types of impact and measures, often referred to as altmetrics, include the amount of income and number of new jobs generated from licensing software, patents, and other intellectual property; inclusion of a theory in government policy; the number of times a paper or software tool has been accessed or downloaded; visits and links to a researcher's web pages or online profile; programs and articles about a theory published in social and traditional media (and audience-reach measurements); and prestigious awards given in recognition of theoretical work by scholarly societies, universities, and governments.

TRAVERSING THE STAGES   A simplistic, linear perspective on the theory development process involves traversing the three stages one after the other, beginning with elaborating a focus. The conducting-research stage would only begin after a focus has been fully developed. Similarly, the results would be used to make an impact after the research has been fully concluded.

However, there is churn and reflection within each stage and fluid movement between stages. A simplistic, linear traversal of stages seldom actually occurs. Instead, the stages are more typically traversed in a nonlinear fashion, as evidenced by the descriptions of theory development in this book. For example, a focus can be reconsidered and refined while one is conducting research; in fact, Thelwall recommends this approach. Impacts can occur before research is completed, and subsequently influence the research process. For example, study participants frequently comment that they learn from the reflection they are asked to do during research interviews, and responses to presentations describing preliminary research results can inspire new interview questions and other changes to the research process.

When you are first learning about and attempting theory development, it can be useful to consider the stages sequentially; however, you should not become discouraged when you discover you cannot traverse them sequentially. The theory development process is a dynamic process that includes the iterative refinement of ideas and plans, as well as multiple executions of tasks.

RESOURCES

Throughout the book authors describe various resources that provide inspiration when they are elaborating a focus or assistance when they are conducting research. Resources can also be transformed by theory. This reciprocal relationship intuitively makes sense; if a resource can inspire and assist our efforts, it is perhaps natural that the resource is, in turn, interested in our results. Resources mentioned by chapter authors are literature, personal experiences, their own research, colleagues, technology, institutions, and societal issues (fig. 1.2). Not every author mentions all of these; rather, the authors discuss resources relevant to their focus. Resources and their potential role in each theory development stage are discussed below.

LITERATURE   That literature often plays a role in all stages of theory development is not surprising. When you are elaborating a focus, it is important to read literature deeply in order to develop a clear understanding of its strengths and weaknesses (Bates, Saracevic). A beginning focus or framework can emerge by contrasting and synthe-

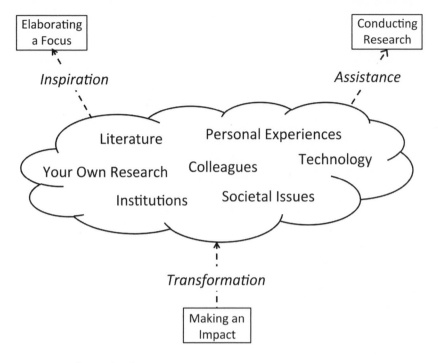

FIGURE 1.2. Theory development resources

sizing literature (Bawden, Chang). Questions and suggestions raised in the literature can inspire new research directions (Meadows), and successful examples of theoretical papers can encourage related work (Thelwall). In addition to current literature, older, historical literature can provide inspiration and insights (Olson and Olson).

Many of the authors (Bates, Chang, Crew, Dillon, Kuhlthau, Nardi, Olson and Olson) comment that literature originating in other disciplines can inspire and inform your focus. However, using this literature brings challenges. Different disciplines often use different terminology for similar concepts, while using similar terms with different meanings. Thus, finding relevant literature emerging from other disciplines and understanding its relationship to your focus may require additional work. One strategy to help identify relevant literature is to employ creative analogies that relate your focus to topics discussed in other disciplines (Chang, Meadows).

Dissatisfaction and disagreement with existing literature can also inspire theory development (Dillon). Dissatisfaction may emerge because the literature has omissions or gaps, or because it diverges from personal experiences or observations.

Literature can also help guide us when we are conducting research. It can inform our research design and methods, as well as help us interpret our results. However, it can be challenging to compare results reported in the literature in order to build cumulative knowledge when those results are based on different theories and methods (Bawden). For example, theories based on qualitative research cannot always be easily reconciled with theories based on quantitative research (Meadows). Furthermore, relying too much on literature to provide answers can stifle our creativity and problem-solving abilities. As Boulding (1961) points out, students often operate on the principle of learning the least amount necessary, and this approach should be more frequently recognized as acceptable in order to promote creativity and problem solving.

As discussed previously, a traditional way to make an impact is to present your theory at conferences or to publish in journals and books. The impact possible through these formats continues to be debated; Chang found that publishing in a highly ranked peer-reviewed journal had the greatest impact for her work, even though her book was published by a prestigious publisher. Although English is the dominant scholarly language used today, translating your theory into other languages can help have an impact on specific audiences (Chang). Using social media such as blogs, videos, and Twitter to present and discuss your work can also help you reach audiences (Chang).

PERSONAL EXPERIENCES   A second resource frequently reported in these chapters is personal experience (Bates, Bawden, Chang, Crew, Dillon, Kuhlthau, Saracevic, Thelwall). That is, experiences and observations that either were not discussed in the literature or did not match discussions in the literature inspired authors.

Observations and work experiences gained in organizations, especially non-academic organizations, can provide insights into problems and phenomena that inspire theory development (Bawden, Kuhlthau, Saracevic). Doctoral degree programs that typically do not require applicants to have recently completed undergraduate and master's degrees can be more welcoming to individuals who have work experience which may inspire theory development. With demands for academics to become more engaged with organizations and societal problems outside academia, these prior experiences are increasingly relevant.

Personal challenges can also inspire theory development. Bates notes that her struggles to complete search tasks assigned as homework led to her highly regarded work in information search tactics. Similarly, Thelwall discusses how challenges in getting his work published led to his new theory, information-centered research (ICR). Personal challenges experienced by others may also inspire theory development.

When you are conducting research, personal experiences can help shape how you collect data and interpret data (Bates, Crew, McGann). Embracing this and understanding the advantages and biases personal experiences contribute can strengthen your work.

Developing theory also has an impact on the developer. It creates new personal experiences that are, ideally, learning opportunities that can help us enhance our existing skills and develop new ones. For example, Nardi reports that creating and mastering a theory makes it easier for us to subsequently create and master additional theories. Invitations to present your theory, join projects, and evaluate other research can also emerge as a result of your theory. These types of activities provide new opportunities to network with others.

YOUR OWN RESEARCH   Your own research can be considered a subset of personal experiences, but it merits a separate discussion due to its unique roles in theory development. Both positive and negative results from your ongoing and previous research can inspire a refinement of or an extension to your focus (Chang, Crew). For example, early results from data analysis may help clarify your focus.

Results from your previous research may also be utilized when you are conducting research. For example, Olson and Olson used a database of cases and detailed case studies that they had created with colleagues when developing their theory of remote scientific collaboration. Järvelin uses results from interviews and observations to propose new concepts and relationships in interactive information retrieval. He then investigates the concepts and their relationships through experimentation to develop theory.

As discussed previously, there is often an iterative nature to research, with research and theory development leading to additional research and theory development. That is, your theory may impact your subsequent research by serving as a foundation for additional research (Järvelin, Kuhlthau, McGann, Olson and Olson, Saracevic). For example, Kuhlthau has transported her theory, the information search process (ISP), to primary and secondary school education. Chang invites graduate students to work with her to test and extend her theory of browsing in different domains, and suggests that continuing to work with your theory and linking it in real-world applications is one of the most effective ways to make an overall impact.

COLLEAGUES   Engagement with colleagues, including professors when you are a student and students when you are a professor, can provide inspiration when you are elaborating a focus (Chang, Kuhlthau, McGann, Nardi, Olson and Olson). Discussing evolving ideas can help clarify them, especially when colleagues listen well and ask constructive questions (Nardi). Engagement with colleagues can occur in a variety of forums, including opportunistic and planned discussions at work, workshops, and conferences.

Colleagues can also provide valuable feedback on our research as we conduct it. For example, feedback can identify what is missing or inconsistent (Crew). Usually feedback from colleagues is given in a constructive manner; however, this is not always the case. It can be challenging, but important, to recognize valuable insights embedded in feedback not presented constructively.

Your theory may also impact colleagues. Colleagues can help disseminate and apply your theory, particularly in new domains (Kuhlthau), use your theory to teach new concepts to students (Dillon, Kuhlthau), and use your theory when interpreting and explaining their research results (Dillon) and developing new theory (Thelwall).

New forms of research output and social media can encourage engagement with colleagues. Examples include blogs, videos, slides, datasets, and digital tools that are shared widely (Chang, Olson and Olson).

TECHNOLOGY   Technology can inspire, or motivate, new theory development (Dillon, Meadows, Olson and Olson, Thelwall). Emerging technology can influence behavior and create phenomena we have not previously encountered or considered (McGann). For example, theory in human information behavior and collaboration continues to be impacted by existing and emerging mobile platforms (Olson and Olson). Furthermore, new types of data (e.g., Twitter) may extend our ability to investigate human information behavior across geographic distances (Thelwall).

Of course, technology can assist in various ways when you are conducting research, including collecting, managing, and analyzing data; creating and exploring visualizations of results; and engaging with colleagues. However, it can be challenging to procure essential technology in settings where such technology has not been previously required (Järvelin).

Technology can also be impacted by theory. This includes theory for the unprecedented that describes how technology can create new practices and services (Carroll); theory that increases our understanding of human information behavior (Bates, Järvelin) and human-computer interaction (Dillon, Nardi) and that informs technology design; and theory creating research methods that lead to new software applications (Thelwall).

Nowhere are the costs + the negative possibility of tech mentioned; among this + how ethical research

INSTITUTIONS   Institutions are not frequently discussed in the literature but are noted by the authors in this book as a resource (e.g., see McGann, Meadows, Olson and Olson, Saracevic). Decisions made by institutions regarding the establishment and allocation of resources can influence the focus of theory development. For example, McGann discusses how computer equipment assigned to another department at his university and subsequently transferred to his department provided an impetus for digital humanities work and subsequent theory development. Meadows mentions that a research center located at his university influenced his focus. In addition, institutions such as funding agencies, universities, and foundations carefully design and construct calls for proposals to provide inspiration and influence the focus of theory development (Olson and Olson).

Institutions often provide access to various experts who can assist when we conduct research, including experts in literature searching, research design, data management, data analysis, data visualization, and writing for publication. Such experts provide specialized knowledge that can help solve problems that emerge, increasing the validity of our theory. In addition, institutions may facilitate access to study participants (e.g., students or employees), technology, or data (Kuhlthau, McGann, Saracevic).

Theory can also impact institutions. For example, Olson and Olson developed an instrument to help organizations determine whether they need additional resources before attempting remote collabora-

Are new practices always a good thing? What is the quality of this impact?

tion. Theory developed by Bawden, Buckland, and Kuhlthau has led to new and revised library services, and theory developed by Carroll, Dillon, and Nardi has led to new design practices in institutions.

SOCIETAL ISSUES   The chapter authors also report that societal issues have informed their focus. For example, the link between illiteracy and poverty inspired Dillon to focus on developing theory about reading. Political economics inspired Nardi to investigate new ways to design technology. Other resources, such as personal observations and experiences, may also be exemplars of societal issues (Kuhlthau).

When you are conducting research, societal issues can also function as a resource providing assistance or introducing constraints. For example, the American Recovery and Reinvestment Act of 2009 was a government initiative in response to an economic recession that provided increased funding to research. This allowed new research to be undertaken in the United States. In comparison, funding for research was reduced in the Republic of Ireland in response to the recent economic recession, and an important evaluation criterion for much research in Ireland became its potential for and actual impact on job creation. This facilitated some types of theory development while constraining others.

The authors in this book did not explicitly claim that their theoretical work has had an impact on societal issues. Yet theories presented in this book have provided new understandings of phenomena, improved practices, informed policies, influenced research directions, and led to new technologies. These types of impact may also affect societal issues in the longer term. Information is an integral component of society, and challenges with respect to sharing, locating, accessing, storing, and understanding information as individuals, organizations, and nations remain central in today's society.

Connections between resources and stages in theory development mentioned by the chapter authors are summarized in table 1.1. The stages and resources, and their connections, synthesize and represent the collected wisdom shared by the authors throughout this book.

FORMAT OF THE BOOK

The chapters in this book are organized into four parts: behavior of individuals and groups, evaluation, design, and cultural and scientific heritage.

Table 1.1. Summary of connections between resources and stages in theory development

	Examples		
Type of resource	Inspiration for elaborating a focus	Assistance in conducting research	Transformation through making an impact
Literature	Prior research results; suggestions for new research; cases of successful theory, omissions, or gaps	Information about methods, results from prior research for comparison	New publications in English and other languages, citations within other publications, publication downloads, discussions of publications in social media
Personal experiences	Prior work experiences, personal challenges	Knowledge regarding collection and interpretation of data	Skill development; networking; invitations to make presentations, join projects, and review research
Your own research	Your positive and negative research results	Data for re-use, new concepts	Foundation for new research, transportation of your theory to other disciplines, application of theory to additional contexts
Colleagues	Help in clarifying ideas	Identification of omissions and inconsistencies	Adoption and use of your theory in teaching, research, and practice
Technology	New types of phenomena and data	Tools to support data collection, management, and analysis; tools to interact with colleagues	Methods to design technology, knowledge to inform technology design decisions, scenarios that inspire technology, new research software tools
Institutions	Allocation of resources	Access to experts, study participants, technology	New and revised practices and services
Societal issues	Social problems	Research funding and research evaluation criteria	Job creation, potential longer-term impacts

Part 1 has four chapters. Chapter 2, authored by Marcia J. Bates, discusses skills and practices that help convert creative ideas into meaningful theory. Bates illustrates the value of these skills using examples from her work focusing on online search tactics. She further suggests promising ideas that could be investigated and possibly lead to new theories. In chapter 3, ShanJu Lin Chang reflects on how she developed a theory of browsing originally presented in her PhD dissertation. She shares her insights and lessons learned regarding major challenges she encountered during this process. In chapter 4, Carol Collier Kuhlthau reflects on her journey developing the information search process (ISP) theory. Kuhlthau discusses how she began with a theory from a cognate discipline, and how her theory is now being transported to other cognate disciplines. Chapter 5, authored by Gary M. Olson and Judith S. Olson, discusses how they have drawn on four types of resources to develop their theory on long-distance collaboration, and how their ideas and theory evolved over time.

The four chapters in part 2 discuss theory development related to evaluation. In chapter 6, Michael K. Buckland illustrates how he used visual techniques to develop theories in bibliometrics and information retrieval. Buckland asserts that theory is a way of viewing phenomena, and thus visual techniques can be helpful in theory development. In chapter 7, Kalervo Järvelin presents his personal view on theory development for interactive information retrieval (IIR), which has two stages. The first stage investigates real-life IIR at workplaces to develop a conceptual framework; this framework is tested in the second stage using controlled experiments that include simulation of human behavior. In chapter 8, Tefko Saracevic discusses theoretical aspects of information relevance, including manifestations and models of relevance that have emerged in the information sciences and relevance theories that have emerged in cognate disciplines, describing what a theory of relevance for the information sciences should encompass. Mike Thelwall, in chapter 9, reviews webometric research using Gregor's theory taxonomy and discusses two webometric theories he developed: information-centered research and the theoretical framework for link analysis.

Part 3 focuses on theory development in design. Chapter 10, authored by John M. Carroll, discusses how the information sciences address unprecedented phenomena, creating technology and human interactions that did not exist earlier. He suggests that scenarios are useful for developing theories for the unprecedented, and presents several examples. In chapter 11, Bonnie Nardi focuses on the scholar's appropriation of theory and how it can lead to developing new theory. She describes how she came to appropriate activity theory, and how the theory and the journey have influenced her thinking. In chapter 12, Andrew Dillon reflects on his journey developing a theory for design that focuses on reading and information use, and provides a framework for understanding, creating, and evaluating interfaces to support information use.

Part 4 focuses on cultural and scientific heritage theory. In chapter 13, Jerome McGann shares his personal journey pursuing theory and developing the theory of texts and textuality. This journey includes editing Byron's work and developing the Rossetti Archive, an "internetwork." In the next chapter, Hilary S. Crew reflects on her theory development process while writing her PhD dissertation. Her work illuminates the daughter-mother relationships portrayed in young adult fiction. David Bawden discusses his approach to theory development, which employs qualitative conceptual analysis and synthesis to develop theories to understand and explain phenomena. He provides several examples of his approach, including work on the negative information phenomenon and digital literacy. Jack Meadows reflects on navigating the different theoretical traditions found across the natural sciences, social sciences, and humanities, all fields he has worked in. He describes how these traditions have influenced his research focusing on scholarly journals.

Each section of the book includes chapters in which authors reflect on theory development from at least two different career time spans or vantage points, and whose authors have substantial educational or work experiences on at least two different continents.

CONCLUSION

This book presents multiple perspectives on theory development in the information sciences written by authors with diverse research expertise, careers, and cultural backgrounds. This diversity helps to broaden our understanding of theory development. It provides evidence that theory development is not limited to a specific type of research expertise, gender, career time span, educational background, place of employment, or cultural context. Each chapter is worthy of careful, multiple readings.

REFERENCES

American Recovery and Reinvestment Act of 2009, H.R.1, 111th CONG. (2009). Washington, DC: Government Printing Office. Retrieved from http://www .gpo.gov/fdsys/pkg/BILLS-111hr1enr/pdf/BILLS-111hr1enr.pdf.

Boulding, K. E. (1961). *The image: Knowledge in life and society.* Ann Arbor: University of Michigan Press.

D'Andrade, R. G. (1986). Three scientific world views and the covering law model. In D. W. Fiske and R. A. Shweder (Eds.), *Metatheory in social science: Pluralisms and subjectivities* (pp. 19–39). Chicago: University of Chicago Press.

Feyerabend, P. (1993). *Against method.* New York: Verso.

Gregor, S. (2006). The nature of theory in information systems. *MIS Quarterly, 30*(3), 611–642.

Kuhn, T. S. (1970). *The structure of scientific revolutions.* Chicago: University of Chicago Press.

Lewin, K. (1951). *Field theory in social science: Selected theoretical papers.* New York: Harper and Row.

Polanyi, M. (1974). *Personal knowledge.* Chicago: University of Chicago Press.

Reagan, R. (1987). Letter to the American Society of Information Science, 12 August 1987. In *Information: The transformation of society: ASIS 50th Anniversary Conference Program* (p. 6). Washington, DC: ASIS.

Simon, R. I. (1992). *Teaching against the grain.* New York: Bergin and Garvey.

BEHAVIOR OF INDIVIDUALS AND GROUPS

CHAPTER 2

MANY PATHS TO THEORY: THE CREATIVE PROCESS IN THE INFORMATION SCIENCES

MARCIA J. BATES

THE CREATIVE PROCESS, by its very nature, is unpredictable and surprising. Nonetheless, one can develop skills that will promote and enhance creativity, and will increase the likelihood of producing fruitful ideas. My present purpose is to say something about this process, based on my own experience. Also, I will describe several research ideas that I think are promising and that I wanted to develop but did not have the time to pursue before my retirement. I hope that readers will draw on both the skills and the ideas presented here to produce further progress in the information sciences.[1]

PART 1: BEING OPEN TO, AND USING, IDEAS

FIRST SKILL: LEARN TO BE OPEN TO IDEAS

First, be open to ideas and research possibilities. It is here, at the beginning, that many people get stopped before they really get started. It helps to recall Sigmund Freud's psychological concepts of the id, the ego, and the superego in the human mind. The id is the child, the autochthonous root of behavior, unpredictable and seemingly uncontrollable. The ego is the adult manager, seeing you through life safely—judicious and mature. The ego does experiment, but cautiously and thoughtfully. The superego is the controller, the guilt-tripper, the part of your mind telling you to follow social rules and religious edicts.

All of these parts of the mind develop in their own way and time, and work together, more or less well, to produce the acting adult that one becomes. Ideally, when one is doing research, the id produces ideas, the ego manages the ideas productively for the benefit of the individual and society, and the superego ensures that the work is done and reported on ethically.

Unfortunately, what happens more often than not is that the superego clamps down on the idea production by the id, along with all the other things in the id that the superego suppresses, as people grow from childhood to adulthood. We have all seen the "uptight" individual, afraid to try anything, super-polite and tightly regulated. In this age of looseness and ease about so many things, we tend to pity these people and wish they would tell that superego of theirs to lighten up. However, other people who are not uptight generally and are quite normal in behavior can still be uptight when it comes to idea generation. It is not so easy sorting out just how you do and do not want that id to be allowed to influence your life. Unfortunately, as we "put away childish things," we often put away as well the wonderful fecundity of the id.

I have observed a number of researchers in my life who, I believe, would never, ever allow a stray idea to wander up from their id into their ego as they work. In these people, *everything is controlled*; perhaps a better term would be *locked down*—so tightly that a fleeting creative thought would never be allowed into the thinking mind. The result is a predictability, a dryness, a purged-of-color-and-personality quality to their work. If there is an obvious interpretation, they will find it. They are not just analytical; they are analytical/boring. In most cases analytical is good; analytical/boring is not.

Now, in order to let in ideas from the id, one needs to be confident one can handle the ideas and not make a fool of oneself. This is usually one of the biggest reasons for suppressing that id. But here is where we can apply a really valuable idea, and that is this: keep in mind that when you are coming up with wild, silly, ridiculous ideas, *no one else ever has to know*. You have complete control over what you do and do not say or write. You can try out ideas, play with them, even write about them, but, still, no one else need ever know, if you conclude that these ideas are non-starters. In other words, do not slam the door on the ideas from the id, but let them in, sit down with them, play with them, and then decide whether you want to do anything further with them, such as taking them out for a visit with the rest of the world.

So how do you become aware of the ideas from the id (or from anywhere in your creative psyche)? At first they may come to you as just fleeting—the sort of thing you ordinarily knock out of your mind without thinking. Well, do not knock them out. Stop and think. Why does this occur to me now? What connection can there be between this goofy thought and the research I was just thinking about? The idea that floats into your mind often constitutes an analogy. People have asked me where I got the idea of "berrypicking" for my paper of that name (Bates 1989). But moving around through different information sources, getting a bit here, a bit there, reminded me of picking huckleberries in the forest with a boyfriend of mine when I lived in Washington state. I allowed that thought in, instead of dismissing it.

Another thing to keep in mind is that creativity requires fecundity, abundance. In her lifetime, a woman produces several hundred eggs, and their associated menstrual cycles, and men produce billions of sperm, all in order to produce just the one or two or three children they ultimately have. Think of how much you and your spouse produced, in order to have just a few children. Ideas are like that, too. You will have *many* ideas in order to produce the few that you actually concentrate on. There may be a thousand ways to think about a particular issue, but only three ways to solve it. To have any hope of solving it, you need to think of a lot of ideas, not just one or two.

Once you allow ideas in, you should have many; more and more should start coming, once you are open to them. It should not be necessary for you to think that every good researchable topic you come up with must be the result of years of striving to find and shape just one or two ideas. If so, you are doing something wrong—such as not letting those ideas in when they first appear. Generally, research does not do well on a paucity model. After all, research and the development of theoretical concepts require multiple big and little moments of creativity to reach fruition. What may look like a single idea at the end is actually often the result of many successive original thoughts and insights.

And if an idea does not work out, do not beat yourself up about it. You are not *wrong* because an idea does not work out. The idea just did not work out. Most of them do not. Move on. That is another advantage of having lots of ideas. You have plenty to spare.

SECOND SKILL: DRAW ON A VARIETY OF RESEARCH TRADITIONS

I often encounter doctoral students who, with a laser-like focus, want to know exactly and only the courses they need to take to get through the doctoral program in the shortest time possible. Given the expense, and the time away from other work and family, this is an entirely understandable sentiment, but, in fact, I do not think this approach is productive for the rest of one's career. Doctoral work should be a time to explore intriguing areas, to take courses that may not be obviously related to your work. This should be a time to trust, and to follow up on, that tickle of interest you feel in anything from whole other disciplines, specialties within disciplines, or simply a research question that has been studied by someone in one or more other fields—or our own. To pursue those interests often involves taking or auditing courses in other departments, or taking not-obviously-relevant courses in your own department, or doing an independent study course. Again, your unconscious mind may be directing you toward research and theory that you may not only have a talent for but that you may also be able to combine in new and creative ways with other knowledge that you already have.

I emphasize this idea of wide exposure to research areas and topics because I believe that this is one of the most productive ways to gain new insights and identify intriguing new topics for research. Each specialty and discipline necessarily brings a whole set of assumptions and established knowledge with it; these are the "paradigms" (Kuhn 2012) that we hear so much about, which are particularly important in the social sciences. When you are exposed to several different paradigms in your studying, you may well see important inconsistencies or conflicts between those ideas. Thinking about these conflicts can point to new questions that neither paradigm is addressing. There can also be a valuable synergy between the different approaches. It is not uncommon for two disciplines to address essentially the same topic, but from their separate perspectives—and often without being aware that the other discipline has a long line of research on that very question.

Here is a case from my own life history. I wrote about "information search tactics" (Bates 1979b) and "idea tactics" (Bates 1979a) after bringing together ideas from several fields. I originally became interested in techniques of information searching when I found myself to be rather incompetent and slow-witted in reference practice exercises in my library education program. A doctoral student serving as a teaching assistant for our reference-lab class took fiendish delight in crafting test reference questions whose answers could not be found in any of the "obvious" places. Other students were much quicker in finding answers to these difficult questions than I was. One day, my friend found answers to twenty-two questions in an hour; I found answers to just two! I was an excellent student in general; why was I so

poor at this core librarian task? I soon found that there was little instruction available on this topic in the library literature. Ability to do
good reference work seemed to be just assumed by everyone. Note the
research opening here: a topic that had not been much addressed in
the literature, and yet that was crucial to professional performance as
a librarian. Note also that I did not slink away in shame at not being
as good as my classmates at this skill; instead I took it as an interesting challenge to find helpful ideas on the matter.

I gathered together everything I could find in the library literature,
and then I branched out to psychology, because thinking of other
places to look for hard-to-find information was a kind of creative process, and I knew that psychology addressed creativity. I had long been
interested in military history and had read books on the subject and
liked to watch war movies. So I was aware of the concepts of strategy
and tactics. It made sense to me that one should have a strategy for
the overall search, and then, as one made various moves to complete
the search, one would apply various helpful tactics within the search
to increase the chance of success in finding the desired information.
So, improbably, I brought military theory together with psychology
to address a topic in library and information science. Another word
for helpful tactics is "heuristics," a term that cropped up in various
fields, such as psychology, computer science, and operations research.
(I had taken courses in all those areas, by the way, as a doctoral student.) So looking at that concept was productive as well.

The insight about tactics and strategies to promote effective
searching provided the framework for my thinking on steps to improve searching. Once I had that idea, I explored all the ways I could
think of that would help promote good searching, ending up with several broad categories of tactics: monitoring, file structure, search formulation, term, and so on (over thirty tactics in total). Note that I also
drew on my knowledge of librarianship, specifically, the organization
of information, in suggesting tactics, for example, that involved ex-
perimenting with different terms for a subject—going broader, nar-
rower, and so forth. Thus, several literatures were brought to bear on
the topic. These ideas also proved productive for several subsequent
articles I wrote (one of which received the Association for Information Science and Technology Best *JASIST* Paper of the Year Award)
and led to others in the field doing research on tactics (e.g., Hsieh-Yee
1993; Xie 2000).

Incidentally, around the time I was working on these papers, I had an experience that further supports my argument about the value of exposing yourself to varied fields when you are researching a question. In the late 1970s, I was teaching at the University of Washington, and used to sit in on some of the lectures of visiting speakers in the Philosophy Department. One time, Paul Grice, an eminent philosopher of language and reasoning, came to speak. What he described in his lecture was his developing work on logical reasoning. He distinguished between formal reasoning and the informal tricks we use to get to an answer to what we are reasoning about. He said he was currently working on the informal reasoning aspect. During the question period, I asked him if he would say that he was working on a conception of the *heuristics of reasoning.* "Well," he said, "'heuristics' is not exactly a term that comes tripping off my tongue." Clearly, he did not know the term. This was a classic example of different fields addressing the same topic under different names. This is not to question in any way Grice's very important and original contributions to this area in philosophy. But might his thinking have changed in any way had he been aware of the several other fields also studying heuristics, each from its own distinctive perspective?

So far, I have presented the idea of drawing on a variety of research traditions as a way to enrich your own work and generate interesting new ideas. But in some cases, the work in related fields is so highly relevant that to *not* address that related work constitutes intellectual failure. A prime example of relevant material typically not referenced in our field is, ironically, the work on relevance by a psychologist and an anthropologist. Dan Sperber and Deirdre Wilson's book *Relevance: Communication and Cognition* (Sperber and Wilson 1995), originally published in 1986, has generated an enormous amount of interest and debate in many social science fields, as well as in philosophy, and has been cited about 1,500 times, according to the Thomson Reuters Web of Science (wokinfo.com). Only a handful of those citations, however, are from the field of information science, despite the hundreds of articles that address the subject of relevance in information science. Two information scientists who have recognized the significance of the Sperber and Wilson work, and incorporated it into their thinking, are Stephen Harter (1992) and, more recently, Howard White (2007a, 2007b). Otherwise, however, despite occasional references, information science seems to have ignored this high-impact work. Given the recent popularity of "soft," more humanistic approaches to library and information science (LIS), it is puzzling that their subtle approach has not been generally taken up in the field. As long as we in information science like to feel that we "own" the idea of relevance, we had better deal with the many implications of the work on this topic elsewhere in academia. The longer we avoid it, the more behind the curve we will appear to be when we finally do take it seriously.

THIRD SKILL: READ DEEPLY, NOT JUST WIDELY

As I have argued, familiarizing yourself with research traditions in several fields can lead to productive new ideas and approaches in your thinking. However, this suggestion comes with a caveat: if you want to use the ideas drawn from other disciplines in your own work, take the time to really understand what you are reading. As noted earlier, one of the things that makes these encounters between disciplines productive is that the disciplines take different approaches to the same questions. But you cannot just borrow the vocabulary, discuss your own field's work using the new vocabulary, and be successful in making a contribution. The conflicts between the ideas as pursued in the different disciplines often lie at a deeper level than merely the vocabulary. In short, when you study a different approach from another field, you need to understand that approach all the way down, that is, all the way to the underlying philosophical perspective driving that field. Different worldviews and philosophical assumptions separate the various fields. If you want to contribute to the information sciences using those models from other fields, you have to do some serious thinking about how to adapt and integrate those ideas with those of your home field. You need to understand deeply the other field's worldview and how it plays out in the specific topic of interest before you can successfully adapt it to (one of the several) information science paradigms operating (Bates 2005).

Jenna Hartel's (2010a) work on the use of ethnographic methods in the information sciences represents a recent example of reading deeply and working hard to integrate a methodology widely used in the social sciences with the needs of information-seeking research. Ethnographic techniques are well developed in anthropology and sociology, and have been used by some researchers in the information sciences. What Hartel has contributed to this important methodological philosophy is a deep understanding of information seeking, keeping, and using. The ethnographic methods are not native to the information sciences, and the information orientation is not well known to the other social sciences using ethnographic methods. Her interest in the extensive information gathering and collecting of passionately devoted gourmet cooks surprised some of her sociology professors. As sociologists, they had not ever thought much about *the ethnography of information*. Bringing those two together is a difficult task, requiring extensive reading in philosophy and theory, and years of analytical work. Hartel described her experiences in a series of articles (Hartel 2010a, 2010b, 2011) that are combinations of research results and expositions of ethnographic methods as applied to the information worlds of the people being observed.

FOURTH SKILL: RELATE YOUR WORK APPROPRIATELY TO THAT OF OTHERS

One of the standard requirements of an academic article is that the author should show how the work fits in with other research and thinking in the area. This is not an idle requirement of fussy journal editors; it is done for a reason. Work that is published should not only be new but also be *shown* to be new. One does this by describing prior work and explaining how the current work relates to the prior work and yet advances beyond it. The literature review in an article (1) *contextualizes the research* presented in the article, so the reader can see where the work fits with other work in the field; (2) demonstrates that the author is *current with other work in the area*, and so is not rediscovering things already known; (3) *affords recognition* to those authors for the earlier work; and (4) *claims its own new territory*.

So the literature review, which may be seen superficially as a boring prelude to the real action of the article where the research is described, is actually a socially very significant part of the article, and needs to be thought about carefully.

I bring this up here in a chapter on creativity in the information sciences because the creativity that produces new ideas or methods can come into conflict in a variety of ways with providing recognition to others for their work. How much credit is due to my thinking, and how much credit is due to others for their thinking?

Why is recognition important? The currency of business is the bottom line—the amount of money made. No matter how clever your product or service, if you do not make money on it, you are not a successful businessperson. The currency of science, on the other hand, is *recognition* for work done and discoveries made. People go into research to discover new things and advance science or scholarship. The mark of success, therefore, is to have other talented people, who also know that research area well, recognize and esteem your work, and value your presence in the field. Esteem is shown, for academics, through successful publication in good venues, through promotions, through awards, through naming things after their discoverer, and so on. It is all about recognition for one's talents by one's respected colleagues.

I got a lesson in this importance early in my career. I was writing the article to be later titled "Rigorous Systematic Bibliography" (Bates 1976). After the article was, for the most part, finished, I was reviewing it and realized suddenly that I had drawn throughout the article on the work of Patrick Wilson, one of my professors at UC Berkeley, where I got my doctorate. In effect, the article represented a way to operationalize, or put into practice, the much more theoretical ideas to be found in Wilson's book *Two Kinds of Power* (Wilson 1968). I had so thoroughly absorbed Wilson's ideas that I did not recognize that I was working through methods of applying his ideas to the practice of bibliography in the article. I had not submitted the article yet, and, somewhat embarrassed, I rewrote it to include full and repeated references to his work. After a bit, I realized that I had gone too far, and was not highlighting what was original in my own contribution in the article, so I rewrote it again, with what finally felt like a good and accurate balance.

The relationship between our own work and that of others can be a very touchy matter, and it is better to recognize that, and work it through, than to deny what is happening. One makes a good-faith effort at reviewing the earlier literature, and one cites it when it is relevant. I suspect that the intense hostile animus that shows up in some journal article reviews arises from the reviewer feeling that you have somehow violated, wittingly or unwittingly, his or her intellectual turf. Perhaps I take this matter of giving credit where credit is due a little too seriously, but I have seen many occasions where people did not deal well with the challenge of getting the credit right.

One time a senior professor wrote to me enthusiastically about how much he liked one of my articles and how influential it had been for him. Later, he wrote a whole book on the subject, and I looked to see the role my work played in it. He cited the reference to my paper seriously incorrectly, and, to read the relevant section, you would think my work had virtually no effect on his, and was at best peripheral to his work. In another case, I was asked to review an article for a double-blind journal (i.e., neither author nor reviewer knows the identity of the other) in which the author had used a research design and research question virtually identical to one in a major research project of mine but had not related it to my study or referenced it. I pointed to the articles that I had published out of my study and asked that they be appropriately referenced and related to the results of the work in the article being reviewed. Later, after the article had been published, I saw that the senior professor who wrote it now cited my article but still did not reference or discuss any of the parts that actually overlapped. The reader would have no idea of the similarities.

I have read many articles that used my work but did not reference it or that referenced my popular article "The Design of Browsing and Berrypicking Techniques" (Bates 1989) instead of referencing the article of mine that actually dealt with the content of the referencing article. When someone's irrelevant article is referenced, recognition appears to have been given when, in fact, it has not. The new work presented in the article is not connected at all to the actual relevant prior work that should have been discussed in the article. One reviews prior work in order, among other things, to compare the results and discuss any differences. By citing a different article than the relevant one, one avoids addressing altogether the actual relationship between the current and cited research. This happened to me so many times that I once sat down, with the help of the Thomson Reuters Web of Science, to review every reference to my work in the literature in order to tally the actual frequency of this problem. However, not wanting to be the skunk at the garden party and offend my professional colleagues, I gave up on this endeavor.

It can be disappointing to discover that someone else has been there before you—but they did get there, and you owe it to them to acknowledge it. Further, if the works differ in results, some discussion of this is in order; such discussion and debate is what science is supposed to be about. If your own work is any good, you will also be contributing work of value; it does not undermine your own contribution to recognize those who have gone before.

Let us turn now to those promising ideas to be put forward. I will have more to say about being creative in information science research as I go along.

PART 2: PROMISING IDEAS

In this section, I discuss a number of ideas that I think have promise, and that I am unlikely to be able to pursue in my lifetime. I encourage students and established researchers to take up these ideas and see where they lead. Keep in mind that these are *ideas*; they are not fully researched or substantiated. There will be gaps, unreferenced literature, and so on. Actual in-depth work with these ideas might lead to different conclusions than I anticipate. In short, much remains to be done, but most of these should have the potential to be good dissertation or other research project topics.

AREA 1: INFORMATION SEEKING AT THE HUMAN AND MACHINE INTERFACE

Here I will describe just three of many topics that could be mentioned as promising ideas to follow up in the area of information seeking at the human and machine interface. However, to introduce those ideas, I need to pick a fight—just a little one—with my colleagues, in this book and elsewhere, from the field of human-computer interaction (HCI). I believe that the full contribution that information science can make to this area is generally not recognized outside the field, particularly by researchers in HCI. Many in HCI come from a psychology background, and when they address the experience of people at a computer interface, they bring a psychologist's desire to discover fundamental principles about human psychology in carrying out the work of using computers. The objective is to understand the whole HCI experience; it is assumed that the most fundamental discoveries will apply across most or all application areas. From that standpoint, *information seeking* on computers is just a single application area, and therefore not of much intrinsic interest to HCI researchers.

I would argue, in reply, that information seeking is a much larger area than generally recognized and has distinctive, important features that need to be understood and designed for in order to produce the best HCI in information-seeking contexts. General HCI principles are not enough for optimal results.

Gregory Bateson (1968) made an interesting distinction between what he called "value seeking" and "information seeking" (pp. 178–179). In value seeking, a person has an idea in mind and goes out into the world to shape that world so as to produce a result that matches the idea in mind. If one wants bacon and eggs for breakfast, one does certain things in the world with pigs, chickens, and a stove, with the end result that one has a plate of bacon and eggs. In information seeking, on the other hand, one goes out into the world to discover things so as to create the idea in mind to match or reflect what is in the world. This is a simplified distinction, obviously, but a powerful one.

The nature of our actions in the world will be very different when we have a plan in mind to impose on the world, versus when we are open to the world imposing some part of its character or shape on our own minds. If we move to a part of the world where bacon and eggs are not to be found, and we are hungry, we face a very different type of challenge in our effort to learn about things that might satisfy our hunger.

Information seeking is not just an application field, like engineering, or retail services; rather, it is the other side of action. It is about gaining knowledge, and there are many characteristics of that behavior that distinguish it from value seeking. First, information seeking makes one vulnerable. Information, by many definitions, is surprise. Not all surprises are fun or desirable. Therefore, the seeker opens him- or herself up to risk, to the potential need to reorganize or reorient his or her hard-earned knowledge. The consequences of this risk ripple throughout the behavior we call information seeking. The behavior ranges all the way from avoiding information to actively seeking it out in cases where our lives are on the line or our passions are engaged with a fascinating subject.

Second, by definition, *you are seeking something that you do not know*. How, then, does one specify the sought information? Whole courses in information science are devoted to this question. Not only the designs of classifications and indexing vocabularies are at issue, but also courses on the interaction between people and information. We know quite a bit about what people do to their own queries to make them understandable to information systems and to information professionals. These propensities have huge consequences for the design of the information-seeking interface in information systems.

Some years back in the Department of Information Studies at the University of California, Los Angeles (UCLA), one of my colleagues taught a course on HCI in information systems, and I taught a course on user-centered design of information systems. By then, information systems were overwhelmingly online, so one might expect quite a bit of overlap in the contents of the two courses. But there was, in fact, virtually no overlap, because I emphasized the design issues that were specific to information seeking/searching, and she taught about HCI in general. *There is a distinct body of knowledge in information science around information seeking on computer interfaces.* Approaches assuming that general HCI knowledge applies without an understanding of the information-seeking part are underperforming in the quality of design for this central human process. My objective in the following sections is to describe some HCI areas involving information searching and retrieving that have interested me, and that I believe would be of value to pursue further.

TOPIC 1: DESIGN FOR REAL BROWSING   What is generally called a "browsing capability" in online systems is nothing of the sort. Overwhelmingly, as currently manifested, this capability in online systems consists of being able to *scan* down the page, with the help of the scrolling function. That systematic, top-to-bottom or left-to-right scanning behavior is not browsing. Think about standing in a bookstore or at a magazine stand, or shopping in a bazaar, for that matter; it is not about systematic scanning. Your eyes dart all around. You glimpse here, then there, then way over there. Things catch your eye. You look at one, then at another. If something is really interesting, you pause and take a serious look at it, then select it, or move on. Rarely do you run your finger along the books, or items in the bazaar, in a systematic way, studying one, then the one right next to it, then the one right next to that, and so on. The eye darts around in browsing; it does not scan, as I have argued in detail (Bates 2007b). Things catch your eye because you first do a gross glance that does not analyze the visual scene in detail; then you put your closer attention to the things that pass your crude filter (Wolfe 1994).

I have argued that "browsing is seen to consist of a series of four steps, iterated indefinitely until the end of a browsing episode: (1) glimpsing a field of vision, (2) selecting or sampling a physical or informational object within the field of vision, (3) examining the object, (4) acquiring the object (conceptually and/or physically) or abandoning it. Not all of these elements need be present in every browsing episode, though multiple glimpses are seen to be the minimum to constitute the act" (Bates 2007b). Thus, design for browsing in online systems would necessarily be very different from the current provision of the capability to scan. First, the screen needs to be large enough to allow the eye to take glimpses, attending to one part, then to another part. Second, there should be a variety of options available to the user—and not just on pull-down menus, which require choosing to pull down the menu! Instead, the many options should be available *at the same time* on the screen—just as a scene glimpsed by our forebears in the forest contained many points of interest. Icons scattered on the screen, representing different types of search capability, could simultaneously present to the user a rich array of options for searching. A single search box, à la Google, has been viewed as the sine qua non for searching—the easiest, most simplified approach. But what if we found a way to make the search itself interesting? Let people browse through different capabilities, and different classes of metadata or taxonomies. There are many ways to structure such a system; the problem is that *we have not ever taken seriously the desirability of designing for true browsing.*

TOPIC 2: INTERFACE DESIGN SPECIFIC TO SEARCHING   For a very long time, there has been a pervasive assumption among computer scientists that an information system search interface can simply be superimposed on any body of searchable data. Set up the information so that various elements can be searched, then superimpose some sort of search engine—most any kind will do—and you have your information system. But, as I argued in "The Cascade of Interactions in the Digital Library Interface" (Bates 2002), there are, in fact, many layers of design needed beneath and in front of the interface that culminate in design imperatives for the resulting interface. The information itself—its content, structure, medium, types of indexing and metadata, and so on—influences how one can best find desired results within the body of information, and therefore how search should be designed in the interface for the user, as well as behind the scenes in the computer. Likewise, everything on the searcher side of the interface—subject area of interest, type of query, level of skill as a searcher, and so on—interacts with the interface design in a productive or unproductive way. Bad design at just one of these several layers can block the effective functioning of all the other layers (Bates 2002).

Here is an example contrasting two situations. In situation A, you have a database of biological reports addressing the various concerns of biologists, from studying animals in their natural habitats to using parts of nature for research in other areas, such as agriculture, animal breeding, and environmental concerns. In situation B, you have a database of articles published in the humanities literature on the several fields encompassed by that term—national literatures, philosophy, religion, and so forth.

Extensive research and practical experience have demonstrated that faceted vocabularies provide the most appropriate means for indexing humanities articles (for the explanation, see Bates, Wilde, and Siegfried 1993). The Getty Research Institute (associated with the

Getty Museum) consequently committed itself to creating faceted vocabularies, using them to index its extensive database production. In contrast, scientific databases do best with the one- to three-word phrases known as descriptors, which have been prompted by classical indexing theory and embodied in the technical standards developed for them (National Information Standards Organization 2005). With faceted indexing, the whole query is composed of terms drawn from each of several distinct facets, while with scientific literature, the search is composed of descriptors presented to the system in Boolean combinations, either implicitly or explicitly. If searchers are to take advantage of these differences, the interfaces must be designed differently for the two systems—a single simple search box, in particular, will not do.

Examples of this sort could be proliferated indefinitely. If the one database contains technical reports with a certain standard structure in introductory matter (author, affiliation, abstract, etc.), and the other database consists of humanities articles using typical bibliographic rules for humanities articles (e.g., University of Chicago Press rules rather than American Psychological Association rules), then there are different ways of coding and representing these bibliographic entities that can either promote successful search or get in the way of it. And I have not even mentioned other types of information, such as video, image, multi-lingual, and other variant forms of data.

When designing for search, one must design the interface all the way down to the actual content itself. A single, standard search interface, superimposed on the huge actual variety of types of information and information organizational schemes, can just about be guaranteed to sub-optimize. Furthermore, there is a huge variety of types of queries characteristically associated with different types of needed information. For example, art databases are searched not only by art history scholars but also by designers and artists looking for inspiration in the images they find, and by schoolchildren for their assignments. The kinds of search interface design features that each of these groups could most benefit from differ. Different capabilities are needed for each. To optimize information search, all these various design layers need to be recognized, understood, and designed for in an interface that nonetheless feels simple and natural to the end user. This is a high standard, and one that has been mostly ignored outside of information science. There are abundant opportunities here, with the right funding and sufficient imagination, to see how complex much of information searching actually is.

TOPIC 3: QUESTION AND ANSWERING—THE 55 PERCENT RULE   Up through the 1990s, there was considerable interest and research in library and information science on what was called the "55 percent rule." Researchers addressed the question of whether the answers provided at library reference desks were accurate. This was usually done by sending testers to library reference desks or by calling library reference departments to ask typical reference questions of the librarians, then checking the accuracy of the answers provided. To the researchers' horror, in study after study, the accuracy rate came out, surprisingly, to a fairly consistent figure of around 55 percent. How could this be? Responding to reference queries is the bread and butter of a substantial portion of professional librarians, the so-called public services staff, and to compile an accuracy rate so low was concerning, to say the least. Why did study after study get results around 55 percent?

I first got interested in this question when asked to review a book by Frances Benham and Ronald Powell (1987) that reported results of two separate such studies. The bottom-line results, the accuracy rates for answering questions in the two studies, were 52.73 and 58.73 percent—remarkably similar, considering variations in the sampling of the two studies (Benham and Powell 1987, p. 136). (There is a large literature on this subject, which will not be reviewed here.)

Something about the consistency of these results across many studies troubled me, however. If training in the reference interview and teaching reference librarians about the typical reference resources available to provide answers to these questions really were the chief influencing factor in performance, then why was there not *more* variation? Surely, smaller libraries with poor reference collections and, probably, staff with less or no professional training should produce poorer results, and the larger, better-staffed and -stocked libraries should produce much better results. Yet the patterns were very similar.

Then I learned about the US Internal Revenue Service call sites, where people can call the agency to inquire about aspects of the tax laws. Studies had been done over several years, and there was some controversy about the nature of the sampling and test questions; these questions were resolved through a thorough review of methodology. By 1989, with good, verified methodology, the test call survey report stated: "IRS' overall . . . results for the 1989 tax filing season showed that IRS telephone assistors responded correctly 62.8 percent of the time to the survey's tax law test questions" (US General Accounting Office 1990, p. 1).

That result rang a bell for me. *If this completely different context could produce a result so similar to that for libraries, then the problem was likely due to something other than simply inadequate library resources or professional training.* As I explored the literature around this question, I came to suspect that the problem concerned any information question-asking situation that was at all complex. In other words, I was forming the hypothesis that in *any* situation where there is a lot of detail or context necessary to fully understand the issue, there will be a 55 percent general rate of accuracy. Indeed, another of the reports on the IRS tests states: "For questions that required IRS assistors to probe callers for more information in order to sufficiently understand the question, the accuracy rate was 56 percent compared to 90 percent for questions where probing was not required" (US General Accounting Office 1987, p. 2). *I hypothesized that this is a general human communication problem, not a library-specific problem.*

This rate is a source of embarrassment wherever it crops up, because it seems so low. I suspect, however, that the error rate is high because it is impractical for both questioner and assister or librarian to carry out the necessary amount of probing needed to ensure that the question is actually understood in all relevant respects, and can therefore be answered correctly. The questioner has in mind a vast amount of context surrounding the question, and, often, has no way of knowing which particular elements of that context the assister needs to know in order to produce a correct answer. On the other hand, the assister does not know that context, and may not realize that some key invalidating characteristic of the context might, if the assister knew about it, change the assister's response to accommodate it. There is probably no easy answer to this situation, because to fully ensure that all factors have, in fact, been taken into account might require a very long interaction. Most of the time—say, about 55 percent of the time—that extra-long interaction would be wasted or unnecessary, because the initial response would be correct, but the rest of the time, a much higher investment might be needed to provide higher accuracy. (This is not to suggest, however, that more complex questions will not, in themselves, and apart from context, be more subject to error, on the part of both assister and requester, just due to their complexity.)

My research assistant and I did quite a bit of literature searching around this question, looking at informational interactions in law and medicine, as well as in general. There is a whole subliterature about inaccuracy and failure to communicate in physician-patient interactions alone! I planned to devote part of the summer of 1994 to explicating this whole issue of question-asking accuracy. Unfortunately, I was not able to follow up, because that spring the campus administration proposed shutting down our school, and two miserable years followed, wherein I served as department chair as we fought back to keep the program alive, though, ultimately, as a part of a new, combined entity: the Graduate School of Education and Information Studies.

On the basis of what I had found in the literature, and on what, to me, seemed the uniting themes of that research, I planned to further research the hypothesis about information-seeking interaction that summer, and would probably conclude by making the argument stated above. I felt that one particularly telling argument would be this: notice that in cases before a court, where absolute accuracy in all respects is the goal of the questioning of witnesses, a long string of questions is posed to the witness, probing, in numbing detail, every aspect of the situation being discussed. "Was the stop sign visible from where you stopped? Were there any leaves or tree branches blocking your line of sight to the sign? Was the overhead streetlight shining on it?" And on and on and on. The practice of law has demonstrated the need to go far beyond the basic initial interaction in order to get all the relevant facts, to get the details needed to push the answer beyond the point of being just 55 percent accurate. Indeed, even when this probing is done, there may be still much more to the story than comes out in court (Finnegan 1994).

The relatively poor accuracy results were embarrassing for librarians and for the IRS. I think it is important to realize that in dense, complex question-asking situations, this accuracy problem is probably built in to the nature of human knowledge and interaction. We have no hope of improving the librarian success rate without attributing the problem to its likely true sources in general human communication, rather than to library training and resources alone. This topic needs to be further explored, argued, tested . . .

AREA 2: INFORMATION ORGANIZATION: EVENT INDEXING

At its very heart, all indexing theory is built around the core idea that we index *nouns, or conceptual objects.* As the technical standard for thesaurus development states, an "indexing term" is "the representation of a concept in an indexing language, generally in the form of a noun or noun phrase" (National Information Standards Organization 2005, p. 6).

I wish to challenge that core assumption to produce a result that can still fit within the larger framework of indexing but that might enrich the possibilities available now. Indexing is generally described as an effort to identify and flag the "subjects" of a document. Those subjects are, implicitly, the topics "covered" or "discussed" in the document. As I write, workers for the San Francisco Bay Area Rapid Transit, or BART, are striking to get more favorable contract terms. Conventionally, a newspaper index would index articles on this event as "strikes and lockouts," "labor unions," or "collective bargaining." These are all noun phrases and certainly represent the topics addressed in the articles, as per our usual understanding of indexing.

But a strike is also an *event* that takes place in time and spools out through time. A little bit of reflection will suggest that while an event can be considered a topic of discussion, if we really want to understand the event, and be able to search for it, should we not develop a way of indexing that is more true to the nature of that event?

Here is one way to think about it. Compare *narrative* and *expository* writing. A *narrative* is a story that takes place through time. It may be fiction or nonfiction. *Exposition* of a topic elaborates and explains that topic. *Standard indexing theory is designed for exposition, not narrative.* Indeed, the question of how to index fiction has been raised many times, and there are no easy answers regarding either the ease of indexing fiction or the value of doing so (Beghtol 1994; Pejtersen 1978; Saarti 1999).

However, here I want to stick to questions of indexing nonfiction, as in newspaper and magazine indexing. Compare topic indexing and event indexing (see table 2.1). In the *topic-indexing* condition, we are addressing a document or document portion devoted to expounding on a topic. The bulk of the text involves description and explanation. If the text is reasonably coherent, it can be considered to be addressing one or more particular topics. Classical indexing attempts to identify those topics and provide good, consistent descriptions of them through the development, control, and application of appropriate index terms.

Now, what do we have in the *event-indexing* condition? First, we have narrative, which is the telling of a story of some sort, spooling out in time. Furthermore, the narrative describes, above all, a *situation*. A situation is a complex of conditions, circumstances, events, and actors existing at a point in time, and often, through time. Within the context of a situation, one or more events may occur. An event is an occurrence, a complex of actors and circumstances that change one condition to another within a noticeably short time frame.

In the example of the Bay Area transit strike, the *situation* is that of contract negotiations between the labor union and BART management. The strike is an *event* that occurs during the contract negotiations.

Now, suppose we are a newspaper needing to index the ongoing events associated with the contract negotiations. We create a template specifically for situations and events. We use the classical aspects for event description that have been identified in journalism: who, what, where, when, why, how. *When* should include duration, that is, beginning and ending times.

Thus, within the larger *situation*, we code for various *events* that occur within it (table 2.2). In indexing, the newspaper creates a situation name and assigns a code number to that situation. At the beginning of contract negotiations, an indexer fills in the names of the parties—the union and the management—and notes the dates, location, and so on. Then, as the negotiations continue through various events, the coding and names automatically populate over to the next event, except where the event itself changes things, and then those features are changed by indexers.

Since events are about *things that happen, that is, action,* we should explore what indexing might look like if verbs were actu-

Table 2.1. Contrasting topic and event indexing

Topic indexing	Event indexing
Exposition	Narrative
Topic	Situation
Description/explanation	Event

Table 2.2. Situation and event coding for indexing

Situation: BART contract negotiations 2013		Code: 54025	
Event	Initiate talks	Go on strike	Return to talks
Who			
What			
Where			
When			
Why			
How			

ally indexed, too. So, verb indexing terms might be words like "initiate [talks]," "strike," "settle," "conclude [talks]," and so on. Alternatively, a separate set of index terms that are nominalized verbs could be carved out to be used specifically to index events. These would be terms like "initiation of talks," "strike," "settlement," "conclusion [of talks]," and so forth. For a newspaper, or for legal, law enforcement, or medical records, having a separate action category of verbs or of verb-based nouns might be useful for identifying contents and enabling discovery by searchers. For example, an ongoing lawsuit is between two parties, and the case name and parties involved will be scattered throughout the records of the suit. But if one is looking for a particular action—say, to discover when a request was made to enjoin someone from acting—then a search on "enjoin" or "injunction" might be helpful. Such event-indexing terms might be extracted from existing thesauri or created anew as specifically verb index terms to draw attention to the sequence of actions that characterizes events and situations that spool out through time. In a certain sense, events have been masked, or submerged, within the broader scope of classical subject indexing. The approach suggested here highlights the distinctive features of events and situations, that is, of *narratives*, as distinct from *exposition*.

AREA 3: INFORMATION DENSITIES

The term "information densities" actually covers a number of possible areas to pursue. I will develop them here as well as I am able, given that I have not actually pursued this area in depth.

TOPIC 1: INFORMATION WHOMPS   In March 1977, Marilyn Levine published an article in the *Journal of the American Society for Information Science* called "The Informative Act and Its Aftermath: Toward a Predictive Science of Information." Levine argued that important events in a society have an impact that can be quantified in (among other ways) the number of books written on that subject or event. The event has an emotional, economic, political (etc.) impact, and people respond by adapting to the event, discussing it, and reorganizing their thinking and their lives in order to accommodate the event and move on. One of the important ways that human beings do all these things is to produce new information expressing their reactions, ideas, and solutions. They then share these ideas with the rest of society through publications, which promotes the absorption and integration of the collective experience into society and people's thinking. Today, unlike in 1977, we see some of this reaction process through the immediate production of tweets and other forms of brief communication. But the process of reacting occurs in a deeper and more thorough way as well through the publication of books, articles, and other written communications.

Levine compared the resignation of President Nixon to the resignations of a New York City mayor and of several state governors. She calculated the information "whomps," or the collective impact of the news, as a multiple of the number of people affected in the country, state, or city by the resignation times the level of stress associated with the resignation and the single hard bit of information, namely, that the resignation had occurred. Obviously the resignation of a US president affects more people than the resignation of a governor or mayor. She then looked at the number of books that appeared in subsequent years in the then-standard listing, the *Cumulative Book Index* (H. W. Wilson Company 1898–1999; the index ceased publication in 1999), and she found that the number of books subsequently appearing about each of the events was roughly proportional with the calculated number of whomps. In other words, societies reflect the impact of important events through publication; the higher the impact, the more publications that result.

Now, I hasten to point out that, in my opinion, there are many methodological and theoretical problems with Levine's article. The initial literature review is superficial and does a poor job of linking the various theories and bodies of research that she cites. Further, there are methodological issues with how she counts whomps. One might argue that a resignation of a state governor affects more than the citizens of that state, and challenge her basis for calculating the amount of hard information and the degree of stress associated with each type of event. In short, there are a lot of issues with this article, and I doubt that it would be published today in this form. But I am glad that the editor (Art Elias) published the article, because the core idea is a powerful one and deserving of more attention.

The discussion and disputation of ideas and events are core to any literate society. It seems to be a reasonable hypothesis that the amount of writing and discussion around certain events or issues would be roughly proportional to their importance to our social discourse. Why is there no bibliometric science today focusing on the measurement and discussion of the number of information whomps associated with various events, or debates about why a particular event produced fewer or more publications than one might have expected? Surely, this kind of measurement would be of interest to historians, social scientists, and information scientists. (We may be returning to these questions through another route, for example, the growing attention recently to discovering the significance of various trends in social media. See, e.g., Mike Thelwall's work on Twitter [Thelwall, Buckley, and Paltoglou 2011; Thelwall et al. 2010].) Thousands of articles have been produced on scientific reputations as measured by number of citations. Though our academic egos are no doubt involved in such questions, surely the study of publication rates as reflections of societal upheaval, stress, and progress is of at least as great importance?

The situation with Levine's idea illustrates another point about creativity in research. Yes, the ideas could have been better developed, and perhaps the colloquialism "whomp" put some people off. But this scrappy little diamond in the rough of an idea is still a diamond—waiting (for the past thirty-five years!) for someone to take it seriously and develop it well and thoughtfully. The lesson: learn to differentiate the several parts of an issue or topic, and select out and develop the good parts. Do not just reject the whole package because some parts of it make you uncomfortable. Derek J. de Solla Price (1975, 1986) studied some basic statistics about publication in the history of science and came up with a remarkable range of important new knowledge about the nature of science and scientific publication patterns. Levine had the great insight to introduce the concept of whomps; whomps are still waiting for their Price for full development.

One final point: I am sure that many people would reject this topic out of hand because of the age of the article. In some contexts, materials that are more than a few months or years old are derisively rejected as being hopelessly out of touch. That is a common way that people unnecessarily limit themselves. In fact, some older things are out of date, and other older things are highly relevant, and can still be the stimulus for further creative developments. One must develop discrimination and selectivity, not just wave something away because it is not currently trendy. *Look for the intrinsic value, not just the current fashion, then reshape the material for the present.* Given the current social media context, and the constant attention to "trending" topics, Levine's idea seems even more relevant—and possibly more easily measured—today than it was at the time of original publication. Even with the demise of the *Cumulative Book Index*, one can still measure the societal impact of various issues and events in book publication, as well as in many other media. Take the earlier idea and adapt it to the current context. Bingo! You have a new area of research.

TOPIC 2: INFORMATION INVESTMENT   As many in the information sciences know, Fritz Machlup (1972) argued that a very large portion of all human economic activity centers on the production and use of information. The book blurb on the publisher's website for his book *The Production and Distribution of Knowledge in the United States* summarizes it nicely: "Machlup's cool appraisal of the data showed that the knowledge industry accounted for nearly 29 percent of the U.S. gross national product, and that 43 percent of the civilian labor force consisted of knowledge transmitters or full-time knowledge receivers. Indeed, the proportion of the labor force involved in the knowledge economy increased from 11 to 32 percent between 1900 and 1959—a monumental shift" (Princeton University Press 2013).

Robert Hayes, professor and former dean at the Graduate School of Library and Information Science at UCLA, produced some research in the early 1980s that I have long felt has much more potential than has actually been developed. A much more recent discussion of this area can be found in Koenig and Manzari's (2010) encyclopedia entry entitled "Productivity Impacts of Libraries and Information Services." Hayes and Erickson (1982), according to Koenig and Manzari, used

> the Cobb-Douglas production function to estimate the value added by information services. In the basic Cobb-Douglas formula, the value

of goals [*sic*: goods?] and services sold is calculated to be the product of a constant times the values of different inputs, labor, capital, and so forth, each raised to a different power (exponent). The exponents are solved for by seeing which exponents best fit a number of separate cases. In the Hayes and Erickson formulation, the value added V in manufacturing industries is a function of labor L, capital K, purchase of information services I, and purchase of other intermediate goods and services X. (Koenig and Manzari 2010, p. 4311)

Hayes and Erickson found that those industries that thrived best over the period he studied were those, such as pharmaceuticals, that had very much larger investments in information relative to the other Cobb-Douglas factors than other industries had. Koenig and Manzari note that Yale Braunstein continued the work, making some modifications in the formula, yet still came out with much the same result—that there is "substantial underinvestment in the purchase of information" (Koenig and Manzari 2010, p. 4311).

I leave it to economists to explicate these ideas—but if the premise holds true that there is huge underinvestment in information in the economy, this should have huge implications for many disciplines, including ours. The argument should be researched and developed further, and the results published in the economics literature, as well as the information sciences literature.

TOPIC 3: DISTILLED INFORMATION   There is yet another sense in which we seldom discuss information, yet that may have interesting implications for theory in the information sciences as well as, ultimately, for practice. This sense concerns the idea of information as a distilled product of thought and communication.

Books, journal articles, newspaper articles, blog entries—even micro-messages such as tweets—are all different forms of work products. Often, they have serious economic value or economic implications. Someone put some brainpower into the creation of them. Furthermore, having created the text, images, and so on, human beings have engaged in various forms of economic production to make them available, whether investing in a printing press and paper or in a computer server to hold this work product ready for access on the Internet.

Both the intellectual investment and the physical investment made so these products will be available represent the information economy in the Machlup and Hayes and Erickson senses. We invest a substantial portion of both our cognitive and physical energies as a society in creating, distributing, and maintaining (in libraries, on the web) these intellectual products. The quantity and quality of the work that goes into these information products vary tremendously, of course. But the same thing about quality and quantity of work could be said of retail clothing, drugs, or many other products of human activity.

But let us focus particularly on these intellectual products. An academic book, for example, may represent a decade, or a lifetime, of research, study, analysis, and writing. We may think of the resulting book as a distillation of all that massive amount of work by an individual. The encyclopedia that I recently edited with Mary Niles Maack (Bates and Maack 2010) had about seven hundred authors, each of whom spent some substantial chunk of time in the preparation and writing of journal-article-length entries. I was retired and spent four years full-time as editor-in-chief of the encyclopedia, while Maack spent many weeks and months as co-editor, taken from her otherwise hectic schedule as a professor, to produce the resulting seven-volume, 5,742-page encyclopedia. On the usual rule of thumb of two thousand hours of work for an individual for a year, the editing alone took five or more person-years. If each of the 565 articles took a month of person-time, which may be an underestimate, forty-seven or more years of person-time went into the creation of the encyclopedia entries. The resulting seven-volume set, taking up a little more than a cubic foot of volume, represents over fifty full-time person-years of human thought, writing, and editing effort.

In fact, each book or other information product can be thought of as such a distillation. *In the network of human relationships and social activity, each document is a node of distillation, a point of intensification of human labor and intellection.* We have developed means of condensing much thought into small packages, and we store those nodes of information all around us. Picture one of those economic atlases that shows the countries of the world, with clear plastic layers that may be laid over the map, each layer representing something of economic interest, such as agricultural production, manufacturing production, and so on. Lay over that map an additional layer that shows the location of information stores. If this is done, then server farms, libraries, bookstores, websites, and many more resources all become points of great intensification of information in the economic map of society.

In my view, the huge amount of energy invested in bibliometric studies of various kinds should include the study of the distribution of these information densities in society, followed by the study of the amount of use that is made of them, where they are underutilized according to formulas such as Cobb-Douglas, and so on.

CONCLUDING THOUGHTS

The role of information in the economy and in social relations is so integral to all we do that it is like the air we breathe. Sometimes we do not see it at all because we take it so much for granted. But it has great meaning and social impact in terms of the mental and physical processing and organizing of our world. There are so many more ways to think about and study the role of information than we have fully engaged in; we have the prospect of huge disciplinary development in the information sciences if we can only start to see the (informational) air we breathe.

NOTE

1. At this time of fluidity in disciplinary boundaries, I use several terms to describe the fields to which these ideas apply, depending on the orientation and emphasis of the work described. "Library and information science (LIS)," "information science," and "the information sciences" are all used here. I discuss these field distinctions in several other publications (see, e.g., Bates 1999, 2007a, 2015).

REFERENCES

Bates, M. J. (1976). Rigorous systematic bibliography. *RQ, 16*(1), 7–26.

Bates, M. J. (1979a). Idea tactics. *Journal of the American Society for Information Science, 30*(5), 280–289.

Bates, M. J. (1979b). Information search tactics. *Journal of the American Society for Information Science, 30*(4), 205–214.

Bates, M. J. (1989). The design of browsing and berrypicking techniques for the online search interface. *Online Review, 13*(5), 407–424.

Bates, M. J. (1999). The invisible substrate of information science. *Journal of the American Society for Information Science, 50*(12), 1043–1050.

Bates, M. J. (2002). The cascade of interactions in the digital library interface. *Information Processing and Management, 38*(3), 381–400.

Bates, M. J. (2005). An introduction to metatheories, theories, and models. In K. E.

Fisher, S. Erdelez, and L. McKechnie (Eds.), *Theories of Information Behavior* (pp. 1–24). Medford, NJ: Information Today.

Bates, M. J. (2007a). Defining the information disciplines in encyclopedia development. *Information Research, 12*(4), paper colis29. Retrieved from http://InformationR.net/ir/12–4/colis/colis29.html.

Bates, M. J. (2007b). What is browsing—really? A model drawing from behavioural science research. *Information Research, 12*(4), paper 330. Retrieved from http://InformationR.net/ir/12–4/paper330.html.

Bates, M. J. (2015). The information professions: Knowledge, memory, heritage. *Information Research, 20*(1), paper 655. Retrieved from http://InformationR.net/ir/20-1/paper655.html.

Bates, M. J., and Maack, M. N. (Eds.). (2010). *Encyclopedia of library and information sciences* (3rd ed.) New York: CRC Press.

Bates, M. J., Wilde, D. N., and Siegfried, S. (1993). An analysis of search terminology used by humanities scholars: The Getty Online Searching Project Report No. 1. *Library Quarterly, 63*(1), 1–39.

Bateson, G. (1968). Information and codification: A philosophical approach. In J. Ruesch and G. Bateson (Eds.), *Communication: The social matrix of psychiatry* (pp. 168–211). New York: Norton.

Beghtol, C. (1994). *The classification of fiction: The development of a system based on theoretical principles.* Metuchen, NJ: Scarecrow Press.

Benham, F., and Powell, R. R. (1987). *Success in answering reference questions: Two studies.* Metuchen, NJ: Scarecrow Press.

Finnegan, W. (1994). Doubt. *New Yorker, 49*(48), 48–67.

Hartel, J. (2010a). Managing documents at home for serious leisure: A case study of the hobby of gourmet cooking. *Journal of Documentation, 66*(6), 847–874.

Hartel, J. (2010b). Time as a framework for information science: Insights from the hobby of gourmet cooking. *Information Research, 15*(4), paper colis715. Retrieved from http://InformationR.net/ir/15–4/colis715.html.

Hartel, J. (2011). Visual approaches and photography for the study of immediate information space. *Journal of the American Society for Information Science and Technology, 62*(11), 2214–2224.

Harter, S. P. (1992). Psychological relevance and information science. *Journal of the American Society for Information Science, 43*(9), 602–615.

Hayes, R. M., and Erickson, T. (1982). Added value as a function of purchases of information services. *Information Society, 1*(4), 307–338.

Hsieh-Yee, I. (1993). Effects of search experience and subject knowledge on the search tactics of novice and experienced searchers. *Journal of the American Society for Information Science, 44*(3), 161–174.

Koenig, M., and Manzari, L. (2010). Productivity impacts of libraries and information services. In M. J. Bates and M. N. Maack (Eds.), *Encyclopedia of library and information sciences* (3rd ed., pp. 4305–4314). New York: CRC Press.

Kuhn, T. S. (2012). *The structure of scientific revolutions* (4th ed.). Chicago: University of Chicago Press.

Levine, M. M. (1977). The informative act and its aftermath: Toward a predictive science of information. *Journal of the American Society for Information Science, 28*(2), 101–106.

Machlup, F. (1972). *The production and distribution of knowledge in the United States*. Princeton, NJ: Princeton University Press.

National Information Standards Organization. (2005). *Guidelines for the construction, format, and management of monolingual controlled vocabularies* (ANSI/NISO Z39.19–2005). Bethesda, MD: NISO Press.

Pejtersen, A. M. (1978). Fiction and library classification. *Scandinavian Public Library Quarterly, 11*(1), 5–12.

Price, D. J. S. (1975). *Science since Babylon*. New Haven, CT: Yale University Press.

Price, D. J. S. (1986). *Little science, big science—and beyond*. New York: Columbia University Press.

Saarti, J. (1999). Fiction indexing and the development of fiction thesauri. *Journal of Librarianship and Information Science, 31*(2), 85–92.

Sperber, D., and Wilson, D. (1995). *Relevance: Communication and cognition* (2nd ed.). Malden, MA: Blackwell.

Thelwall, M., Buckley, K., and Paltoglou, G. (2011). Sentiment in Twitter events. *Journal of the American Society for Information Science and Technology, 62*(2), 406–418.

Thelwall, M., Buckley, K., Paltoglou, G., Cai, D., and Kappas, A. (2010). Sentiment strength detection in short informal text. *Journal of the American Society for Information Science and Technology, 61*(12), 2544–2558.

US General Accounting Office. (1987). *Tax administration: Accessibility, timeliness, and accuracy of IRS' telephone assistance program* (GAO/GGD-88-17). Retrieved from http://www.gao.gov/assets/210/209820.pdf.

US General Accounting Office. (1990). *Tax administration: Monitoring the accuracy and administration of IRS' 1989 test call survey* (GAO/GGD-90-37). Retrieved from http://www.gao.gov/assets/220/211963.pdf.

White, H. D. (2007a). Combining bibliometrics, information retrieval, and relevance theory, Part 1: First examples of a synthesis. *Journal of the American Society for Information Science and Technology, 58*(4), 536–559.

White, H. D. (2007b). Combining bibliometrics, information retrieval, and relevance theory, Part 2: Some implications for information science. *Journal of the American Society for Information Science and Technology, 58*(4), 583–605.

Wilson, P. (1968). *Two kinds of power: An essay on bibliographic control*. Berkeley: University of California Press.

Wolfe, J. M. (1994). Guided search 2.0: A revised model of visual search. *Psychonomic Bulletin and Review, 1*(2), 202–238.

Xie, H. (2000). Shifts of interactive intentions and information-seeking strategies in interactive information retrieval. *Journal of the American Society for Information Science, 51*(9), 841–857.

CHAPTER 3

REFLECTIONS ON THEORY CONSTRUCTION IN HUMAN INFORMATION BEHAVIOR: A THEORY OF BROWSING

SHANJU LIN CHANG

THIS CHAPTER IS A REFLECTION ON how I developed a multidimensional theory of a common phenomenon—browsing. It describes the formation of the research questions, the various stages of a comprehensive literature review, and the analysis. Also delineated in this chapter are the thought processes on one of the major challenges in the construction of theory—how to develop data collection and analysis methods that will eventually lead to a theory. Some lessons learned from this process conclude the chapter.

PREFACE

When a student engages in scholarship at the PhD level, she usually starts with an inquiry about a phenomenon that is both intriguing to herself and important to the scientific community. Initially, she might not think that she will build a theory or anything close to it. It is the process of knowledge creation that leads her to develop relevant constructs and relationships for understanding that phenomenon, which in turn leads her to the development of a theory.

THE FORMATION OF A RESEARCH TOPIC

I picked up on the topic of browsing from informal talks with faculty members over the course of several years in the school where I was studying. "Why is browsing important?" I asked.

Before going further, I observed that browsing was an interesting phenomenon commonly experienced in library use and online public access catalogs (OPACs), and it was also a common experience during window shopping. However, the notion of browsing was not well understood, and the importance of it increased as the development of hypertexts emerged in the technological arena. With that, I went on to conduct a literature search, trying to get a general picture of how browsing activities were conceptualized and studied.

THE LITERATURE REVIEW: A JOURNEY TO THE UNKNOWN

The first step in conducting the literature review was to examine what the literature had to say about browsing, the topic to be studied. After a preliminary survey, I realized that the central goal of my research was to clarify the notion of browsing—that is, to identify the underlying dimensions of browsing, if any.

The literature review was crucial, allowing me to identify some important constructs across different literatures from various disciplines. I repeated the process of searching, reading, discussing, and reflecting on the materials found. From time to time, it was necessary to create an imaginative space in my mind and compare what I observed in real life to what the literature said.

SEARCHING

Using my professional training in searching, I surveyed every database I considered relevant to finding out how authors in the research literature conceptualized the notion of browsing, or how they conducted related studies. I used only a simple keyword search term—"browsing"—and its variants. The results quickly indicated many studies in the field of library and information science, but there were also some potentially relevant resources that emerged in unexpected areas.

DETERMINING RELEVANCY OF DIFFERENT LITERATURES

I first delved into the universe of browsing discourse in library science, information retrieval, and consumer behavior. After discussion with my adviser, Ron Rice (well known for his research in communication), I also looked at audience research in mass communication and social browsing research in organizational communication. Finally, through snowballing, that is, seeking out and reading materials mentioned in a relevant resource, I delved into the discourse of way-finding in environmental design.

It seemed a little odd for a library and information science (LIS) student to search in media communication, organizational communication, and environmental design research on this topic. However, a media viewer is like a book reader. Channels are like book chapters or journal articles. Using a control panel to switch channels is functionally similar to using a hand to turn the pages to different sections of a book. Furthermore, a person can be considered a book, to be read by another person through conversation. Looking for the right person to talk to by arranging a meeting or bumping into one another is like a planned or unplanned search for a book of interest.

In the way-finding literature, I saw another good metaphor: the physical structure of a space is akin to the invisible information structure in cyberspace. There are physical highways that lead to physical destinations, and there are information highways that lead to intellectual destinations. That is, trying to find a physical destination or to explore a new place is analogous to trying to navigate through various hyperlinks on a website in order to find a specific page or to see the contents of the website. The distinction between search path and content viewing emerges from this analogy.

ORGANIZING AND REFLECTING

I started to see that the notion of browsing, although not necessarily identified and discussed using the same vocabulary in all disciplines, refers to a kind of behavior involving scanning something, such as looking through magazines or books on a bookshelf, citations on a computer screen, objects in a shop window, channels on a TV, people in their offices, and so on. Then the idea emerged that browsing does not have to be strictly visual, but can also be audio. Is there something in common between a person pushing a scan button and trying to select a radio station to listen to and looking through some books in order to select what he or she desires to borrow or buy?

My task was to describe the nature of this common phenomenon. While reading the literature, I asked myself: How can I organize the reading notes in a meaningful and useful way? By discipline or by the research questions I raised? It seemed more straightforward to do so by discipline and then break it down by research questions within each discipline. When I read the literature within a discipline, I asked the author of each document to answer my research questions: What is browsing? Why do people browse? What influences browsing behavior? What are the consequences of browsing? I took notes on the definitions, the motivations, the consequences, and the influential factors.

Checking the dictionary during the literature review turned out to be more crucial than I had imagined. Through comparing and contrasting different definitions, I started to identify important aspects of the browsing phenomenon. For one, there were behavioral characteristics (e.g., eye movement), and for another, there were cognitive characteristics (e.g., without real knowledge) and motivational characteristics (e.g., in order to select for reading or purchasing). All involved some sort of resource (e.g., books, products, etc.) or object.

I used similar "compare-and-contrast" strategies to identify the common dimensions of browsing in the literature from each discipline. For example, in the literature from library science, Apted (1971) discusses three forms of browsing: (1) specific browsing—when a user makes a literature search through a bibliographic tool, but does not start with a formal search strategy; (2) general purposive browsing—a planned or unplanned examination of sources, journals, books, or other media in the hope of discovering unspecified new information; and (3) general browsing—random, nonpurposive, passing-time browsing.

Herner (1970) derives three similar categories that he labeled directed browsing; semi-directed, or predictive, browsing; and undirected browsing. To synthesize Apted and Herner, different forms of browsing emerge according to

1. the types of *resources* the user interacts with (bibliographic tools, books, journals),
2. the *purpose* of examining a resource (discovering information, passing time),
3. the specificity of the search *goal* (unspecified, vague search, low in document specificity), and
4. the presence or absence of a *plan* (random, planned, unplanned, without planning).

Levine (1969) characterizes browsing according to the browser's *knowledge or familiarity with the external information store or environment* he or she interacts with, as follows. Browsing as a sensory intake of information seems to take a number of forms: (1) random browsing through an *unknown* collection; (2) quasi-random browsing through an area of a building or a *collection previously explored*; and (3) semideterministically in a *limited physical area or bounded intellectual area*.

This description, like Herner's, implies that the way people go about browsing (i.e., directed, patterned, or undirected movement) is influenced by their external knowledge (including experience) within the information space. Thus, one additional dimension for the categorization of browsing is *knowledge* about resources and their locations.

In summarizing from each disciplinary review of literature, I explained what additional dimensions were identified and pointed out the outstanding, or missing, subdimensions within each dimension as well.

THE RESULT OF THE LITERATURE REVIEW:
A PRELIMINARY THEORY

The literature review resulted in a preliminary theory that identified salient dimensions from multiple disciplines for understanding browsing. The preliminary theory described four dimensions important to understanding the phenomenon: behavioral, cognitive, motivational, and resource. Each of these included two subdimensional aspects: scanning and movement, knowledge and plan, goal and purpose, and form (e.g., information or representation) and focus (e.g., content and structure), respectively. This preliminary theory, published as chapter 4 in my thesis (Chang 1995), became a milestone for my research. The identified dimensions served as the basic concepts to be analyzed with empirical data, thus becoming the guideline for later data analysis.

Although I had completed a comprehensive literature review, which was later published as a chapter in the *Annual Review of Information Science and Technology* (Chang and Rice 1993), I was still in search of a definition of browsing. There was no consensus in the literature because each study either used its own definition of browsing or did not offer an explicit definition.

DESIGN OF AN EMPIRICAL STUDY: THE MOST CHALLENGING STEP

The next question was how I could empirically investigate the phenomenon. To start an empirical investigation, I needed a definition of browsing, but I did not have one.

Several authors indicated that it was difficult to devise an empirical study for investigating the phenomenon of browsing, noting that the absence of a widely accepted definition and normative data on browsing habits in existing libraries renders problematic their description, measurement, and evaluation. Questionnaires, record keeping, personal diaries, user choices between alternatives, and subjective estimates of probabilities or costs involved in browsing had all been suggested as sources for data collection. Licklider (1965) advised researchers to look at the user's account of browsing activities and to define the conditions or courses of action in the domain of browsing.

One thing consistent throughout the literature was a call for the investigation of people's goals and motives during the information-seeking process in general (Belkin et al. 1990; Roberts 1982) and browsing in particular (Ayris 1986; Boll 1985; O'Connor 1993). Thus, the design of my empirical study of browsing behavior focused on the identification of browsing activities, and the conditions—including goals and motives—that lead people to engage in those activities. It sought to answer the following two fundamental questions: What is the nature of browsing? What motivates people to browse?

What should one investigate in order to answer questions such as "What constitutes browsing?" or "Is there an underlying structure of browsing?" or "What motivates people to browse?" One way is to point to a set of behaviors with some characteristics, label or define them as browsing, and then ask people what they did and the motivation behind it. This approach is taken by most researchers conducting empirical studies in the literature. In this way, one may be able to determine the motivations of some forms of browsing that were already preconceptualized, because those behaviors were selected beforehand. However, this approach would not lead me to an analytical language to describe the browsing phenomenon.

Another approach is to observe what people do with a resource in a library and ask them what they intend to do, that is, to investigate the information-seeking behavior as a whole, with an attempt to identify some common characteristics manifested in browsing activities. I realized I needed to look at all sorts of information activities and adopt a broad concept extracted from the literature that is shared among all disciplines—scanning a resource, to start with.

DATA COLLECTION STAGE: A QUALITATIVE START

On the basis of my decisions regarding the empirical study design and preliminary theory, I identified the interaction between a person and an information object (broadly defined) as the focus of data collection in my investigation. In addition to observable behaviors, a person's motivation, intent, and knowledge and the characteristics of the interacted resource were all important elements in describing the phenomenon under study.

Thus, in my empirical investigation, I followed library visitors who agreed to participate and reveal the purpose of their visit and the resources to be used. After approaching each participant, I recorded on a separate form the purpose of his or her visit and resources he or she intended to use that day. I observed what the participants did, recorded their behaviors with as much detail as possible, and interviewed them at the end of their visit. During the interview, for each behavior I observed, I asked participants what their intent was, how successful they were, and why they felt that way about it.

Since it was important to consider a person's motivation (purpose and intent) and the resources she or he interacted with, it was also important to include different types of libraries as locations for data collection. That is, because different types of libraries target different types of users, participants with various purposes of visit or motives in interacting with resources could be drawn from different types of libraries, such as academic, public, and special libraries. Thus, I collected data at academic, public, and special libraries to maximize participant diversity.

Those participants whose stated purpose of visit was irrelevant to the study, such as returning books, were eliminated from further data collection. The data collected from all other participants were descriptions of the participants' behavior and transcripts from each interview, as well as answers to the questions on the form recording the purpose of visit.

DATA ANALYSIS STAGE: THE LONGEST JOURNEY

I looked at the data collected to understand what people did in the library, what they intended to do, and how successful they were in achieving each intention, along with the reasons for their perceptions regarding success. At this stage, I had to ponder about what was to be analyzed and how. With the data in hand, the answers to these questions were not as obvious as they had seemed when I planned the study.

There were several ways to analyze the data. First, I needed to decide what the unit of analysis was. Initially, one might intuitively think to divide the text from the transcripts by the interviewer's prompts, such as "I observe you doing X; what was your intent?" "How successful were you?" and so forth. However, one instance of observation could include more than one object, such as repeating the act of retrieving a book, flipping through it, and putting it back. Should the unit of analysis be each of the books retrieved? Or should the unit of analysis be the intention behind retrieving a book or books? Once again, the literature review provided meaningful insight.

The literature review revealed several important concepts. Different motivations or intents/goals tend to lead to different browsing activities. Similarly, interacting with different objects also points to a potential change in a person's intention. Thus, the unit of analysis was determined not by the interviewer's questions but by the object examined or when an intention shifted. The important role of the two constructs, object and intention, was also suggested in the preliminary theory constructed through my literature analysis. For me, this was a major breakthrough in investigating this phenomenon at the data analysis stage.

So here is what I had in mind. For each case, an obvious unit of analysis was a person's movement around the library, moving from one place to another as laid out by the library structure, such as the OPACs station, the journal section, and so on. Such movements were considered the higher level of a unit of analysis. Within each movement, a unit of analysis at the lower level, an episode, was considered present when an intention or an object changed.

Thus, the relationships between a case, a movement, and an episode were described as follows: A case is composed of one or more movements, which are indicated by either a physical place (e.g., from an information retrieval section to a section of bookshelf) or a logical place (e.g., from one article to the other). A movement is composed of one or more episodes, which are defined by either an intent/goal or an object. For each movement, the episodes that were considered as browsing in its most general sense (as discussed in the preliminary model) were first identified. That is, the episodes that involved "scanning a library resource" were considered as potential browsing activities to be further analyzed.

Once I had identified the unit of analysis, I needed to decide what was to be analyzed. For the purpose of conceptualizing the notion of browsing, data analysis was guided, but not limited, by my preliminary theory, and browsing activities were identified and analyzed within the whole spectrum of library activities in which people engage. That is, in order to understand what constitutes browsing behavior, other kinds of information activities or nonbrowsing activities were also identified and examined. Specifically, in order to verify and clarify those constructs in the preliminary theory, empirical evidence was established by examining the study participants' scanning behavior, their motivations, the resources they interacted with, and the participants' cognitive aspects.

THE THEORIZING STAGE: AN INTELLECTUAL LEAP

At this point, the procedures of data analysis were developed, and I used a bottom-up approach to identify and define relevant constructs from the empirical evidence. The results were grounded independent *constructs* within each *dimension*, in the sense that each construct was substantialized with identifiable *categories*.

For example, the motivation dimension—the intent or goal for scanning a resource—included seven categories. These were as follows: to locate, to confirm, to evaluate, to keep up, to learn something, to satisfy curiosity, and to entertain oneself. Similarly, in the cognitive dimension, a new construct—object, which refers to what the patron scanning a resource is seeking or expecting—contained five categories (something *specific*, things with *common characteristics*, things in a *location*, something *in general*, and *none to be specified*).

It is not enough to just identify some meaningful categories or facets of a construct. To build up a theory, the researcher needs to ask what the relationships are among the categories of each construct. That is, what are the properties that connect these categories within that construct? Similar inquiries were also applied to other constructs.

Take the *object* construct as an example. The object that a study participant intended to interact with may be a specific item, multiple items that share some common characteristics, a specific location, something in general, or nothing specific. Again, I needed to ask myself, "What is the relationship that connects each of the categories (i.e., specific, common, location, general, none) within the *object* construct?"

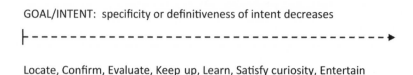

GOAL/INTENT: specificity or definitiveness of intent decreases

Locate, Confirm, Evaluate, Keep up, Learn, Satisfy curiosity, Entertain

FIGURE 3.1. The goal/intent construct (Chang 1995, p. 146)

Day after day, I pondered about the phenomena I had observed in the data. After I had considered every category of each construct, the underlying essence finally dawned on me: *specificity*. I described my understanding of this in my dissertation as follows.

The construct of the motivational dimension (intent or goal) involves differing degrees of open-endedness to the criteria for valid information acquisition. The terms "specificity" and "vagueness" are both often used in the literature in regard to this characteristic of browsing. The left end of the continuum in figure 3.1 reflects the nature of the goal when the object intended is predetermined and well specified. As we move along the continuum, the specificity of the patron's goal decreases, as what the patron intends to accomplish is increasingly determined by the information encountered during the scanning process. Thus, "satisfying curiosity" is a goal that is primarily indefinite, to the extent that it is determined by external information objects. The prototypical browsing appears to occur when the patron's goal is to evaluate whether or not an item is of interest, is worth looking into, is useful, or has the right level of information on a topic.

The notion of object refers to what the patron scanning a resource is seeking or expecting. At one extreme, the patron's object is a specifically identified object, such as a book or a journal. That is to say, the specified item is the one and only item sought, which can be a specified logical item, such as an article seen before, or a piece of information, such as the "size of a protein enzyme." At the other extreme, the object to be sought has not been defined beforehand, and no specific location or content was determined at the outset. In between these two extremes, the patron knows that the type of object sought is at a specific location, but no item at that location is specified. Rather, the patron intends to scan the items of the location to see what is in there. A typical browsing activity often involves ob-

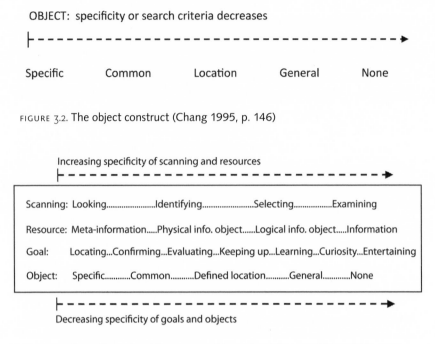

OBJECT: specificity or search criteria decreases

Specific Common Location General None

FIGURE 3.2. The object construct (Chang 1995, p. 146)

Increasing specificity of scanning and resources

Scanning: Looking......................Identifying.......................Selecting.................Examining

Resource: Meta-information.....Physical info. object......Logical info. object.....Information

Goal: Locating...Confirming...Evaluating...Keeping up...Learning...Curiosity...Entertaining

Object: Specific............Common...........Defined location...........General...........None

Decreasing specificity of goals and objects

FIGURE 3.3. Four-dimensional taxonomy of browsing (Chang 1995, p. 147)

jects with common characteristics. That is, although patrons may or may not bring with them a specific idea of what will be of interest, no specific documents are sought. Rather, some attributes of a resource are examined upon encounter. Thus, as one proceeds along the object dimension toward the right, the specificity of the object decreases. As with the *goal* dimension, object specificity involves differing degrees of open-endedness to the criteria for valid information acquisition. That is, vagueness about what to look for increases as one travels rightward from point to point (fig. 3.2).

In this manner, the four constructs, with associated elements (or categories), that can be utilized to describe the process of browsing are (1) the specificity of the *scanning* activity, (2) the specificity of information provided by the *resource*, (3) the specificity of the patron's *goal or intent*, and (4) the specificity of the *object* sought.

Thus, a four-dimensional taxonomy of browsing can be developed according to the level of scanning, the kind of resource scanned, the type of goal, and the object. Figure 3.3 illustrates the continuum for each construct.

The categories, or elements, identified within each construct can serve as an analytical language to describe various types of browsing. Take an example. In my study one participant responded to my question about his intent behind an activity I observed him doing as follows: "[I was] scanning the bookshelf to find new biographies to read," which can be described as *examining information objects* to *locate* items that have *common* characteristics. This is a frequently observed instance of shelf-browsing in the public library to select a nonfiction book to read (Ayris 1986).

Scanning as a "nonverbal behavior" (where there is no need to express intent or make any statement in words) is considered a browsing activity, especially when it involves the more attentive acts of identifying, selecting, and examining. Behaviorally, browsing is increasingly easy to recognize as the level of scanning activity increases, that is, when a patron's behavior involves selecting and examining an item after looking through a series of items. The "resource scanned" refers to a series of information items under consideration. Four levels of a resource are identified according to the specificity of information provided for examination. The goal construct involves differing degrees of open-endedness to the criteria for valid information acquisition. The object construct refers to what the patron scanning a resource is seeking or expecting (table 3.1).

Table 3.1. The four constructs and elements within each construct in the taxonomy of a browsing process

	Construct			
	Scanning	*Form of resource*	*Goal*	*Object*
Categories in constructs	Looking	Meta-information	Locate	Specific item
	Identifying	Physical information object	Confirm	Common items
	Selecting		Evaluate	Defined location
	Examining	Logical information object	Keep up	
			Learn	General
		Information	Satisfy curiosity	None
			Entertain	

Source: Based on Chang (1995, p. 147).

BREAKING NEW GROUND

After identifying the four dimensions that can be used to describe the underlying constructs of a browsing process (i.e., scanning, resource, goal, object), I realized that a major problem in the previous literature was the ambiguity between the constructs of the browsing process itself and those that affect the process of browsing.

For example, knowledge about the object sought appeared to be an important construct both in the literature and in my empirical analysis. According to the literature (Levine 1969), the most relevant knowledge about a resource is related to two salient facets of the resource: knowledge of the structure or search paths of a resource, and knowledge of the content of a resource. However, my analysis of the empirical data showed that knowledge as a construct of the cognitive dimension is an influential factor of a browsing process rather than one defining it. In other words, through the empirical data analysis, I found that some constructs are useful to describe patterns of browsing rather than being types of a browsing process themselves. That is, patterns of browsing can be characterized by the type of browsing that the patron engages in, along with four additional constructs—movement, knowledge, purpose, and information organization. On the basis of the identified constructs, an important finding emerged: different patterns of browsing can be identified.

Take *situational browsing* (identified in my research as pattern 2) as an example. Situational browsing is characterized by examining other unknown items during the process of locating a specific item, once the general area containing the needed item is identified. One patron in my study looked for geotechnical information for his projects, searched in the OPAC by author, and found the specific author's work listed. He then went to the book stacks in order to retrieve it. While he was approaching the specific area of the book stacks (as identified in the OPAC), he was exposed to a related section of interest and decided to look for some books on a topic of interest—groundwater. The type of browsing involved in this episode can be described as *examining physical information objects to evaluate items with common characteristics*, which supports his original *purpose*. Another pattern of browsing—pattern 3, *opportunistic browsing*, involves scanning other items "incidental to the original purpose" during the process of locating a specific, intended item.

Situational browsing thus differs from opportunistic browsing in the entry point of browsing: situational browsing starts near the location of a known item on a given path in the same resource area to support the original goal, whereas opportunistic browsing occurs on some path taken toward finding a specified item. Thus, while the *structure of information organization* influences situational browsing, *movement* between resources influences opportunistic browsing.

It is also worth noting that with respect to knowledge, my analysis of empirical data showed that a browser's "plan" as a construct discussed in the literature is not an essential element in defining browsing, but the construct of *object* is.

PUTTING IT ALL TOGETHER: THE ENTIRE THEORY

My theory construction process thus yielded a theory that documented why, how, and what people browse. The theory suggests that four dimensions characterize browsing: behavior, motivation, cognition, and resource. Specifically, four constructs within each dimension are useful to describe any browsing process. A taxonomy of browsing, with empirical evidence on the first set of four constructs in the model (i.e., scanning, form of resource, goal, object), was proposed.

Along with the second set of four other constructs (movement, purpose, knowledge, and focus of resource), nine patterns of browsing were identified. Together with a follow-up study on the consequences of browsing (Chang 2000), I proposed a theory for understanding the influential factors in the process of browsing and the process of browsing itself, as well as the consequences of browsing.

This theory suggests that movement, purpose, knowledge, and focus in the behavioral, motivational, cognitive, and resource dimensions, respectively, influence the browsing process in which people engage. In turn, the browsing process (described by the four constructs—scanning, goal/intent, object, and form) helps to determine general themes and specific types of browsing. Note that the "plan" construct in the preliminary framework was eventually dropped from the final theoretical framework.

In seeking the answer to the questions "How does browsing occur?" and "What motivates people to browse?" nine specific patterns of browsing within each of five general themes were identified: (1) looking for a specific item—includes *situational browsing* and *opportunistic browsing*; (2) looking for something with common characteristics—includes *systematic browsing, evaluative browsing,* and *focus browsing;* (3) keeping up to date—*monitoring browsing;* (4) learning or finding out—includes *indicative browsing* and *preparatory browsing;* and (5) goal free—*invitational browsing.*

For example, *situational browsing* is characterized by examining unknown items during the process of locating a specific item, once the general area containing the needed item has been identified. *Opportunistic browsing* is differentiated from situational browsing because it is characterized by "scanning other items" incidental to the original purpose during the process of locating a specific, intended item. Details regarding these and the other patterns are provided in Chang (1995) and Rice, McCreadie, and Chang (2001; see esp. pp. 171–297).

On the basis of my research findings, I could now answer the question "What is the definition of browsing?" Browsing in essence is an examination of unknown items of potential interest by scanning or moving through an information space in order to judge the utility of the items, to learn something of interest, or to satisfy curiosity about something. Browsing is often associated with the vagueness of information objects sought. The nature of browsing is fundamentally evaluative and inclusive. At the micro level, the nature of a browser's goal/intent and the specificity of the object sought are the two most important factors influencing the way people browse.

FINAL REMARKS

At the end of this theory construction process, I suggested that the concept of browsing is multifaceted. It serves as a search strategy when people are exposed to many alternatives in looking for useful or interesting documents or when trying to locate information items not considered beforehand or not found with the bibliographic tools available. It also serves as a screening technique to help people decide what not to read, to filter out unknown items that are of potential interest but actually not interesting or useful upon examination. Browsing also serves as a viewing pattern in that the browser intends to identify something to read by glancing through (or "reading") the unknown items encountered in the process, but he or she stops reading as soon as he or she realizes the item holds no interest. Such an evaluative viewing process can often result in a learning effect simply because of the opportunity of encountering the unknown. Finally, browsing is also a recreational activity that people engage in to satisfy the need for enjoyment or diversion.

The fact that browsing behavior is characterized by this idea of examining unknown items by scanning or moving through an information space seems to explain why people so frequently browse; we are often surrounded (physically, intellectually, and increasingly, virtually) with unknown items—all kinds of information objects and information, or even meta-information—in this complex and fast-changing world.

There are several implications of this research for systems design and evaluation; for example, personal attributes and "browsability" should be considered in systems design and evaluation. The findings also suggest that information providers such as librarians should arrange physical layouts and displays in a way that encourages successful and enjoyable browsing. Future research might test the browsing theory in alternative settings, such as shopping malls or websites.

My research also has implications for further study. In *Accessing and Browsing Information and Communication*, coauthored with Rice and McCreadie and published by MIT Press, I describe the theory I developed in my dissertation and report additional results of a continuing study to answer another research question—"What are the consequences of browsing?"—by analyzing study participants' responses to the questions "How successful were you?" and "Why do you feel that way about it?" (Rice et al. 2001).

In my work, I have identified the following means of disseminating theory: present it at relevant conferences; publish it in peer-reviewed journals or monographs; recruit graduate students to test and subsequently modify your theory or methodology when applicable; publish your theory, including related research, in other languages; use social media such as blogs and videos to present and discuss your work; and investigate your theory in other settings or with different types of study participants.

For example, one of my graduate students is testing the browsing theory with consumers at an online bookstore, comparing how the patterns of browsing differ in physical and virtual spaces. I also published translations of my theory and wrote papers describing related work in another language (Chinese). This, of course, has had little influence on Western scholarship as a whole, but it served to widen my audience.

Among the various options for presenting my work, I have found that publishing in a peer-reviewed journal is more useful than publishing in a monograph, although publishing a monograph with a prestigious publisher is helpful in gaining recognition. My article on browsing, coauthored with Rice and appearing in the *Annual Review of Information Science and Technology* (ARIST; Chang and Rice 1993), has been cited much more often than the MIT book mentioned above or the chapter on browsing that I wrote for the ASIST monograph, *Theories of Information Behaviors* (Chang 2005). From my personal experience in using and developing theory, the most important step for its effective dissemination is to emphasize linking the theory to applications in the real world and to publish it in the right venues, depending on the audiences you want to reach.

Publishing your work gives you the opportunity to engage in scholarly discussions about your ideas. In 2007, Marcia Bates published an article titled "What Is Browsing—Really?" In response to the notion of browsing proposed in our book, she argued that browsing is better conceived as a behavioral concept. Hjørland (2011) took Bates's argument as an example of a theory-based interdisciplinary approach to understanding an important concept in information science. My own continuing research, however, indicates that the defining characteristic of browsing is closer to a cognitive concept than to a behavioral one.

Thus the discussion regarding browsing, at least in the information sciences, is not concluded. My journey as a PhD student led to a contribution to this discussion but, as usually happens in theory development, not the final word.

REFERENCES

Apted, S. M. (1971). General purposive browsing. *Library Association Record, 73*(12), 228–230.
Ayris, P. (1986). *The stimulation of creativity: A review of the literature concerning the concept of browsing, 1970–1985* (CRUS Working Paper No. 5). Sheffield: University of Sheffield, Center for Research on User Studies (CRUS).
Bates, M. (2007). What is browsing—really? *Information Research, 12*(4), paper 330. Retrieved from http://www.informationr.net/ir/12–4/paper330.html
Belkin, N. J., Chang, S., Downs, T., Saracevic, T., and Zhao, S. (1990). Taking account of user tasks, goals and behavior for the design of online public access catalogs. In D. Henderson (Ed.), *Proceedings of the 53rd annual meeting of the American Society for Information Science* (pp. 69–79). Medford, NJ: Learned Information.
Boll, J. J. (1985). Shelf browsing, open access and storage capacity in research li-

braries. *Occasional Papers No. 169*. University of Illinois, Graduate School of Library Science.

Chang, S.-J. L. (1995). *Toward a multidimensional framework for understanding browsing* (Unpublished doctoral dissertation). Rutgers University, New Brunswick, NJ.

Chang, S.-J. L. (2000). Research on browsing behavior in the libraries: An empirical analysis of consequences, success, and influences (in Chinese). *Journal of Library and Information Studies, 15*, 37–68.

Chang, S.-J. L. (2005). Chang's browsing. In K. E. Fisher, S. Erdelez, and L. E. F. McKechnie (Eds.), *Theories of information behavior* (pp. 69–74). Medford, NJ: Information Today.

Chang, S.-J. L., and Rice, R. E. (1993). Browsing: A multidimensional framework. *Annual Review of Information Science and Technology, 28*, 231–276.

Herner, S. (1970). Browsing. In A. Kent and H. Lancour (Eds.), *Encyclopedia of library and information science* (Vol. 3, pp. 408–415). New York: Marcel Dekker.

Hjørland, B. (2011). The importance of theories of knowledge: Browsing as an example. *Journal of the American Society for Information, 62*(3), 594–603.

Levine, M. M. (1969). An essay on browsing. *RQ, 9*(1), 35–36, 93.

Licklider, J. C. R. (1965). Appendix I: Proposed experiments in browsing. In C. Overhage and R. Harman (Eds.), *INTREX: Report of a planning conference on information transfer experiments* (pp. 187–197). Cambridge, MA: MIT Press.

O'Connor, B. (1993). Browsing: A framework for seeking functional information. *Knowledge: Creation, Diffusion and Utilization, 15*(2), 211–232.

Rice, R. E., McCreadie, M., and Chang, S.-J. L. (2001). *Accessing and browsing information and communication*. Cambridge, MA: MIT Press.

Roberts, N. (1982). A search for information man. *Social Science Information Studies, 2*, 93–104.

CHAPTER 4

REFLECTIONS ON THE DEVELOPMENT
OF A THEORETICAL PERSPECTIVE

CAROL COLLIER KUHLTHAU

A THEORETICAL PERSPECTIVE PROVIDES a lens for seeing patterns and understanding principles that allows interpretation for meaningful action. In this chapter I reflect on the development of a theoretical perspective based on research that resulted in the well-regarded information search process (ISP) model. The journey began with a theoretical perspective from an allied field that disclosed the "big problem": from the user's perspective, complex information-seeking tasks involve a holistic process of seeking meaning rather than merely retrieving information. Kelly's personal construct theory was influential in developing a hunch for framing the initial qualitative study that opened the black box of student research. The journey next included deciding how to portray the sequence of experience that resulted in the ISP model; using a combination of methods over many years to verify, refine, and expand the model; proposing a statement of theoretical principle from the core concepts; and developing a theoretical approach to intervention for library and information services. Conversations with colleagues all along the way fostered and encouraged the work. Current collaborative work on Guided Inquiry applies ISP research to designing schools to engage students in learning and creating with vast sources of information, relieving the narrow dominance of skills and testing. The chapter closes with the challenge that the insights and wisdom of library and information science be transported to allied fields to provide solutions to entrenched problems as well as open equal opportunities for innovation in the expanding technological information environments.

BEGINNING WITH A THEORETICAL
PERSPECTIVE FROM AN ALLIED FIELD

"Theory" seems like such a grand word. I certainly didn't set out to develop a theory. I did start out with a theoretical perspective from the allied field of education. As I reflect on how I acquired a theoretical perspective, I realize that my undergraduate work was firmly grounded in John Dewey's philosophy of education, along with the work of other learning theorists, particularly the constructivists. I was strongly influenced by Dewey's (1944) experiential learning, the view that optimal learning is a holistic constructive process actively involving the whole person.

As I became more reflective in my own education, I began to experience learning as a process of construction. I saw that learning at its best is holistic, active, and engaging. Learning can be fun, sometimes flowing along effortlessly, but it is also a struggle requiring dogged perseverance.

In my early years as a teacher I experimented with ways to engage my students in their own learning. I looked through a constructivist lens to judge successful learning. My goal was for my students to be interested in what they were learning, motivated to learn more, and eager to tell others about their learning. When they weren't, I adopted other ways to engage them in their own learning. My constructivist view of learning was a theoretical perspective that directed my teaching practice.

INFORMATION SEEKING AS LEARNING

Later, while studying for my master's degree in library and information science (MLIS), and in light of my experiences as a teacher, I realized that I was most interested in information seeking that resulted in learning. Information seeking that a person pursues for the purpose of learning seemed to me both interesting and important. Studying the traditions and knowledge of the library profession along with the research and concepts of the information sciences expanded my expertise and broadened my vision for creating an environment for independent learning and inquiry. This vision melded with my constructivist view of learning.

This theoretical perspective became an internal lens for assessing the effectiveness of my work as a librarian in a secondary school. Were students interested and engaged in the ideas they were encountering? Were they motivated to go further into their investigation and inquiry? To my mind, a librarian collected and organized sources for efficient retrieval and also provided access to multiple quality resources for independent learning and inquiry. I enjoyed my work and was very good at it. But over time I was confronted with a disturbing problem. I discovered that the traditions and knowledge of the library profession and the research and concepts of the information sciences couldn't address some troubling questions that my constructivist view of learning revealed in my everyday library practice.

THE BIG PROBLEM

I was quite successful at teaching students to locate sources and helping them to retrieve information for research assignments. But I had a lingering sense that something was missing. After students found some information, the real learning was ahead of them. Could they manage that on their own? I really didn't know what went on between the time they left the library with some information sources and the time they handed in their research paper. Even when a class was scheduled for several days in the library, I didn't seem to get much beyond information location for the ideas they needed to grapple with to actually learn something. My research was grounded in this lingering sense that something important was going on that I wasn't getting at in my everyday library practice.

I also noticed a recurring problem. No matter how well students were oriented to the library and its resources or how bright they seemed, there was a common pattern of behavior when they came to the library for the first days of their research. Students became confused and uncertain in the early stages of a research project, often expressing annoyance at the assignment, the library, and themselves.

I needed to understand how students learned from multiple sources and why it was so hard for them to engage in their own inquiry before I could more effectively assist them. I felt compelled to dig more deeply into their experience in the process of learning from information. I was driven to research by the "big problem" that had emerged before me.

Thus my research into the user's perspective of the process of information seeking began in the early 1980s with my experience with students as a secondary school librarian, and it continues to this day. This was the research problem that got me started on my scholarly journey, and it is a problem that still fascinates me.

STARTING WITH A HUNCH

In the early 1980s, I discovered Taylor's (1968) levels of information need, Saracevic's (1975) work on relevance, Belkin's (1980) work on the anomalous state of knowledge, and Bates's (1979) idea tactics. But it was George Kelly's (1963) personal construct theory that really struck a chord with me at the time.

Kelly analyzes the experience of constructing meaning from new information, explaining that information is assimilated in a series of phases, beginning with confusion. Confusion increases as inconsistencies and incompatibilities are confronted between new information and the constructs the person already holds. As confusion mounts, it frequently causes doubt. The disruption caused by the new ideas may become so threatening that the new information is discarded and construction of new meaning is abandoned. At this point, Kelly proposes an alternative to move the process of construction along. The person may form a tentative hypothesis to move toward incorporating the new construct into the existing system of personally held constructs.

I wondered whether, from the user's perspective, information seeking might not be a process of construction, as described in Kelly's personal construct theory, and whether the confusion I was observing in my students was a natural phase in this process. I had a hunch that I was observing the emotional struggle that underlies the constructive process related to information searching and meaning making. How could I find out whether my hunch was correct?

OPENING THE BLACK BOX OF STUDENT RESEARCH

My first challenge was to design a study that would get inside the black box of students' experience during their progress through a research assignment. I needed to be able to get their perspective on what they were thinking, feeling, and doing. I realized that I came from the library profession, which had a long tradition regarding how searching should be done and how research assignments ought to be approached. In addition, teachers generally thought that research papers should begin with a fully articulated thesis statement. However, I wanted to capture the students' experience from their own perspective and to investigate without too many preconceived notions. I needed to get inside the students' experience from their point of view, without "oughts" or "shoulds." This determined my research methodology as ethnographic observer.

I read the literature on grounded theory and naturalistic methodology. I devised a number of different methods to study two groups of students over one academic year. A perceptions questionnaire was designed to gather baseline data. Conceptual maps, time lines and flowcharts, short written statements, source logs, journals, and observations tracked progress throughout the study. Multiple open-ended interviews were conducted with eight case study subjects. Teachers assigned grades and assessed the focus on final papers. These qualitative ethnographic methods opened up the students' thoughts, feelings, and actions in the process of learning from a variety of sources.

In that initial study, I found that students' information seeking did indeed involve construction that was experienced with thoughts shifting from confusion to clarity and feelings changing from uncertainty to confidence as the search progressed. The students referred to the shift as finding a focus, a theme, a main idea, or a thread. I picked up on their terminology to explain their experience and used the term "focus" for the turning point in their search process. I found that I could identify six stages in the students' description of their experience. Most important, they described two critical stages of exploring and formulating between collecting information and accomplishing their task that were being overlooked in the traditional research process. When they confronted these stages, they thought they were doing something wrong. They expected to simply collect information and accomplish their task. When their expectations did not match their experience, they felt uncertainty, anxiety, and frustration, as Kelly had predicted. I had been observing them in the library when these feelings were coming to the fore. At this point they were encountering information that was inconsistent and incompatible with their preconceived notions. They were in the most difficult stage of the constructive process.

This was an important discovery. As my research unfolded I could see the black box opening. Students welcomed the opportunity to talk about their research process. In the confusing early stages, they thought they were procrastinating or doing something wrong, using negative terms to describe the most challenging and possibly most creative phase of learning. They thought of the process as independent work and thought it "cheating" to ask for help. They were surprised to find that others were experiencing a similar struggle.

My dissertation advisor called it a "breakthrough study." Recently I was giving a lecture, and one of the students remarked, "But haven't we always known that?" Well, no. When I first started writing about the holistic experience in the stages of the information search process (ISP), many people were put off by the idea of emotions having anything to do with information seeking. Now it is integrated into the commonly held theoretical perspective of the field.

HOW TO PORTRAY A SEQUENCE OF EXPERIENCE?

The next challenge was to find a way to portray the process experienced by the students. I found that I could identify students' thoughts, feelings, and actions in a series of stages. How do you show a sequence of holistic experience? The stages were named for the main task undertaken to move on to the next stage: task initiation, topic selection, focus exploration, focus formulation, information collection, and search closure. I made detailed charts of the thoughts, actions, and feelings in each stage (Kuhlthau 1983, 1994).

The next step was to summarize the charts into a model that could be displayed on one page (table 4.1). One of my data collection methods was a time line on which students described their thoughts, actions, and feelings during the entire research process. I adopted the time line to capture the sense of the sequential process to display the three realms of experience. The model summarized the thoughts, actions, and feelings commonly experienced by students in the six stages of their research process. Later, following the verification studies, the model was refined and simplified to initiation, selection, exploration, formulation, collection, presentation, and assessment, and was named the "information search process." This work was published in a paper in *JASIS* that continues to be highly cited (Kuhlthau 1991).

STICKING WITH THE PROBLEM

The initial study opened the black box of student research and revealed the complex, constructive process underlying student information-

Table 4.1. Information search process (ISP) model

	Initiation	Selection	Exploration	Formulation	Collection	Presentation	Assessment
Feelings (affective)	Uncertainty	Optimism	Confusion Frustration Doubt	Clarity	Sense of direction/ confidence	Satisfaction or disappointment	Sense of accomplishment
Thoughts (cognitive)	Vague ——————————————→ Focused —————————————→ Increased interest						Increased self-awareness
Actions (physical)	Seeking relevant information Exploring —————→			Seeking pertinent information Documenting —————→			

Source: Kuhlthau (2004, p. 82).

seeking behavior. I had found something important and interesting about this group of students. There was more research to be done to see if the model applied to other students or even to these same students at some later time. I was able to verify the model in follow-up studies with this same group of students and in extensive longitudinal case studies. I conducted large-scale studies of diverse samples of secondary and middle school students, undergraduates, public library users, and, later, information workers. Through these studies, the model was verified and developed. I ended up staying with the problem for three decades, and I am still working on it.

A combination of qualitative and quantitative methodology has been an important component of this research, as have longitudinal methods. Initially, I used qualitative methods to open the process for examination. When quantitative methods enabled verification of the initial model in a large sample of diverse users, I realized the power of using the combination of methodologies. I continued researching the ISP, applying a range of methods over the years depending on the aspect of the problem that I was studying at the time. Qualitative methods opened an inside view of the ISP, and quantitative methods revealed patterns that held in larger populations. Studying different types of information users enabled me to see if the model held in different situations of information seeking.

Longitudinal methods have been an important component of my research. I used longitudinal methods at three points of data collection to capture data before formulation, during formulation, and after formulation within studies and semistructured interviews in longitudinal case studies for comparative analysis across studies—one over the course of fifteen years.

As the ISP model held across studies, I gained increasingly more insight into the process of learning from a variety of sources of information. I stayed with the "big problem," driven by my own compelling interest and curiosity. The work never seemed done, with the findings of one study leading to the research questions for the next. Most of my subjects were students; when I expanded my subject pool to study adult public library users and then later information workers, I recognized some commonality with subjects' experience in the ISP, but also noticed some important differences.

It became clear that most public library users were engaged in a different type of information-seeking behavior that didn't quite fit the ISP model. These users didn't seem to have the time pressure of pursuing a task with a definite beginning and end. They were engaged in more open-ended information seeking, such as looking for information related to an ongoing interest in a hobby, an area of personal study, or a health concern that didn't fit the time-limited task described in the ISP (Kuhlthau et al. 1990).

Later, my conversations with Katrina Byström (1999), Pertti Vakkari (1999), and Kalerva Jävelin (Byström and Järvelin 1995) at the University of Tampere in Finland about their work on task complexity broadened my understanding of the ISP in work tasks. I looked into when and why the ISP applies in information-seeking tasks in work situations. In these studies I found that the complexity of a task associated with uncertainty related to when the ISP model applied. I found that it wasn't the innate complexity of the task that was important, but the complexity of the task for that person. Routine tasks, no matter how innately complex, did not require constructing from new information and did not prompt the stages of the ISP. When comparing expert with novice experience in the ISP, I found that both novices and experts experienced increased uncertainty in the preformulation stages of the ISP, with uncertainty decreasing after formulation. However, a complex task for the novice often was considered a routine task for the expert. It was clear that it was not the inherent complexity of the task but the person's perception of complexity that prompted that person's experience in the stages of the ISP. A task that is complex for one person may be routine for another person. The ISP model applies where the information-seeking task requires considerable learning and construction from new information.

In addition, I found that the novice and the expert approached the ISP with different moods, or attitudes. The novice expected to encounter uncertainty in order to learn in the new environment and willingly entered the ISP stages with an open mind—what I call an "invitational mood." The expert tried to avoid situations of uncertainty, knowing from experience the time and effort involved in the process of construction, a more "indicative mood." The reason for this may be that the novice's work allowed for the learning time involved in the ISP. The expert's work often encompassed added responsibilities that left less time for projects requiring extensive new learning (Kuhlthau 1999).

These were among the many important insights into the ISP model that were revealed by staying with the problem and developing a research agenda that extended over many years and that expanded my thinking about the theoretical perspective of library and information services (Kuhlthau 2004).

SOME THOUGHTS ON THE ISP MODEL

The ISP is a task model with a discrete beginning and end. Occasionally someone misunderstands the model as linear. The ISP is a multidimensional model that displays the holistic sequential experience of the constructive process of learning from a variety of sources from the user's perspective. The ISP model describes a sequential constructive process, occurring in life and proceeding with a beginning and an end, as life is experienced—as linear only in a chronological sense. Of course a constructive process draws from something that has gone on before and may continue on well after. The model, however, describes only the information search process within the task, albeit extensive and complex. Recursion may occur within each phase, particularly in the exploration stage. Nevertheless, the process goes from one stage to the next as the person progresses toward accomplishing the task. It is likely that when a person returns to an earlier stage, the stages of the process will be repeated. For example, by returning to selection to select a different topic after exploration rather than moving on to formulation, the person will progress through exploration again with the new topic.

The ISP model does not purport to describe all information-seeking behavior but rather models a particular type. The ISP model displays the patterns of thoughts, feelings, and actions in a sequence of stages that users (such as students working on a research project) commonly experience in a task with a discrete initiation point and due date. The ISP describes users' experience as learning progresses over time and shows the formulation of focused ideas from information as the turning point in the learning process. It essentially reveals three different phases of learning: before formulation, formulation, and after formulation. It is applicable in time-sensitive situations of information seeking where learning is required to enable the accomplishment of the task, such as school inquiry and academic research, and in information work tasks with a steep learning curve and definite deadline, such as those of journalists, lawyers, and securities analysts. I found the ISP to be consistent across groups and over time under "certain circumstances," and something that the changing technological environment didn't seem to affect.

CONVERSATIONS—NOT A LONELY JOURNEY

This has not been a lonely journey. I have had conversations all along the way. When I joined the faculty at Rutgers University, I found it was an especially fruitful environment for exploring ideas. The Department of Library and Information Science (LIS) had recently merged with the Department of Communication and Journalism, bringing a wide range of converging theoretical perspectives into lively discussions. Tefko Saracevic and Nick Belkin joined the LIS faculty as senior professors. Betty Turock partnered with me on an Institute of Museum and Library Services (IMLS) grant for a large-scale verification study. In those early years, I met with each senior faculty member to talk about my thinking and get advice. Just articulating these ideas was a challenge at first. The short explanation of an "elevator talk" was hard for me. I kept my eyes on the "big problem," both conceptually and practically.

When I began traveling, my conversations broadened with my increased contact with new research colleagues at LIS schools across and outside the United States, first in Finland at Tampere and in Sweden at Gothenburg and Borås, then in Brazil at Minas Gerais, and later at numerous other locations where I gave presentations and held visiting lectureships. I joined the Information Seeking in Context (ISIC) conference and grew with it. The Association for Information Science and Technology annual meeting was, of course, always a conversation of sharing and learning.

Important to my evolving thinking were continuing conversations with librarians I had known for years, as well as conversations with new colleagues. I chose American Library Association committees that related to my research interests. My time on the Committee on Accreditation and my colleagues in the Association for Library and Information Science Education influenced my vision of library and information science education for the future. I was president of the New Jersey Association of School Librarians (NJASL) when I joined the faculty at Rutgers and have continued to maintain close contact with school librarians in New Jersey as well as throughout the country through the American Association of School Librarians, and with international contacts through the International Association of School Librarianship. I was involved in the early days of the information literacy initiative through Patricia Brevik's work, which pulled in leaders across the spectrum of education as well as key library players; this initiative has developed into an international community for thoughtful conversations.

Over the years, conversations about research into student information-seeking behavior with Louise Limberg and so many others brought fresh ways of looking at my work and created lasting friendships. Ross Todd, who joined the faculty at Rutgers as a research colleague, became a partner in founding the Center for International Scholarship in School Libraries (CISSL). I have gleaned considerable benefit from working with the talented students at Rutgers, many now noted leaders in the field, including the editor of this volume, Diane Sonnenwald. Conversations all along the way challenged, inspired, and deepened my work.

PROPOSING A THEORETICAL PERSPECTIVE
FOR LIBRARY AND INFORMATION SCIENCE

I had successfully applied my theoretical perspective from an allied field to my research into the user's perspective of information seeking and incorporated the results into the ISP model. I wondered if I could develop a statement that would meld the theoretical perspective revealed in the ISP model into a principle for library and information science.

The important core idea that emerged from the ISP studies is that in complex information-seeking tasks, users' thoughts are charged with emotions that influence their actions in the process of constructing meaning from new information. They are seeking meaning rather than merely collecting information. Users experience an increase in uncertainty and a dip in confidence in the early stages of the ISP, when more information commonly increases uncertainty rather than reducing it. The turning point of the ISP is the formulation of a focus, with uncertainty decreasing and confidence and interest increasing.

I identified uncertainty as the operative emotion. I decided to begin with the concept of uncertainty as the critical affective experience and to build a statement of the findings of the research around that concept. The theoretical statement would need to be based in my research premise that information seeking is a holistic process of evolving stages of construction, with increasing uncertainty before focus formulation and decreasing uncertainty after focus formulation.

The concept of uncertainty had been introduced into library and information science by a number of scholars, but it was not working as a central concept at the time. Library and information science was solidly based on certainty and order, although a number of scholars were working on breaking out of these confines. Two examples are Marcia Bates, with her innovative ways of thinking about searching associated with uncertainty (her influential work on berry picking [1989] and, one I particularly like, hitting the side of the barn [1986]), and Tom Wilson, with his introduction of the affective dimension in 1981.

I decided to lay out a statement for library and information science, adopting Kelly's format of a principle supported by a number of corollaries. The principle centered on uncertainty with six corollaries drawn from concepts underlying the research findings. I smiled a bit at the play on Heisenberg's physics principle, but realized that library and information science could use an uncertainty principle as well.

The principle states that uncertainty is a cognitive state that commonly causes affective symptoms of anxiety and lack of confidence (Kuhlthau 1993). Uncertainty and anxiety can be expected in the early stages of the information search process. The affective symptoms of uncertainty, confusion, and frustration are associated with vague, unclear thoughts about a topic or question. As knowledge states shift to more clearly focused thoughts, a parallel shift occurs to feelings of increased confidence. Uncertainty due to a lack of understanding, a gap in meaning, or a limited construction initiates the process of information seeking.

The central principle is supported and expanded by six corollaries:

Process corollary: The process of information seeking involves construction in which the user actively pursues understanding and meaning from the information encountered over a period of time.

Formulation corollary: Formulation is thinking, developing an understanding, and extending and defining a topic from the information encountered in a search.

Redundancy corollary: The interplay of seeking what is expected and redundant and encountering what is unexpected and unique results in an underlying tension in the search process.

Mood corollary: Mood, a stance or attitude that the user assumes, opens or closes the range of possibilities in a search.

Prediction corollary: The search process may be thought of as a series of choices based on predictions of what will happen if a particular action is taken.

Interest corollary: Interest increases as the exploratory inquiry leads to formulation in the search process.

By developing the uncertainty principle and corollaries, I had summarized my research findings in a completely different way than I had in the ISP model. As a theoretical statement for library and information science, the uncertainty principle was never as well received as the ISP. I still find it helpful as shorthand for the main findings of my research and the lasting insight into implications for the field of library and information science that are easily overlooked.

THE ISP IN THE USER'S WORLD: ZONE OF INTERVENTION

My research had opened up the black box of student research and indicated that intervention and guidance could be helpful at particular times within the process. I began thinking about how this might work in practice. Librarians hovering over people while they are searching for information would be overwhelming and annoying to users and an unrealistic requirement of professionals' time. I needed to pinpoint when intervention would be most helpful.

Uncertainty was the operative emotion in the ISP, and uncertainty was the key to intervention. When a high level of uncertainty occurs is when some kind of intervention is most likely to be needed. The ISP model describes when uncertainty is likely to increase and when it is likely to be at its ebb.

Vygotsky's (1978) zone of proximal development gave me an idea for applying intervention in library and information services. The core idea is that increased uncertainty indicates a need for assistance and guidance. The zone of intervention is that area in which a student can benefit from advice and assistance on what he or she cannot do alone or can do only with difficulty. Intervention within this zone enables students to progress in their learning. Intervention outside this zone is inefficient and unnecessary, experienced as intrusive or overwhelming. These concepts formed the foundation for implementing a process approach to library and information services, particularly for students.

Taken together, the uncertainty principle and zone of intervention constitute a theoretical perspective for advancing library and information practice. It offers a lens for viewing the user's dilemma but does not prescribe a particular kind of intervention. This development raised the professional question of how to intervene when people are seeking meaning, not simply seeking information. How does the practice of librarianship shift when information searching is viewed as a process of seeking meaning rather than simply seeking information? Over the years the ISP model developed into a well-regarded theory in the information sciences and a foundation for academic and school library information literacy initiatives. I summarized this work in *Seeking Meaning*, proposing a process approach to library and information services. The first edition was published in 1994, and the updated second edition in 2004.

THEORETICAL PERSPECTIVE IN A CHANGING INFORMATION ENVIRONMENT

I came to library and information science with a theoretical perspective from another field. Library and information science was about organization and classification, that is, order and certainty, for locating and retrieving. My theoretical perspective made me notice the gap between locating information and seeking meaning.

Is library and information science about seeking meaning or about retrieving information? Can the field be about both? This is still something of a debated question. What is library and information science about? Library science is still having the fiction versus nonfiction debate. Information science is still having the retrieval versus uses debate. For me these debates seem unimportant. From the user's perspective, information is not genre bound, and retrieval is always about use. Library and information science is about ideas, about constructing understanding from information and ideas. Information facilitates interest, curiosity, and inquiry.

A theoretical perspective can offer an illuminating lens. But it also can be a limiting blinder that actually closes down one's view to new ways of looking at things. One might fall into the trap of thinking, "This is the way we have always done it or viewed it." A theory sometimes runs its course and needs a fresh approach to meet new challenges.

There have been vast changes in the information environment since my first study back in the mid-1980s. I have been particularly aware of changes in technology that may affect users' experience in the information search process. Theories need to be continually tested, refined, and adapted to changing environments. At this juncture I find that the ISP continues to be a useful model in technological information environments for describing users' experiences in complex information-seeking tasks with a beginning and an ending that require considerable construction. A constructivist perspective on seeking meaning from multiple sources of information endures for understanding people's experience in a dynamic information world. The model seems in some ways even more applicable in today's overloaded information environment than in the contained library collection prior to the Internet.

TRANSPORTING INFORMATION THEORY: ISP MODEL AS A FOUNDATION FOR GUIDED INQUIRY

The information environment has been completely transformed in the thirty years since I first took on this research. The theoretical perspectives of library and information science that have developed over these years are based on a wide range of research and practice. Taken together, the research and theories of library and information science offer a solid foundation of insight needed outside the field to address the many problems facing a changing world. We don't have all of the answers, but we do have some useful collective wisdom. The challenge remains, however, for the work of library and information science to cross over into those fields that are directly impacting information seeking, retrieval, and use in the context of people's everyday lives.

One example close to my heart is kindergarten through grade 12 (K–12) education. As information technology opens up learning to broad areas of investigation and creativity, schools, particularly in the United States, have become more skill bound and test driven. Educators all over the world are seeking new ways to prepare their students for creating and innovating with vast sources of information. Over the past decade I have become increasingly concerned that schools are off the mark for preparing students for the future.

As an emerita professor I have turned my attention to a project we call Guided Inquiry, based on the findings of the ISP research. This initiative developed over several years of conversations. I have had the wonderful opportunity to create this work with two of my

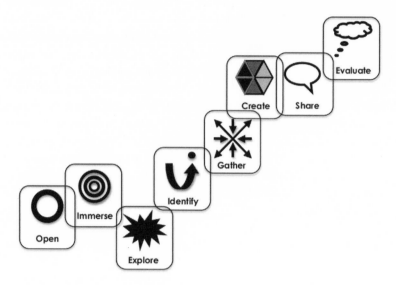

FIGURE 4.1. Guided Inquiry design framework (Kuhlthau, Maniotes, and Caspari 2012, p. 31)

daughters, Leslie Maniotes, master teacher in the Denver Public Schools with a PhD in instructional design, and Ann Caspari, museum educator with the Smithsonian's National Air and Space Museum. Although the ISP model is well known in library and information science, it is not as familiar in education, where the shift to information-centered learning is extremely difficult for teachers. Using the ISP model, we set out to address the problem of redesigning learning for students in the technological information age. Some of the most challenging work of my career has been to translate the findings of ISP research into a design framework for constructivist learning in today's schools.

It has been thirty years since I came to library and information science with a theoretical perspective from the allied field of education. This was extremely fruitful for broadening an understanding of the user's perspective of information retrieval and librarianship at a time when it was crucial to open up new ways of viewing information-seeking behavior. The theoretical perspective of library and information science can facilitate an understanding of the new environment of learning as information-seeking behavior. Guided Inquiry (Kuhlthau, Maniotes, and Caspari 2007, 2012) offers a theoretical perspective for the information-age educator and a practical framework to take the theory into enlightened practice. Guided Inquiry is all about creating and sustaining the engagement in the process of learning from multiple sources that prepares students for living and working in the twenty-first century (fig. 4.1).

Library and information science has become an increasingly important discipline in the first decades of the twenty-first century, with theories and research to address the most pressing problems of societies around the world. The theoretical perspectives of library and information science offer a lens for understanding the complexities of everyday life in the changing information landscape. I am convinced that the insight and wisdom of our field can provide solutions to entrenched problems as well as open equal opportunities for innovation in the expanding technological information environment.

REFERENCES

Bates, M. (1979). Idea tactics. *Journal of the American Society for Information Science, 30*(5), 280–289.

Bates, M. J. (1986). Subject access to online catalogs: A design model. *Journal of the American Society for Information Science, 37*(6), 357–376.

Bates, M. J. (1989). The design of browsing and berrypicking techniques for the online search interface. *Online Information Review, 13*(5), 407–425.

Belkin, N. (1980). Anomalous state of knowledge for information retrieval. *Canadian Journal of Information Science, 5*, 133–143.

Byström, K. (1999). *Task complexity, information types and information sources* (Unpublished doctoral dissertation). Tampere University, Tampere, Finland.

Byström, K., and Järvelin, K. (1995). Task complexity affects information seeking and use. *Information Processing and Management 31*(2), 191–213.

Dewey, J. (1944). *Democracy and education.* New York: Macmillan.

Kelly, G. (1963). *A theory of personality: The psychology of personal constructs.* New York: Norton.

Kuhlthau, C. (1983). *The research process: Case studies and interventions with high school seniors in advanced placement English classes using Kelly's theory of constructs* (Unpublished doctoral dissertation). Rutgers University, New Brunswick, NJ.

Kuhlthau, C. (1991). Inside the search process: Information seeking from the user's perspective. *Journal of the American Society for Information Science, 42*(5), 361–371.

Kuhlthau, C. (1993). A principle of uncertainty for information seeking. *Journal of Documentation, 49*(4), 339–355.

Kuhlthau, C. (1994). *Teaching the library research process* (2nd ed.). Metuchen, NJ: Scarecrow Press.

Kuhlthau, C. (1999). The role of experience in the information search process of an early career information worker: Perceptions of uncertainty, complexity, construction and sources. *Journal of the American Society for Information Science, 50*(5), 399–412.

Kuhlthau, C. (2004). *Seeking meaning: A process approach to library and information services* (2nd ed.). Westport, CT: Libraries Unlimited.

Kuhlthau, C., Maniotes, L., and Caspari, A. (2007). *Guided inquiry: Learning in the 21st century.* Westport, CT: Libraries Unlimited.

Kuhlthau, C., Maniotes, L., and Caspari, A. (2012). *Guided inquiry design: A framework for inquiry in your school.* Santa Barbara, CA: Libraries Unlimited.

Kuhlthau, C., Turock, B., George, M., and Belvin, R. (1990). Validating a model of the search process: A comparison of academic, public and school library users. *Library and Information Science Research, 12*(1), 5–32.

Saracevic, T. (1975). Relevance: A review of a framework for thinking on the notion of information science. *Journal of the American Society for Information Science, 26*(6), 321–343.

Taylor, R. (1968). Question-negotiation and information seeking in libraries. *College and Research Libraries, 29*(6), 178–194.

Vakkari, P. (1999). Task complexity, problem structure and information actions. *Information Processing and Management, 35*(6), 819–837.

Vygotsky, L. (1978). *Mind in society: The development of higher psychological processes.* Cambridge, MA: Harvard University Press.

Wilson, T. (1981). On user studies and information needs. *Journal of Documentation, 37*(1), 3–15.

CHAPTER 5

CONVERGING ON THEORY FROM FOUR SIDES

GARY M. OLSON AND JUDITH S. OLSON

IN OUR WORK ON LONG-DISTANCE COLLABORATION, we have developed our ideas about what makes such collaboration successful by drawing on four resources. On the one hand, we've been very empirical, having studied scores of such collaborations and looked for generalizations about what differentiates successful from unsuccessful collaborations. We also mine the literature, since we are not the only researchers studying these issues. The third source of ideas for theory came from our compilation of basic data on more than seven hundred collaboratories,[1] some of which were successful and some not. Our fourth source of ideas came from an online assessment tool we built called the Collaboration Success Wizard. The Wizard serves two purposes: it is a way to take theory back into practice, with the aim of helping those involved in long-distance collaborations to increase the likelihood that they will be successful, and it serves as a rich source of data that will help us to further refine our theory.

OUR FOCUS

Our efforts have focused on understanding how long-distance collaborations work (or not) given a dizzying array of technologies. It is hardly surprising that there is still a lot of conservatism among collaborators. While almost everyone uses e-mail and some form of audio conferencing, other technologies are currently used more sporadically. But we expect this will change dramatically in the coming years.

In developing our theory, one important framing concept has been the definition of long distance. On the basis of Allen's (1977) seminal work, we have used thirty meters of separation. He found that the likelihood of interaction or communication dropped off rapidly with distance, reaching an asymptote at roughly thirty meters, an observation that has also been reported by others (e.g., Kraut, Egido, and Galegher 1988). Thus, collaborations where the participants are in different buildings on the same campus would qualify as long-distance collaboration. Of course, we commonly think of long distance as meaning different campuses, different cities, or even different countries, and indeed such collaborations are increasingly common. But collaborations involving colleagues on the same campus have many of the same challenges as these more geographically serious dispersions.

TWO SOURCES OF IDEAS

EMPIRICAL FINDINGS AND LITERATURE

As this volume exhibits, many sources feed into theory building. In our work on long-distance collaboration, we have come at it from four sides. We have mined an extensive sample of empirical findings of our own. For almost three decades we have observed long-distance collaborations, primarily in science and business. We have conducted laboratory experiments on various specific aspects of such collaborations. These activities have given us rich material for arriving at empirically grounded generalizations.

But over this same period, we have read extensively in the relevant literature, which is large, diverse, and growing rapidly. These two approaches nicely complement each other in the early stages of theory building. While our empirical findings are by now quite vast, there is always the concern that they may have any of a number of idiosyncrasies. We are unable look everywhere. Often our studies have been opportunistic, taking advantage of things in our physical or intellectual neighborhoods. Mining the literature helps correct such idiosyncrasies. But the literature has its own problems. The study of geographically dispersed collaboration has been carried out in many different arenas—computer-supported cooperative work (CSCW, our home field), communication studies, organizational science, management information systems, and social studies of science, just to list a few. These diverse arenas have their own journals and conferences, and look at different aspects of distance collaboration. Unfortunately, there is little cross talk among them. But at least sampling these diverse areas and being exposed to the different kinds of lenses they use to explore the issues helps ensure that we are not distorting our own observations; it also puts them in a broader context.

In addition, we looked into the historical literature. Long-distance collaborations are not new. In an interesting historical analysis, O'Leary, Orlikowski, and Yates (2002) describe how collaboration worked with the Hudson's Bay Company in the seventeenth century. However, what has made distance collaboration's growth so dramatic is the emergence of communication technologies of great diversity and power. The telephone, of course, was an early such technology, with impressive effects on how work could be organized. Later the appearance of video conferencing gave additional options for collaboration, though as Egido (1988) outlined in an important review article, this technology was plagued with many problems in its earliest days. But in recent decades the Internet has enabled the creation of a stunning array of tools that can be used to facilitate collaborations. E-mail is the earliest example of a highly successful tool, though as has been pointed out several times, it too has been plagued by growing pains as people devise ways to use it for many functions beyond those envisioned by its designers (Fisher et al. 2006; Whittaker and Sidner 1996). Nowadays tools such as web-based audio and video conferencing, chat or instant messaging, shared calendars, document repositories, databases, blogs, wikis, and most recently the cloud (e.g., Dropbox, Google Drive) have offered numerous capabilities to collaborators. And now these capabilities are available on mobile platforms like laptops, tablets, and smartphones, giving collaborators even more flexibility.

OUR INITIAL THEORY

Our initial theoretical ideas evolved over fifteen years as we collected and analyzed empirical data and reviewed relevant current and historical literature. Our first attempt at synthesis was a paper titled "Distance Matters" (Olson and Olson 2000). One interesting aspect of the theory building surrounding this paper was that we had given a talk with this title and content thirteen times before we wrote it up! This may suggest a subthread to our evolving ideas: give-and-take with gifted colleagues. These opportunities to communicate with colleagues have been critical to the evolution of our ideas. In particular, people with experience with large collaborations tested our ideas and offered additional nuances and interactions.

The account we developed in "Distance Matters" grouped the factors associated with distance collaboration into four broad categories: common ground, coupling in work, collaboration readiness, and technology readiness. These factors were drawn from our research findings as well as the literature, and were illustrated with many concrete examples. Here we briefly describe each of them.

Common ground refers to the knowledge that participants have (and are aware they have) in common. As Clark (1996) and more recently Monk (2009) have stressed, common ground is essential to effective communication. Since good communication is key to successful collaborations, having common ground is essential. This can be a major challenge for a collaboration that involves several disciplines, several national cultures, or even different organizational cultures. Some of the multidisciplinary collaborations we have studied have gone so far as to create an explicit dictionary or glossary.

A special issue involving common ground is being aware of what is going on at another site or with a distant colleague. When collocated, we share the same weather, current events, and time of day. It is easy to tell if someone is in his or her office and is busy. Such *awareness* issues have received extensive attention in the CSCW literature (see review in Olson and Olson 2014), and there are now many tools and procedures that can help with being aware of other people and sites.

The second factor is *coupling in work*, which refers to the extent and kind of communication required to carry out the work. Work that can be easily divided into discrete subtasks is much easier to do at a distance than work that requires constant interaction. An example of the latter would be the kind of brainstorming that might be done as part of the early stages of design. We saw examples in some of our fieldwork where after the collaborators started working in a tightly coupled way across locations and found it difficult, the work was redesigned to fit the geographical distribution of the participants so that it could be carried out more easily. Making a complex decision would be another example of a task that would be much easier among collocated participants. Many of the successful scientific collaborations that we have studied were possible because the work could be subdivided in sensible ways.

The third factor is *collaboration readiness*, which refers to the reasons for collaborating and the alignment of goals among the participants. A core issue for collaboration readiness is trust. It is well known that trust can be more difficult to establish and maintain at a distance, though effective use of communication technologies can ameliorate this problem (Bos et al. 2002; Zheng et al. 2002). In our work, we have often observed that when collaborations are established purely for some exogenous reason, such as a funder requiring collaboration, there are many difficulties. Since working with others at a distance requires extra attention to communication, the collaborators have to see some value in working with distant colleagues. It is hardly surprising that successful long-distance collaborations are often ones where there is a history of working together (Cummings and Kiesler 2008).

The fourth factor is *technology readiness*, which refers to the participants' experience with relevant technologies as well as the technical and human infrastructure available to support their use. When we first began studying long-distance collaboration several decades ago, many communities had barely begun using e-mail. This presented some serious challenges when we tried to introduce what were then more experimental collaboration technologies, such as text chat or document sharing. And early users of video conferencing often complained about the numerous problems they had in setting up and using conferencing tools (Egido 1988). The situation is quite different today, as most people who attempt long-distance collaborations are much more comfortable with at least some basic technology tools. But even today, tools such as blogs, wikis, and cloud-based document sharing present challenges, as not everyone is familiar with using these kinds of tools.

We are also often asked what size collaborations fit our theory of what makes for successful distance work. Our answer is that the factors in the theory proved useful for collaborations as small as two or three participants all the way up to collaborations involving thousands. Scale certainly makes some factors more important than others (e.g., engendering trust, finding common ground), but these four factors apply throughout.

A THIRD SOURCE OF IDEAS

DATA ON COLLABORATORIES

Around the time we were writing "Distance Matters," one of us attended an interesting workshop in Vienna that included discussions of scientific collaboration. During this workshop Suzi Iacono of the National Science Foundation asked those of us assembled why it was that some scientific collaborations were successful and others were not. What factors differentiated these two kinds of outcomes? It occurred to us that the story we were developing in "Distance Matters" might be relevant, but this was a preliminary attempt at addressing these matters. So we wrote a proposal to the National Science Foundation that addressed this topic. We were funded, and this led to the launching of a project called the Science of Collaboratories (SOC). Our focus would be on such collaboratories.

The SOC project had several components. One was to assemble a database of as many collaboratories as we could find. This led to the creation of the SOC database, which is still in existence today and has over seven hundred examples in it (soc.ics.uci.edu/Resources/colisting). Another was to carry out further detailed studies of selected collaboratories. This was important, because when a project does not work out, there is seldom a published account of what happened. So we needed to explore a range of projects in more detail to try to dig out answers. We did such detailed studies of about twenty collaboratories.

Another component of the project was to engage our colleagues in the field. To do this we formed an external advisory committee (the editor of this volume was one of the members) and, guided by that group, convened a series of workshops to both explore the questions and try out tentative answers. Reports from these workshops are available at soc.ics.uci.edu/Workshops. One important discussion at the first of these workshops was what is meant by "success" in collaboration. For example, in a scientific research project, the highest form of success would be some kind of breakthrough that would not have been possible without a long-distance collaboration. But other kinds of success could include more rapid progress than might have occurred otherwise, the successful mentoring of younger scientists, or the creation of collaboration tools that are broadly useful.

A THEORY OF REMOTE SCIENTIFIC COLLABORATION (TORSC)

As a result of this work, we published an edited book entitled *Scientific Collaboration on the Internet* (Olson, Zimmerman, and Bos 2008). The chapters, authored by both our research group and a number of other invited researchers, constitute a rich set of case material on geographically dispersed scientific collaboration. There are also several chapters that attempt to synthesize ideas about long-distance collaboration. In particular, chapter 4 of *Scientific Collaboration*, entitled "A Theory of Remote Scientific Collaboration," was the second iteration of our effort toward theory (Olson, Hofer, et al. 2008). We used the term "theory of remote scientific collaboration" (TORSC) to refer to this account. The major change was to introduce a fifth category of factors: management, planning, and decision making. We had observed several times how difficult it is to manage long-distance scientific collaborations, something that has been noted by others who have studied such collaborations in other kinds of venues (e.g., Weisband 2008). Table 5.1 describes the five factors in a bit more detail.

Just recently we authored a third iteration of our theory, in a monograph entitled *Working Together Apart* (Olson and Olson 2014). We brought our account up to date by reviewing additional evidence from both our own work and the literature. We also reviewed much more systematically the current state of technological support for long-distance collaboration, and how the factors that affect success can be impacted by these technologies.

A FOURTH SET OF IDEAS: OUTREACH AND LARGE-SCALE DATA COLLECTION

The fourth important stream in the development of our theory has to do with outreach and large-scale data collection. We turned our theoretical account of successful collaboration into a useful tool called the Collaboration Success Wizard. This is an online survey based on the factors described in TORSC. It has approximately fifty questions related to the factors described in table 5.1. We show what a Wizard screen looks like in figure 5.1 and provide an excerpt from a sample personal report in figure 5.2. The Wizard focuses on a particular collaborative project, and comes in three versions—past, present, and future. The first is for projects that are completed, the second for projects currently under way, and the third for projects being planned. We developed it iteratively, administering it to participants on geographically distributed projects while we sat with them to see if there were questions that puzzled them or that they interpreted differently than we intended. It takes about twenty to twenty-five minutes to complete, and at the end respondents can request an automatically generated report that tells them how the project looks given the responses they made, identifies the strengths and vulnerabilities, and gives guidance about what to do to ameliorate the vulnerabilities. When

Table 5.1. A theory of remote scientific collaboration: Factors that lead to success in distance collaborations supported by various technologies

Coupling in work	The more modular the work assigned to each location, the less communication required.
	The more routine or unambiguous the work, the easier it is to do it long distance.
Common ground	There was previous collaboration that was successful.
	Participants share a common vocabulary. If not, there is a dictionary.
	Participants are aware of the local context at other sites.
	Participants share a common working style, including management.
Collaboration readiness	Individuals tend toward extroversion, are trustworthy, have "social intelligence," and are, in general, good team members.
	The team has "collective intelligence," building on each other's strengths.
	The culture is naturally collaborative.
	The goals are aligned in each subcommunity.
	Participants are motivated to work with each other, enjoy working together, and feel they have a stake.
	Participants trust each other to be reliable and productive.
	Participants have a sense of self-efficacy, believing that they can succeed in spite of barriers.
Management, planning, and decision making	The project is organized in a hierarchical way, with roles and responsibilities clear.
	There is a critical mass at each location.
	There is a point-person at each location.
	The project manager is respected, has real project management experience, and exhibits strong leadership qualities.
	A management plan is in place.
	A communication plan is in place.
	Decision making is free of favoritism.
	Decisions are based on fair and open criteria.
	Everyone has the opportunity to influence or challenge decisions.
	Cultural and time zone differences are handled fairly.
	No legal issues remain (e.g., intellectual property).
	No financial issues remain.
	A knowledge management system is in place.

Table 5.1. (*continued*)

Technology readiness	The technologies fit the work.
	The network has sufficient bandwidth and reliability.
	The architecture fits the need for security and privacy.
	Communication tools have the richness and immediacy to fit the work.
	Coordination tools (calendars, awareness, scheduling, workflow, etc.) are sufficient.
	Everyone has access to shared repositories with sufficient access control.
	Social computing (e.g., micro-contribution systems and social support) are well designed and fit the social as well as work needs.
	Large-scale computation is adequate.
	Virtual worlds are used in appropriate ways.
	The choice of technologies directly considers speed, size, security, privacy, accessibility, richness, ease of use, context, cost, and compatibility.

multiple members of the same project use the Wizard, we manually prepare a summary report for the project leadership.

As of this writing, we have administered the Wizard to more than a dozen projects involving more than two hundred respondents. It is accessible at http://hana.ics.uci.edu/wizard/. We have received very positive feedback from those who have used the Wizard. For example, "This is the first national collaborative that we've ever conducted within the ISRN . . . so this has given us confirmation that the policies and procedures we have created to manage a national, multi-site, quality improvement (research) project are indeed useful to our team of researchers. . . . [It] is a beneficial report back to us, definitely. It really does help us gather information to improve the success of our future collaborations, particularly about managing expectations." This project and another biomedical example are discussed in more detail in a paper by Bietz and colleagues (2012).

This rich set of Wizard data will allow us to pursue a further refinement of our theory. We are often asked about the relative weight of the factors in our theory, and about possible trade-offs among them.

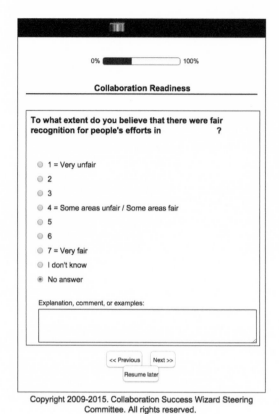

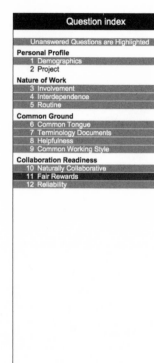

FIGURE 5.1. An example screen with a question from the Collaboration Success Wizard

For example, can good management compensate for weak technology readiness? Our Wizard data will allow us to examine these issues quantitatively. We plan to do a multivariate analysis of the quantitative data collected by the Wizard. This will be a much more sophisticated empirical test of our account. It may even lead to a simplification of the theory if we discover that certain of the factors we identified more qualitatively are so highly correlated that there must be some single underlying factor that explains them.

NOT YET FINISHED

Our theory-building effort has proceeded for over twenty years. We are still not finished. The rich data provided by the Wizard is one

Report for Collaboration Success Wizard

December 16, 2014 1:01 pm

[Print the Report]

Thank you for completing the Collaboration Success Wizard. One of the goals of the Wizard is to provide an opportunity to reflect on your collaborative practices, guided by findings from decades of research on the challenges collaborating across distance.

The Wizard was developed based on the Theory of Remote Scientific Collaboration (TORSC) [1]. Based on studies of over 200 collaborations, TORSC provides a set of five high-level categories that contribute to the success of collaborative projects. In this report, we outline each of the categories and provide feedback and collaborative strategies based on the answers you provided to our questions and best practices that have been successfully used in other projects.

We hope that you find this personal report a useful tool for reflection and discussion with your colleagues. However, we want to point out that as a diagnostic tool, it can only provide part of the picture. This report is generated automatically. It is based on your individual responses and does not take into account how your colleagues answered. The report uses only your numeric answers and cannot capture the richness of your text comments. As such, we can only provide general comments that may be more or less relevant to your particular situation. Also, if you did not answer all the questions, the overview feedback may be less accurate. Once the survey period is complete, we will aggregate the responses and provide customized high-level feedback to the project as a whole. In the meantime, if you have any questions, please do not hesitate to contact us at hana-csw@uci.edu.

Theory of Remote Scientific Collaboration
The Collaboration Success Wizard provides guidance about collaborative practices that tend to lead to successful outcomes. A collaboration that works well is more likely to produce good outcomes. The Theory of Remote Scientific Collaboration (TORSC) identifies five areas of collaborative practice that guide our analysis:

- *Nature of the Work*: How is the work divided among sites, and how interdependent are the collaborators?
- *Common Ground*: To what extend do collaborators share mutual knowledge, beliefs, language and assumptions?
- *Collaboration Readiness*: Are participants motivated to work together? Are goals aligned? Do the participants get along?
- *Management, Planning, & Decision Making*: How is the work organized and carried out? What organizational support is available?
- *Technology Readiness*: Are appropriate collaboration technologies available to the participants, are they comfortable using them, and is support available?

Below, we first provide a summary comment for each of these five categories. Then we provide more specific comments on individual questions that suggest collaborative strengths and areas that may need improvement.

Overview based on your responses

Nature of Work	Overall, your responses here suggest there may be some challenges that should be addressed in the near-term.
Common Ground	There were insufficient responses to create an effective summary for this area (even a single "I don't know" or "No answer" can throw off the calculations). However, your responses to individual questions will be addressed below. If you answered "I don't know" to some of the questions, you may want to have a discussion with your colleagues to make sure you have a common understanding of your project, which is important for successful collaboration.
Collaboration Readiness	Overall, your responses in this category suggest there are some areas you and your colleagues need to work on together to become better prepared to cope with problems that may arise in this area.
Management, Planning, and Decision Making	There were insufficient responses to create an effective summary for this area (even a single "I don't know" or "No answer" can throw off the calculations). However, your responses to individual questions will be addressed below. If you answered "I don't know" to some of the questions, you may want to have a discussion with your colleagues to

FIGURE 5.2. An example report printed at the end of a Collaboration Success Wizard session

new resource that we will mine to refine our account. We are also studying new technologies, such as Google docs, to understand better how collaborations work when supported by such tools. We already know, for example, that the emergence of the cloud as technology infrastructure has been confusing for many users (Voida, Olson, and Olson 2013). The challenges of such technology transitions mean that in many respects our theory will probably never be finished. But that is in fact what almost all theories face.

In sum, four major streams of activities fed (and are still feeding) our theory-building efforts. Our own rich experiences in a number of distance collaborations, including large-scale scientific collaborations, were a major source of insight. The accounts of what made for success from these experiences then was accompanied by a review of the literature, which resided in a number of separate disciplines, all giving insights with their own separate lenses. After publishing several summaries of what the theory was at the time and getting feedback from both audiences in our presentations and attendees at workshops we ran, we added a database of over seven hundred examples of collaborations in science, helping us identify the less successful ones for more scrutiny. Most recently, we turned the current version of the theory into the online Wizard, which both helps people who are in distance collaborations and gathers important data for theory refinement. As is obvious, with a complicated theory about social activity that evolves over time, theory development takes a very long time. But that is the keystone of science: accumulation of knowledge over time.

ACKNOWLEDGMENTS

We have had generous support for our work over the years, and have benefited from many wonderful collaborators. A detailed listing appears in Olson and Olson (2014). Most recently, we have been supported by the National Science Foundation (IIS-0308009, OCI-1025769, ACI-1322304), the Army Research Institute (W74V8H-06-P-0518, W91WAW-07-C-0060), and Google.

NOTE

1. The term "collaboratories" is a neologism for distributed scientific collaborations facilitated by emerging Internet-based technologies (Wulf 1993).

REFERENCES

Allen, T. (1977). *Managing the flow of technology.* Cambridge, MA: MIT Press.

Bietz, M. J., Abrams, S., Cooper, D., Stevens, K. R., Puga, F., Patel, D., Olson, G. M., and Olson, J. S. (2012). Improving the odds through the Collaboration Success Wizard. *Translational Behavioral Medicine, 2*(4), 480–486.

Bos, N., Olson, J., Gergle, D., Olson, G., and Wright, Z. (2002). Effects of four computer-mediated communications channels on trust development. In D. Wixon (Ed.), *CHI '02: Proceedings of the SIGCHI Conference on Human Factors in Computing Systems* (pp. 135–140). New York: ACM.

Clark, H. (1996). *Using language.* Cambridge: Cambridge University Press.

Cummings, J., and Kiesler, S. (2008). Who collaborates successfully? Prior experience reduces collaboration barriers in distributed interdisciplinary research. In B. Begole and D. W. McDonald (Eds.), *CSCW '08: Proceedings of the 2008 ACM Conference on Computer-Supported Cooperative Work* (pp. 437–466). New York: ACM.

Egido, C. (1988). Video conferencing as a technology to support group work: A review of its failure. In I. Greif (Ed.), *CSCW '88: Proceedings of ACM Conference on Computer-Supported Cooperative Work* (pp. 13–24). New York: ACM.

Fisher, D., Brush, A. J., Gleave, E., and Smith, M. A. (2006). Revisiting Whittaker and Sidner's "Email overload" ten years later. In P. Hinds and D. Martin (Eds.), *CSCW '06: Proceedings of the Conference on Computer-Supported Cooperative Work* (pp. 309–312). New York: ACM.

Kraut, R. E., Egido, C., and Galegher, J. (1988). Patterns of contact and communication in scientific research collaboration. In I. Greif (Ed.), *CSCW '88: Proceedings of ACM Conference on Computer-Supported Cooperative Work* (pp. 1–12). New York: ACM.

Monk, A. (2009). *Common ground in electronically mediated conversation.* San Rafael, CA: Morgan and Claypool.

O'Leary, M., Orlikowski, W., and Yates, J. (2002). Distributed work over the centuries: Trust and control in Hudson's Bay Company, 1670–1826. In P. Hinds and S. Kiesler (Eds.), *Distributed work* (pp. 27–54). Cambridge, MA: MIT Press.

Olson, G. M., and Olson, J. S. (2000). Distance matters. *Human-Computer Interaction, 15*(2), 139–178.

Olson, G. M., Zimmerman, A., and Bos, N. (Eds.). (2008). *Scientific collaboration on the Internet.* Cambridge, MA: MIT Press.

Olson, J. S., Hofer, E. C., Bos, N., Zimmerman, A., Olson, G. M., Cooney, D., and Faniel, I. (2008). A theory of remote scientific collaboration. In G. M. Olson, A. Zimmerman, and N. Bos (Eds.), *Scientific collaboration on the Internet* (pp. 73–97). Cambridge, MA: MIT Press.

Olson, J. S., and Olson, G. M. (2014). *Working together apart: Collaboration over the Internet.* San Rafael, CA: Morgan and Claypool.

Voida, A., Olson, J. S., and Olson, G. M. (2013). Turbulence in the clouds: Challenges of cloud-based information work. In W. E. McKay, S. Brewster, and S. Bødker (Eds.), *CHI '13: Proceedings of the SIGCHI Conference on Human Factors in Computing Systems* (pp. 2273–2282). New York: ACM.

Weisband, S. (Ed.). (2008). *Leadership at a distance: Research in technologically-supported work.* New York: Erlbaum.

Whittaker, S., and Sidner, C. (1996). Email overload: Exploring personal information management of email. In B. Nardi, G. C. van der Veer, and M. J. Tauber (Eds.), *CHI '96: Proceedings of the Conference on Human Factors in Computing* (pp. 276–283). New York: ACM.

Wulf, W. A. (1993). The collaboratory opportunity. *Science, 261*(5123), 854–855.

Zheng, J., Veinott, E., Bos, N., Olson, J. S., and Olson, G. M. (2002). Trust without touch: Jumpstarting long-distance trust with initial social activities. In D. Wixon (Ed.), *CHI '02: Proceedings of the SIGCHI Conference on Human Factors in Computing Systems* (pp. 141–146). New York: ACM.

EVALUATION

CHAPTER 6

DRAWING GRAPHS FOR THEORY DEVELOPMENT IN BIBLIOMETRICS AND RETRIEVAL

MICHAEL K. BUCKLAND

DISCUSSION OF THEORY, LIKE RESEARCH, can appear intimidating. For research a good solution is to prefer the phrase "problem solving." Not all problems require research for their solution, but research should be concerned with solving some kind of conceptual or practical problem. As an alternative for "theory," the word "view" has some merit. The word "theory" derives from the same root in ancient Greek as the word "theater," and both share a sense of viewing or of a spectacle. Other terms associated with theory, notably "insight" and "speculation," are also associated with a sense of seeing something.

Theory involves a perspective on something. No view is complete, and what you see (and don't see) depends on where you stand, on what vantage point you choose. To theorize is to try to view something more clearly, more completely, or more usefully.

There are many kinds of problems, many different reasons to want to solve them, and many different ways to look at them, so we should expect theory development to come in a variety of forms. The choice should be pragmatic: whatever works well for the person and purpose at hand.

If we consider theory to be a kind of view, then we might expect that visual techniques could be helpful in theory development. Sketching diagrams when thinking is quite traditional. Since it can be helpful to examine examples, I present two case studies of theory development using a special form of diagram, graphs, which have the advantage of including some calibration. The two examples relate to two very basic areas: library collection development and information retrieval, respectively.

CASE STUDY 1. THE RELATIONSHIP BETWEEN TWO
BIBLIOMETRIC PATTERNS: OBSOLESCENCE AND SCATTERING

The classic theorizing of library collection development is by McColvin (1925), who formulated the problem in terms of two different and potentially conflicting objectives: What would be good for the readers ("value")? What will the readers ask for ("demand")?

In 1969, Alexander Graham Mackenzie, head of Library Services at the University of Lancaster (UK), where I was employed at the time, asked his staff to examine the extent to which quantitative techniques could improve the probability that readers would find books and journals when they wanted them. By that time numerous studies had documented well-established statistical patterns in document use. One pattern was "obsolescence," the tendency for documents to be used less as they became older. Another was "scattering," the tendency for some documents to be used more than others. The classic form of scattering is to take a bibliography on some topic, sort the journal articles by journal title, and then rank the journal titles starting with the title that contributed the most articles, then the next most "productive," and so on, with very many titles yielding very few articles. Samuel C. Bradford found that this dispersion across ranked titles formed a regular curve similar to the patterns found by George K. Zipf in the frequency of the use of words and of many other human activities. There was learned debate regarding the precise mathematical formulation of the curve for both obsolescence and scattering, but the general pattern was not in doubt (e.g., Fairthorne 1969).

Could these empirical findings be put to practical use? The first insight was that these two forms of dispersion of use—across time and across titles—could be viewed as laws of diminishing returns with respect to two dimensions of library holdings: (1) how long volumes were retained and (2) how many additional titles were subscribed to. The second insight was that they could be combined. If space were at a premium and volumes were discarded when usage fell below some low threshold, it would take popular journal titles longer to reach that threshold than the marginal, least popular titles. Retention periods for any given title would be a function of its popularity. I visualized this as a three-dimensional graph with contours of use. Thus the cost and space implications of satisfying any given percentage of demand (a "p% library") could be calculated using mathematical models (Buckland 1975; Buckland and Woodburn 1968). Others published similar studies, but too many simplifying assumptions had to be made for this theoretical approach to be directly useful in everyday library practice.

However, contemplation of the three-dimensional graphs stimulated an intriguing question: if these two well-established forms of dispersion were similar, might they be related in some way? It was well known that the rate of obsolescence varied from discipline to discipline. Variation in scattering between disciplines had received little or no attention. I supposed that it did vary.

My initial assumption, based on thinking of a p% library as a partially inflated balloon, was that scattering and obsolescence would be inversely related. If severely constrained by rapid obsolescence, the literature would be broadly spread over a wide front of titles (wide scattering); or, vice versa, a literature might be concentrated in a few journals but with enduring use, as shown in figure 6.1a. Alternatively, these two forms of dispersion might vary directly, being more or less compact (or diffused) on both dimensions: doubly concentrated or doubly dispersed, as in figure 6.1b.

Published empirical studies of obsolescence had been consistently separate from empirical studies of scattering, but I found a study with raw data for both for eight different science disciplines (Brown 1956). The slopes could be calculated for each and plotted against each other on a graph, shown in figure 6.2.

When plotted against each other, the points clearly form a diagonal line from lower left to upper right. Obsolescence and scattering are clearly related to each other and vary directly, not inversely! Literatures are more or less compact (or dispersed) on both dimensions. But why?

INTERPRETATION

Obsolescence and scattering are surface phenomena reflecting something deeper, something at the core of information science. My colleague Anthony Hindle pointed out that if the eight disciplines are ranked by compactness—from physics to zoology and entomology—the order correlates with subjective perceptions of the hardness/softness of the various disciplines. I believe that these variations are caused by differences between fields of discourse in the degree to which concepts can be unambiguously defined. If so, there should also be discernible linguistic differences, which are also symptoms—this is a conceptual issue, not a linguistic one. If it were a linguistic problem there would be a linguistic solution. In other words, there appear to be fundamental differences in the character of the discourse of each academic field, and the variations in these bibliometric patterns are indicators of these differences.

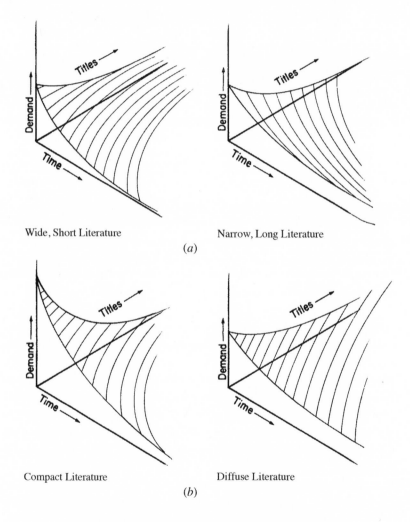

Wide, Short Literature   Narrow, Long Literature

(*a*)

Compact Literature   Diffuse Literature

(*b*)

Note. The thin lines represent 'contours' of demand.

FIGURE 6.1. Alternative relationships between obsolescence and scattering (Buckland 1972)

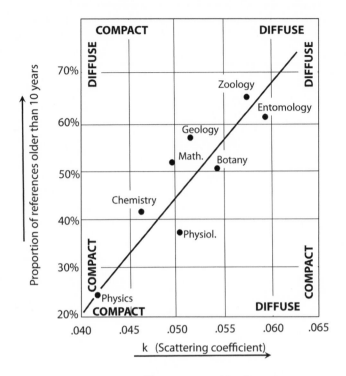

FIGURE 6.2. Compactness of literatures (Buckland 1972)

HISTORY

These findings were published in the *Journal of Documentation* (Buckland 1972) and in recent years have been translated and published in other languages. A complex mathematical restatement was published by Egghe in 2004. Over the years bibliometrics has become a hugely sophisticated specialty in which dazzling quantitative analyses of surface phenomena have not yet been accompanied by any known progress in explaining the deeper causal issues at the core of the information sciences.

CASE STUDY 2. THE TRADE-OFF BETWEEN RECALL AND PRECISION IN RETRIEVAL EVALUATION

When serious studies of retrieval effectiveness started in the 1960s, two measures of performance were used: recall and precision.

Recall is a measure of completeness, of how completely relevant documents were retrieved. Did the retrieved set include *all* the relevant documents? Or, if not, what proportion? The proportion is usually expressed as the percentage of the documents in any given collection that were relevant to a given query and are found by the retrieval system.

Precision is a measure of purity: did the retrieved set include *only* retrieved documents, or were some nonrelevant documents ("false drops") included? "Precision" is used as a technical term for the proportion of a retrieved set that is relevant to the query used.

The ideal is, of course, to retrieve *all* the relevant items (perfect recall) and *only* relevant items (perfect precision). It was soon found, however, that this rarely happened. In practice, efforts to increase completeness in retrieval performance (higher recall) tended to result in an increase in the number of nonrelevant documents included (lower precision). Alternatively, efforts to avoid nonrelevant items to achieve high precision tended to increase the number of relevant items that were not retrieved. Everyone wanted retrieval systems that would retrieve *all and only* relevant documents, but in practice it seemed that one had to choose between seeking *all but not only* relevant items or *only but not all* relevant items, and, either way, results were less than perfect. These empirical results happened often enough to be accepted as typical and thus were included in didactic materials (e.g., Lancaster 1978).

For twenty-five years there was grumbling about this situation (e.g., Cleverdon 1972), but there was a striking lack of published explanation of *why* this unwelcome trade-off was so frequently found or whether it could be avoided if one only knew how. The existence of a trade-off was generally conceded, but without clear published explanations. In 1991 I developed a theoretical explanation by drawing three graphs (Buckland and Gey 1994). Graphs are a convenient way to show relationships because they combine diagrams with calibration.

RECALL GRAPHED

The first step was to make a simple recall graph assuming an imaginary collection of one thousand documents of which one hundred were deemed relevant to a query. The numbers used were perhaps unrealistic, but that should not matter for an examination of relationships, and these quantities were easy to draw.

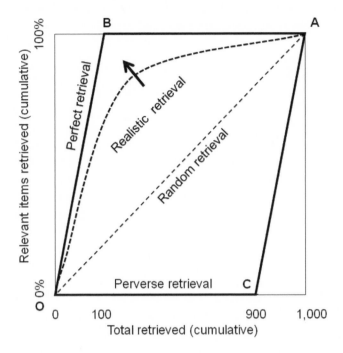

FIGURE 6.3. Recall graph showing lines for random retrieval (OA), perfect retrieval (OBA), realistic retrieval (curve), and perverse retrieval (OCA) (Buckland and Gey 1994)

I drew the initial graph (figure 6.3) as a square and calibrated 0–1,000 on the horizontal axis (the collection) and 0–100 percent on the vertical axis to calibrate the proportion of the relevant one hundred documents retrieved (recall).

If documents are retrieved at random, the recall curve will be a straight line starting at the point of origin (bottom left, O) and ending, when all items, relevant or not, have been retrieved, in the top right corner (A). All recall curves must start at the origin and end at the top right, but only retrieval at random will form a straight diagonal line between these two points.

A perfect retrieval system would retrieve only relevant items until no more were left. If one persisted, any further retrieval would necessarily have to be of nonrelevant documents until no documents remained. This perfect performance was plotted on the graph as a steeply rising line from the origin (O) to the top (at B), which is reached, in our example, when all of the hundred relevant items have been retrieved. If one persisted, further retrieval could only be of the remaining items (all nonrelevant), so the line would turn right along the top margin to the top right-hand corner (from B to A).

We do not need empirical data from retrieval tests to have a general idea about where the retrieval curve for any actual operational retrieval system would lie. It must start at the origin (O) and end at the top right corner (A). It is realistic to assume that any actual retrieval system will perform better than retrieval at random. Therefore, the ratio of relevant items retrieved to nonrelevant retrieved is better than random retrieval, so the "realistic" line rises more steeply than the random line. But a consequence of this early success is that the pool of not-yet-retrieved relevant items decreases more rapidly than with random retrieval. As a result, a realistic retrieval curve must rise faster than the straight diagonal line for random retrieval, and then it must gradually flatten out until it reaches the top right-hand corner (A), where all recall curves must end. Since no operational system is exactly perfect, the curve must also run below the line for perfect retrieval. It must therefore always be within the triangle OBA, and it is likely to be more or less like the curved line drawn. The better the performance of a real retrieval system, the closer its recall curve will be to the perfect retrieval line as opposed to the random retrieval line, tending in the direction of the arrow.

For theoretical completeness we can also draw the recall curve for a perfectly awful retrieval system that insisted on retrieving all and only nonrelevant items until no more were left, and thereafter could retrieve only relevant items. We called this imagined case "perverse retrieval"; the perverse retrieval curve would run straight from O to C, then necessarily rise to A.

Three comments can be made:

1. The parallelogram OBAC defines all possible recall performances.
2. Only systems achieving better than random retrieval will be of any practical interest, so all realistic systems will have recall curves within the triangle OBA.
3. The better the retrieval performance, the closer the recall curve will be to the perfect retrieval recall curve (OBA) and the farther away from the diagonal random retrieval recall curve (OA). Differently stated, the better the retrieval performance, the more its curve will move in the direction of the arrow.

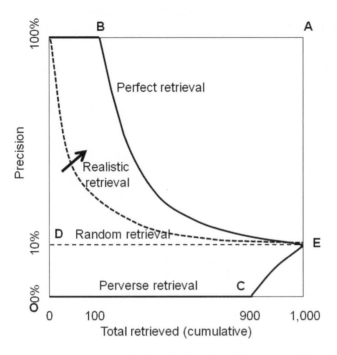

FIGURE 6.4. Precision graph showing lines for random retrieval, perfect retrieval, perverse retrieval, and realistic retrieval (Buckland and Gey 1994)

PRECISION GRAPHED

I next drew a comparable graph for precision (fig. 6.4). Since in our exercise one hundred out of the thousand items in the collection are relevant (10 percent), any selection retrieved at random will tend to be composed of 10 percent relevant items and 90 percent nonrelevant. Precision is expressed as a percentage, so random retrieval has a precision of 10 percent regardless of how many items are retrieved. This is shown by the horizontal dashed line (DE).

A perfect retrieval system would initially yield only relevant items, so it starts and remains at 100 percent until all hundred relevant items have been retrieved (at point B). After that, only nonrelevant items remain, so the retrieved set becomes progressively more diluted with nonrelevant items until, when the entire collection has been retrieved, precision reflects the collection as a whole. The perfect retrieval curve changes direction at point B and follows a concave curve down to point E.

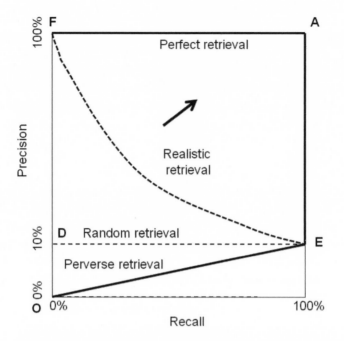

FIGURE 6.5. The relationship between precision and recall for random, perfect, perverse, and realistic retrieval (Buckland and Gey 1994)

Correspondingly, a perverse retrieval system initially retrieves all and only nonrelevant items, so until all nine hundred nonrelevant items have been retrieved, precision remains at 0 percent. After that, at point C, only relevant items remain, so precision can only increase, as shown by the convex curve (CE).

Any realistic retrieval system, being better than random but less than perfect, will lie between the lines for perfect and for random retrieval, starting at or near 100 percent precision, then decaying in a concave curve until it eventually reaches E.

THE RELATIONSHIP BETWEEN PRECISION AND RECALL GRAPHED

Since both recall and precision were plotted against total retrieval, they could be plotted against each other, as shown in figure 6.5. With random retrieval, precision tends to 10 percent regardless of recall, and so it is shown as the horizontal dashed line (DE).

A perfect retrieval system yields only relevant items until no more are left, so precision is at 100 percent until recall is complete, as is shown by the horizontal line across the top of the graph (FA). After that point, since only nonrelevant items remain to be retrieved, precision drops but recall is unaffected, so the line drops vertically (AE).

With perverse retrieval, nine hundred nonrelevant items have to be retrieved before the first relevant item. During the retrieval of those items, both precision and recall are at zero, so the line remains at the origin (O). When, finally, only relevant items remain to be retrieved, both precision and recall begin to rise in a shallow concave curve (OE).

The curve for realistic retrieval, as before, lies between the lines for random and perfect retrieval. The line should start at or near 100 percent precision (near F) and then form a downward, concave curve, eventually reaching E when the entire collection has been retrieved. In this graph, as in the others, the more effective the retrieval system, the nearer the curve will be to the perfect curve indicated by the arrow.

INTERPRETATION

The advantage of delineating curves for both perfect and perverse retrieval is that they bound the space of feasible retrieval performance, and the area between perfect and random retrieval defines the realistic region of all practical retrieval systems. Within this region all retrieval performances that are better than random necessarily have downward-sloping curves, as shown in figure 6.5. In other words, *a trade-off between precision and recall is unavoidable for any retrieval system that performs better than at random.* A corollary is that in the region of retrieval systems performing worse than randomly, that is, in the region DEO, precision and recall are positively related.

CRITIQUE

In hindsight it might be observed that the inverse relationship found is entailed by the way that retrieval effectiveness is formulated: if all items are characterized as either relevant or nonrelevant, then any initial success in picking out relevant items necessarily has the effect of impoverishing the pool of items remaining to be retrieved, so retrieval performance must progressively deteriorate. Further, orthodox retrieval performance is based on simplifying assumptions. The notion of relevance itself is problematic and unscientific. So too is the assumption that all items are independent: the notion that the relevance of one item does not affect the relevance of any other item is open to question. For example, if two are very similar, does one really need both? Nevertheless, the objective was to understand whether the empirically found trade-off between precision and recall was accidental or inherent, and this approach using graphs does provide a theoretical explanation within the conceptual framework of orthodox retrieval performance studies.

HISTORY

This theory development took place in 1991, partly in seminar discussions at the University of California, Berkeley, School of Information (then the School of Library and Information Studies). It was combined with mathematical studies of the slope of retrieval curves by Fredric Gey to form a joint paper eventually published in 1994. Then, in 1998, Egghe and Rousseau published a highly mathematical restatement.

CONCLUSION

Drawing a diagram is a widely accepted way to develop ideas as well as to explain them. This should not be surprising since a theory is a way of viewing something. Graphs are a special kind of diagram with the advantage of calibration, thereby adding quantification. Not being mathematical, I much prefer graphs to equations. These two examples demonstrate the usefulness of graphs in theory development.

REFERENCES

Brown, C. H. (1956). *Scientific serials: Characteristics and lists of most cited publications in mathematics, physics, chemistry, geology, physiology, botany, zoology, and entomology.* Chicago: Association of College and Reference Libraries.

Buckland, M. K. (1972). Are scattering and obsolescence related? *Journal of Documentation, 28*(3), 242–246. Retrieved from http://people.ischool.berkeley.edu/~buckland/obscat.html.

Buckland, M. K. (1975). *Book availability and the library user.* New York: Pergamon. Retrieved from http://openlibrary.org/works/OL4283199W/Book_availability_and_the_library_user.

Buckland, M., and Gey, F. (1994). The relationship between recall and precision. *Journal of the American Society for Information Science, 45*(1), 12–19.

Buckland, M. K., and Woodburn, I. (1968). *Some implications for library manage-*

ment of scattering and obsolescence (University of Lancaster Library Occasional Papers, No. 1). Lancaster, UK: University of Lancaster. (Also published as ERIC report ED 022 502.)

Cleverdon, C. W. (1972). On the inverse relationship of recall and precision. *Journal of Documentation, 28*(3), 195–201.

Egghe, L. (2004). Solution for a problem of Buckland on the influence of obsolescence on scattering. *Scientometrics, 59*(2), 225–232.

Egghe, L., and Rousseau, R. (1998). A theoretical study of recall and precision using a topological approach to information retrieval. *Information Processing and Management, 34*(2–3), 191–218.

Fairthorne, R. A. (1969). Empirical hyperbolic distributions (Bradford-Zipf-Mandelbrot) for bibliometric description and prediction. *Journal of Documentation, 25*(4), 319–343.

Lancaster, F. W. (1978). Precision and recall. In A. Kent et al. (Eds.), *Encyclopedia of library and information science* (Vol. 23, pp. 170–180). New York: Dekker. doi:10.1081/E—ELIS3–120009003.

McColvin, L. R. (1925). *The theory of book selection for public libraries*. London: Grafton.

CHAPTER 7

TWO VIEWS ON THEORY DEVELOPMENT FOR INTERACTIVE INFORMATION RETRIEVAL

KALERVO JÄRVELIN

DISCUSSION OF THEORIES IN information retrieval (IR) tends to focus on mathematical models (e.g., language models) or on user-oriented models (e.g., cognitive models). The primary interest often lies in explaining the quality of the ranked search result list, measured in some way using an experimental design that includes ranking quality metrics such as mean average precision (MAP) or normalized discounted cumulated gain (nDCG) (Sanderson 2010).

The mathematical retrieval models in IR specify the interactions of query and document representations for result ranking, but not for retrieval effectiveness. In this sense, retrieval models are theories on the (functioning of) search engines. Their effectiveness is assessed using a classic experimental design based on test collections (Harman 2011). Borlund (2000), among others, finds that evaluations based on test collections are wanting in realism.

User-oriented models in IR indicate factors affecting retrieval effectiveness, but their effects and interactions are very complex to study systematically. There is a dilemma between realism, control of factors, and enough data. Typical interactive information retrieval (IIR) experiments, trying to establish the best methods for document ranking, are struggling with adequate sample size, participant fatigue, and the effects of learning through repeated interaction with search tasks and search engines (Järvelin 2011; Kelly 2009). Despite these challenges, one should consider whether quality of ranking is the right and sufficient dependent variable in user-oriented IR studies. In other words, does such evaluation offer realism?

Neither the mathematical nor the user-oriented approach provides as much predictive power as one would expect from theories of IR— even in predicting the quality of the ranked list. Robertson (2000) argues that IR is not a very theoretical field but rather pragmatic, driven by pragmatic problems and evaluated by pragmatic criteria. He states that while we may gain insight through theoretical argumentation on whether recall and precision, for example, can be expected to change in a ranked output system, we cannot make a well-founded hypothesis, but need to test the effect.

The present chapter discusses two approaches to theory development for IIR. One is based on building up from an analysis of real-life IIR at workplaces and openly exploring the phenomena related to IIR (bottom-up). The other is based on extending controlled IR experiments by means of simulation of human interactive behavior (top-down). The bottom-up approach is an example of theory development at a pretheoretical stage—work toward a conceptual framework within which theory may be developed and tested. The section entitled "On Approaches to Model and Theory Development" will explain what I mean by theory development at a pretheoretical stage. The top-down approach is an example of theory expansion through incorporation of new concepts, with the aim of improving the explanatory power of the theory under construction.

Working in two directions is motivated by the hope that the two approaches might eventually meet, facilitating the development of a theory of IIR that is informative and realistic in relation to human information access and that is also experimentally testable. This chapter does not provide such a theory but rather describes work in progress toward such a theory.

The chapter is my personal view on theory development for IIR. Readers can assess how far the approach carries. I begin with a few words about conceptions of theories and their development in the next two sections, "On Models and Theories of IIR" and "On Approaches to Model and Theory Development." In the sections "Model Development: Pretheoretical Stage" and "IIR Theory Development through Simulation of Interaction," I discuss the bottom-up and top-down approaches, respectively, to theory development. The conclusions are presented in the section "IIR Theory Development: Discussions and Conclusions."

ON MODELS AND THEORIES OF IIR

This section is based on an earlier paper (Järvelin 2007) and a monograph (Ingwersen and Järvelin 2005), both of which provide longer discussions on models and theories of IIR.

All research has an underlying *conceptual model* of the phenomena it investigates. The model may be tacitly assumed or explicit. Such models, sometimes called conceptual frameworks, or paradigms, often become topics of discussion when the orientation of a research area is debated. An example is the debate between user-oriented and system-oriented models in IR. Conceptual models specify, as far as is known and understood by the IR research community, the following:

- essential objects related to the phenomena studied,
- the relationships of the objects that are recognized or significant, and
- intended goals and valid research methods.

Terminologies vary across conceptual models. Still, there are shared or debated assumptions across models. Shared or debated assumptions are as follows: *ontological* (what phenomena are out there to investigate?), *conceptual* (how to name, structure, and relate them?), *factual* (what to take as established facts?), *epistemological* (what can we possibly learn/know about the phenomena?), and *methodological* (how can we learn about them?). Discussion of conceptual models can be used to expose such implicit assumptions for examination.

Conceptual models are broader and more fundamental than scientific theories in that they set the preconditions of theory formulation. In fact, they provide the conceptual and methodological tools for formulating research questions, hypotheses, and theories.

In general, a theory explains observed regularities and hypothesizes novel ones between objects. Further, a theory provides deeper understanding of phenomena by using theoretical concepts that go beyond immediate observations. Therefore, scientific theories represent reality, systematize knowledge concerning it, and guide research, for example, by suggesting novel hypotheses (Bunge 1967).

Theoretical growth in a research area may result from *theory expansion* (e.g., due to enrichment through new concepts), *improved analytical power* (through formalization or model building), *improved empirical support* (due to confirmed hypotheses), and *proliferation of hypotheses* within the theory (Berger, Wagner, and Zeldith 1992). Theoretically good concepts (and therefore, variables) relate to each other in systematic and fruitful ways. In IIR, theory expansion would mean picking a new concept, say, "human fallibility in providing relevance feedback" (Baskaya, Keskustalo, and Järvelin 2011), operationalizing it in some experimental setting, and demonstrating its interaction with other independent variables and effect on the dependent variable, say, "ranking quality." A possible hypothesis for testing could be "increasingly incorrect manual relevance feedback will progressively deteriorate the search engine's ranking capability."

The goals of theory development for IIR may be classified as follows: theoretical understanding; empirical description, prediction, and explanation; and technology development. While much IR research is driven by the technological interest of developing retrieval tools, the technological interest becomes blind if not nurtured by the other goals.

This conception of theories is quite demanding. Before one can formulate theories, a model is required that gives the concepts (variables) for expressing theories. Personally, I would like to discuss theory development as a broader concept that includes building up and justifying the models underlying the theories of a given domain as well as developing the theories themselves within a given framework. The methods for developing models are different from those for theories. These ideas are discussed in the sections "Model Development: Pretheoretical Stage" and "IIR Theory Development through Simulation of Interaction."

ON APPROACHES TO MODEL AND THEORY DEVELOPMENT

DEVELOPING MODELS

The development of conceptual models involves mapping the ontology of a domain. A typical approach used to develop models includes experience-based contemplation and structuring. This may be based on identifying the components of a physical system, such as an IR system, and listing the system components, such as documents, information need statements, document representation, queries, matching methods, and search. The following discussion on developing models draws on earlier work by Ingwersen and Järvelin (2005; Järvelin and Ingwersen 2010), Järvelin and Wilson (2003), and Järvelin (2007).

Research in the information sciences has proposed numerous models that vary across several dimensions, including the following:

- *Scope*: There are broad and narrow models, for example, models of information behavior versus computational aspects of IR.

- *Processuality*: There are process models (e.g., Kuhlthau 2004) and, in comparison, static models (Wilson 1997) of information seeking.
- *Concreteness*: Some models, like Wilson's (1997) model on information behavior, are abstract; others are concrete models of retrieval system components.
- *Analyticality*: There are summary models on information behavior that list sets of factors affecting behavior (Wilson 1997) versus analytical models explicating the relationships of objects or phenomena that have an impact on behavior (see, e.g., Byström and Järvelin 1995).
- *Specificity*: Some models are specific to domains, and others claim to be more general, or applicable across domains. For example, the early information-seeking models (Allen 1969; Paisley 1968) were specific models for science and engineering domains, whereas some more recent models (see, e.g., Dervin 1983) claim greater generality.

These models are not substantial theories of information science in the strict sense; rather, they are pretheoretical models. For example, Wilson notes that the models of information behavior, among others, "rarely . . . advance to the stage of specifying relationships among theoretical propositions: rather they are at a pre-theoretical stage, but may suggest relationships that might be fruitful to explore or test" (1999, p. 250). Later, Wilson notes that "the limitation of this kind of model . . . is that it does little more than provide a map of the area and draw attention to gaps in research: it provides no suggestion of causative factors in information behaviour and, consequently, it does not directly suggest hypotheses to be tested" (p. 251).

Nevertheless, these pretheoretical models are necessary preconditions for the development of substantial theories in the information sciences because they propose a map of the domain and some central concepts to structure it. Thus their development, comparison, and validation are important. The main criterion in the comparison of models for research is practical: do they generate interesting, informative, and testable hypotheses and theories? Heuristics that can be used to compare and validate models include the following (Ingwersen and Järvelin 2005):

- Does the model comprehensively cover the phenomena it represents?

- Do the phenomena the model covers form a meaningful system?
- Is the model simple, accurate, and explicit in its constituent concepts?
- Does the model propose systematic relationships between its concepts?
- Does the model explain and predict phenomena/relationships reliably?
- Does the model propose relevant problems for solving and hypotheses for testing?

Affirmative answers to these questions are signs of better models. A model about complex phenomena cannot be proven to be correct or true. Either it is an abstraction that leaves many possibly significant factors out, or it is so complex that one cannot manage it; that is, one stumbles on epistemological and methodological problems when attempting to validate it. One way of trying to argue for, or validate, a model is to conduct studies that find positive answers to the heuristics listed above. This can be done through explorative and qualitative studies; see the following section, "Model Development: Pretheoretical Stage," for an example.

DEVELOPING THEORIES

A model, if it is fruitful, proposes relevant phenomena and relationships to study. It offers concepts that can be used as they are or specialized suitably, followed by operationalization, in order to formulate hypotheses and design a study, that is, an experiment to test the hypotheses. The experiment then confirms or refutes the hypothesis and may suggest further experiments. In this way, a theory or several competing ones may be developed within a model. Theory expansion may take place within the existing model by incorporating new concepts offered by the model, or through model revision. The chapter section "IIR Theory Development through Simulation of Interaction" discusses an example in IIR.

MODEL DEVELOPMENT: PRETHEORETICAL STAGE

This section discusses theory development at a pretheoretical stage. As an example, I discuss the motivation and execution of a study on IIR by molecular medicine researchers. The empirical study is joint work with Sanna Kumpulainen (Kumpulainen 2013; Kumpulainen and Järvelin 2010, 2012). Several long-term personal beliefs underlay this project: many information systems are used in coordinated ways in task performance; the task and the properties of the perceived available information systems shape the way the task is performed and the systems used; and all are adapted to each other, and changing any of the components puts new requirements on the other components (Järvelin 1986). Therefore, information (retrieval) systems should not be developed as stand-alone systems for isolated use with no recognition of their use context. This is not a unique idea, but should be considered in information retrieval/science as well. The above is a claim about the existence of a phenomenon (coordinated use of information systems), contains a claim about the existence of some relationships (joint adaptation), and proposes a requirement regarding systems design (systems should not be developed in isolation), but it is far from a hypothesis in the strict sense. In particular, it does not state in precise and testable terms a possible relationship between two or more variables. The requirement on design is a practical conclusion, not a scientific fact.

How does one argue for the existence of the proposed phenomena and their relevance in IIR design? How does such model development advance theory in IIR? Constructive answers to such questions would motivate the phenomena/concepts as relevant parts of an IIR model.

STUDY DESIGN

In an earlier study with Roos and colleagues (2008), we found that the information environment of research in molecular medicine and biotechnology consists of numerous search systems and databases, including web search engines, domain-specific websites, literature databases, and biological databases, all of which are in everyday use. It was thus natural to ask how such information access tools are integrated in work task processes; we decided to study the following questions, among others (Kumpulainen and Järvelin 2010):

- How do work task sessions differ at different levels of task complexity?
- How are various information channels integrated in interaction?
- What problems or barriers are hindering information interaction?

To address these questions, we studied six molecular medicine researchers and collected interview data, shadowing field notes, interaction log data, and SenseCam photo streams of task performance, during six months in 2007–2008. The participants were interviewed at the beginning of the shadowing to find out about their research processes, current tasks, and perceptions of their information access. Field notes were then collected by shadowing the participants for an average of twenty-four hours per person over periods, from three to eight weeks. During the shadowing periods, the participants were performing their regular tasks under familiar conditions and employing their normal practices and orientations. Any aspects of information interaction in task performance could be immediately observed. The log data consisted of 24,360 log entries for the six participants (ranging from 3,130 to 5,760 entries per participant). The photo streams, a still photo taken about twice per minute, totaled up to 72,000 images.

In the analysis, we first identified work task sessions in the data. A total of twenty-four sessions, four sessions from each participant, were analyzed in detail. Work tasks and work goals were analyzed based on the field notes. Sessions were classified into three complexity levels: complex, semi-complex, and routine. The resources used for information retrieval access were classified into channels, including "web search engines," "websites," "literature databases," "bio-databases," "tools on the participants' PCs," and "other resources." The transitions between the channels were counted in the analysis.

FINDINGS

The findings on information system integration in task performance are illustrated in figure 7.1, which represents a sample work task of medium complexity. The top line indicates queries employed, classified as WN = web navigational, WT = web topical, and BR = bioresource. The bottom bar approximates task duration. Each shaded and white section represents fifteen minutes. The middle area is divided into broad horizontal resource channels. Each horizontal line within a channel represents the same unique resource throughout the session. The solid arrows represent the workflow, the dashed arrows represent data flows, and the dotted arrows represent transitions by links. The middle area represents the transitions from resources and channels to other channels. It is apparent that in this almost three-hour-long work task session, many different resources are accessed and integrated. Shadowing revealed that tools on PCs were heavily used to manually harmonize originally incompatible data between resources (Kumpulainen and Järvelin 2010).

The specific content of the illustrated task does not matter here and is therefore not explained: I wish to focus on the abstraction of channels and tools used, and transitions between them. The transition frequencies between various resources are summarized in table 7.1 across task complexity classes. It shows the overall trend that most transitions are concentrated between two channels, biodatabases and tools on a participant's PC. There are some transitions to and from the PC channel between all remaining channels, while transitions from the web search engine channel to the PC channel are rare. Biodatabases belong to the deep web, so some of these transitions are just navigational. Table 7.2, for complex tasks, suggests that transitions in complex tasks are spread more evenly across the channels than in average tasks.

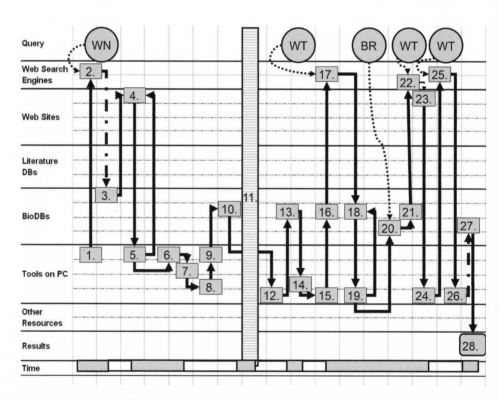

FIGURE 7.1. Workflow chart of a semi-complex session (Kumpulainen and Järvelin 2010, p. 99)

Table 7.1. Transitions in all sessions, percent (*N* tasks = 24, *n* transitions = 754)

	Web search engines	Websites	Literature data-bases	Bio-databases	Tools on PC	Other resources
Web search engines	0.0	5.4	0.2	3.4	0.4	0.0
Websites	2.5	0.0	1.2	2.0	4.4	0.2
Literature databases	0.0	2.0	0.0	1.4	3.4	0.6
Biodatabases	3.7	2.3	2.1	0.0	24.6	2.1
Tools on PC	2.5	2.1	4.8	25.2	0.0	0.4
Other resources	0.0	0.4	0.0	0.2	2.6	0.0
						100.2

Source: Kumpulainen & Järvelin (2010, p. 100)

Table 7.2. Transitions in complex sessions, percent (*N* tasks = 4, *n* transitions = 76)

	Web search engines	Websites	Literature data-bases	Bio-databases	Tools on PC	Other resources
Web search engines	0.0	4.7	0.0	13.6	0.0	0.0
Websites	5.0	0.0	4.7	3.8	2.7	0.0
Literature databases	0.0	5.4	0.0	3.6	0.0	0.0
Biodatabases	10.6	5.4	7.6	0.0	12.5	2.3
Tools on PC	2.7	0.0	0.0	13.6	0.0	0.0
Other resources	0.0	2.3	0.0	0.0	0.0	0.0
						100.0

Source: Kumpulainen & Järvelin (2010, p. 100)

OUTCOMES AND CONSEQUENCES

These findings support the claim regarding the existence of the proposed phenomena (integrated use of information systems in task performance) and their relevance in information access design: transitions between systems involve barriers and require manual integration effort that could be avoided by coordinated design of the systems. Therefore, information system integration belongs to the theoretical model of task-based IIR. It extends the model by introducing a new concept and suggests new relationships, for example, with task complexity. In practical systems design this suggests keeping an eye on the entire information environment and avoiding blind, context-unaware fine-tuning of individual systems. This might lead to suboptimal designs—excellent systems when analyzed alone but not working together well.

IIR THEORY DEVELOPMENT THROUGH SIMULATION OF INTERACTION

I now turn toward theory development in a stronger sense, that is, no more empirical exploration for pretheoretical model building. I assume a model of the domain that allows expressing hypotheses concerning the relationships of phenomena. The empirical study discussed below is joint work with Feza Baskaya and Heikki Keskustalo (Baskaya, Keskustalo, and Järvelin 2011, 2012, 2013).

Information retrieval in real life is interactive; that is, it consists of search sessions. Searchers interact with one or more retrieval systems and carry out a number of subtasks until they are satisfied, frustrated, or lacking further search ideas. These subtasks include query formulation and submission, result scanning, document link clicking, document reading and judgment, and stopping. A range of behavioral factors affect these subtasks. Such factors include the quality of the searcher's topical and searching knowledge, chosen search strategies, search goals and cost constraints, scanning and assessment behavior, and relevance scoring, among others. While most IR researchers hold the view that IR interaction is a key area in IR research, there are many factors at play, and there is no broad consensus on factors or their operationalization. The community does not know which factors dominate or the extent to which they explain behavior and success in IIR. Even success in IIR is debatable; how should success be measured? Interactive experiments involving human test persons are expensive, challenging, and difficult to control due to learning effects and human fatigue. These issues may explain the continued popularity of the traditional Cranfield evaluation approach (Harman 2011; Sanderson 2010), which looks at single-query sessions and abstracts users away as far as possible, and the continued popularity of *log analysis* of interaction, where the searcher's explicit actions toward a single search engine leave a trace in the log of that engine but her or his other actions, intentions, or properties are omitted.

My colleagues and I approach IIR theories through simulation of IR interaction. The idea—developing user-oriented theories of IR without users—may be seen as controversial, but it has nevertheless attracted considerable constructive efforts (see, e.g., Azzopardi 2011; Azzopardi et al. 2010; Baskaya, Keskustalo, and Järvelin 2012; Smucker and Clarke 2012). These efforts can be seen as an extension of the traditional evaluation approach, based on test collections. They employ the traditional IR test-collection experimental design but also include variables related to searchers and their behavior. At the same time, one avoids problems of recruiting large numbers of test persons, their fatigue, and learning effects within a controlled design.

Through simulation we aim to develop theories that incorporate human searcher–oriented factors and determine their effects and interactions in IIR. In order to orient research and development in IR, and to place the research efforts sensibly, it is important to understand which share of variation in IR effectiveness is explained by which factors, including searcher-specific and system-oriented factors. In simulation, it is possible to design and run experiments in which a number of factors, such as the test collection and its topics, the interface characteristics, and the search engine (with its underlying retrieval model), are held constant, and the user-oriented factors are systematically varied. The next sections discuss the design of such simulation experiments and report some sample findings.

STUDY DESIGN

Simulating IIR requires modeling complex behavior and generating sample behaviors. Our simulation approach is based on Monte Carlo simulation and therefore follows probabilistic generation of thousands of sessions for each experiment. We abstract search sessions based on a comprehensive set of subtasks performed during IR interaction, as illustrated in figure 7.2. Each session begins with query formulation, followed by snippet scanning, snippet relevance assessment and possible link clicking, document reading and relevance assessment, and stopping. (Snippets are the few lines of text appearing under every search result in web searching. They are intended to

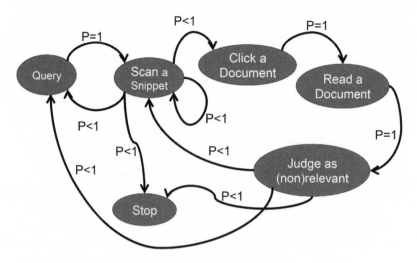

FIGURE 7.2. Session automaton expressing the subtasks and transitions between subtasks (Baskaya, Keskustalo, and Järvelin 2013, p. 2299)

inform searchers about how the linked documents match their queries.) The arcs represent possible transitions, and the probabilities (P) represent the transition probabilities. Therefore, for example, after scanning a snippet, the simulated searcher may with some probabilities click the link, continue scanning, stop the session, or return to query formulation.

The behaviors associated with figure 7.2 are as follows: the use of a range of query formulation strategies, snippet-scanning behavior, setting search goals (how much gain does one require?), setting cost constraints (what is the maximum available time for the session?), snippet relevance assessment (scale and fallibility), and document relevance assessment (scale and fallibility). I introduce these concepts briefly below.

Query formulation strategy determines the pattern of query words and queries in a session of one or more queries. *Snippet-scanning behavior* is either persistent or probabilistic. *Persistent scanning* means scanning all snippets in the specified range top-down. *Probabilistic scanning* means scanning snippets in the specified range top-down with some probability at each step to stop and skip all remaining ones (see, e.g., Carterette, Kanoulas, and Yilmaz 2012). *Search goals* are set as the cumulated gain required before the session is stopped.

Here the found documents are seen to be, to varying degrees, relevant to the information need. Each document accumulates gain to the searcher according to its degree of relevance (Järvelin and Kekäläinen 2002). *Cost constraints* determine the time allotted for the session (Baskaya, Keskustalo, and Järvelin 2012). Time, context, and competence affect assessments of snippet and document relevance (Ingwersen and Järvelin 2005). In *ideal assessment*, snippet and document relevance are correctly assessed with respect to the underlying document relevance, whereas in *fallible assessment* the assessments are fallible following some predefined probability. Consequently, we have two simulated behaviors: *ideal behavior* consists of persistent scanning and correct assessments; *fallible behavior* consists of probabilistic scanning and fallible assessments. The latter better represents real-life behavior.

The operationalizations of the behaviors for IIR simulations should reflect real life. This means that the probabilities (see fig. 7.2) should be given justifiable values with respect to the real-world context that is simulated. Likewise, query formulation strategies, session goals, and time limits should reflect the real-world context. In part such values are available in the literature, but some values may need to be determined empirically through log analysis, observation, or experiments. Once this is accomplished, it is possible to design experiments where these values are systematically varied via simulation to determine the significance of each factor in affecting the dependent variable—say, session effectiveness—in terms of cumulated gain under a given time constraint or session duration under a given gain goal. Figure 7.3 presents the experimental design that we've used.

In our simulations based on the design presented in figure 7.3, the interface properties, test collection, and search engine were held constant throughout, and thus are the *controlled variables*. The test collection was the TREC7-and-TREC8 collection (see http://trec.nist .gov), which had some five hundred thousand documents and forty-one topics with graded relevance assessments (Sormunen 2002). Being constant, their contribution to the *dependent variables* remains unknown. The *independent variables*, to be systematically varied in the design, are search topics, query formulation strategies, session gain goals and time constraints, snippet-scanning behavior, and relevance judgments. The idea is that each of these may be varied separately—and in combination—to show their effect on the dependent variables.

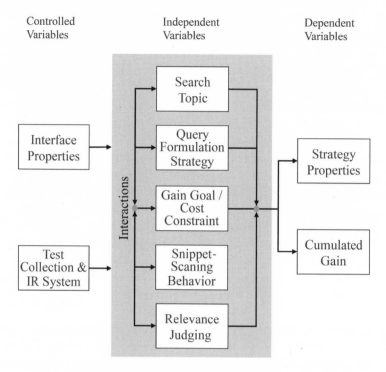

Controlled
Variables

Independent
Variables

Dependent
Variables

FIGURE 7.3. An experimental design for session simulation (Baskaya, Keskustalo, and Järvelin 2013, p. 2299)

The independent variables are explained as follows (for more detail see Baskaya, Keskustalo, and Järvelin 2013):

- *Search topics*: A group of hired study participants generated in a systematic way five ordered query words for each of the forty-one topics of the TREC 7–8 test collection. They had to first think about a one-word query, then a two-word query, and so on.
- *Query formulation strategies*: We logged the queries of real searchers in a task-based IR experiment and then idealized them into five predefined strategies. For example, the strategy S3 ("varying the third word") used up to three queries in a session and the available query words $w1$–$w5$ as follows: Q1: $w1\ w2\ w3 \to$ Q2: $w1\ w2\ w4 \to$ Q3: $w1\ w2\ w5$.
- *Session gain goals*: We defined a range of session goals in terms of the cumulated gain (CG) (Järvelin and Kekäläinen 2002), reflecting situations where searchers desire a smaller or larger amount

of relevant information. The ground-truth relevance assessments were made on a 4-point scale, I to IV, from nonrelevant to highly relevant. The gain (G) for each document "found" depended on its ground-truth relevance as follows: $G(I) = 0$, $G(II) = 1$, $G(III) = 5$, and $G(IV) = 10$ gain units. Another scoring value set used was: $G(I) = 0$ and $G(II) = G(III) = G(IV) = 1$.

- *Time constraints*: We defined session time constraints because real-life searching typically allows only limited time for each session. Alper and colleagues (2001) reported searching times for physicians (family practitioners) ranging from 2 to 6 minutes to obtain an adequate answer, so we used 2, 3, and 6 minutes, as well as an open time (i.e., a session with no time limit) in our simulations. There is a cost involved with each of the subtasks. On the basis of earlier literature (see, e.g., Azzopardi 2011; Smucker and Clarke 2012), we set the cost of entering a query word at 3 seconds, scanning one snippet at 4.5 seconds, reading and evaluating a document at 30 seconds, and entering the relevance judgment at 1 second.

- *Snippet-scanning behavior*: The literature provides several scanning models for single-query result scanning (see, e.g., Carterette, Kanoulas, and Yilmaz 2012), but no models for session scanning. Therefore, we developed a new model that takes into account the session goal, previous query gains, and current query gain in determining whether to continue scanning or to break off. This model was not empirically verified; that is, it was only supported by practical arguments.

- *Relevance judgments*: The probability of clicking (C) a link based on a snippet and judging a document as relevant also depended on the ground-truth relevance (I–IV) of the underlying document as follows: clicking a link: $C(I) = 0.27$, $C(II) = 0.27$, $C(III) = 0.34$, and $C(IV) = 0.61$; judging a document as relevant: $R(I) = 0.20$, $R(II) = 0.88$, $R(III) = 0.95$, and $R(IV) = 0.97$. For example, the simulated searcher will click the snippet of a nonrelevant document (of relevance degree I) with the probability of 27 percent and judge it as relevant with the probability of 20 percent. The probabilities were set on the basis of the literature (Dupret and Piwowarski 2013; Vakkari and Sormunen 2004).

It is obvious that achieving greater realism in simulation makes the experiments very complex. Indeed, even though we have not thus far varied the subtask costs in seconds, or the clicking/judging behaviors, we have simulated billions of sessions to answer a few research questions. Two such questions are as follows:

- How effective is fallible human behavior employing predefined query formulation strategies compared to baselines under various search result gain goals and time constraints?
- How effective is fallible human behavior employing predefined query formulation strategies compared to ideal human behavior under various search result gain goals and time constraints?

We used several baseline behaviors for comparison. One of them was the best possible behavior for each topic as identified by exhaustively examining all possible alternatives of query formulation for that topic (with five words) and conducting result scanning up to ten snippets per query (Baskaya et al. 2013).

FINDINGS

Simulation experiments can be run as soon as session behaviors can be generated, alternative values are available for the independent variables, and a design for systematically combining these values exists. A complex overall design, with several independent variables and several alternative values for each, generates a huge amount of experimental data, which has to be managed in order to be able to extract statistical information for answering the research questions.

Consider the two research questions presented above. Figure 7.4a shows cumulated gain (CG) by session time up to five hundred seconds following ideal behavior, that is, no errors in judgments. There are two curves: The gray one represents the gain achieved by identifying—through exhaustive examination of all possible alternatives, and for each topic separately—which strategy among all possible and which behavior yields the maximum gain over time. The black curve represents how much gain can be compiled over time by consistently following the query formulation strategy S3 (see above) for all topics and making no judgment errors. We can see that S3 delivers roughly 70 percent of the best possible behavior output. The strategy S3 proved the overall best one among the predefined query formulation strategies.

Figure 7.4b shows similar plots for fallible behavior. Here fallible assessments with strategy S3 yield 60 to 70 percent of the fallible best

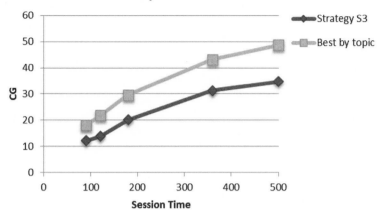

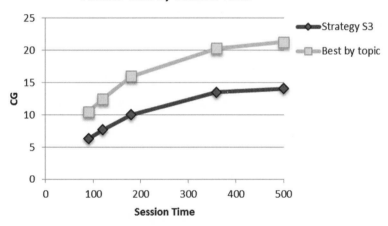

FIGURE 7.4. Gain by session time following (a) ideal behavior and (b) fallible behaviour (adapted from Baskaya, Keskustalo, and Järvelin 2013, p. 2301)

by-topic performance. By comparing figures 7.4a and 7.4b, one notes that the fallible sessions are clearly inferior to the ideal ones, with less than 50 percent of the corresponding performance in the shorter sessions and around 33 percent in the longer ones.

We also found that when we exhaustively examined all possible alternatives, for each topic separately, which query formulation strategy among all possible ones and which scanning/stopping behavior in each result yielded the maximum gain, the same query formulation strategy was never optimal for two or more topics (Baskaya et al. 2013).

From these findings one may conclude that, first, there is no simple model for query formulation in a session that will guarantee optimal performance; each topic requires different interaction. This corroborates Alemayehu's (2003) finding of topic variation being an important factor in explaining IR effectiveness. Second, compared to ideal behavior, fallible behavior regarding scanning and judging has a dramatic effect on session performance. Whether fallibility interacts with, say, ranking methods in producing session effectiveness is not revealed by these data.

OUTCOMES AND CONSEQUENCES

A simulation approach like the one just discussed allows systematic experimentation with a combination of independent variables to examine their effects on one or more dependent variables. For example, we examined session effectiveness in terms of cumulated gain over session time. Through simulations, the significance of each variable, or combination thereof, can be assessed. This allows the development of an explanatory model for (the variance of) IIR session effectiveness. Such a simulation approach is thus an important tool for theory development in IIR. It better supports theory expansion by new concepts than does the traditional Cranfield model of IR evaluation.

The strengths of a simulation approach of the type presented here include control over experimental parameters, unlimited supply of "test subjects" with no fatigue, low cost, no (nonprogrammed) learning effects, and repeatability of experiments (Azzopardi et al. 2010).

IIR simulation has been criticized for lack of realism and lack of utility. The former criticism sees limitations in the lack of fullfledged human subjects, which may lead to unrealistic and biased designs and findings if the simulation model lacks significant parameters or if its range of variation is incorrect or insufficient (Azzopardi et al. 2010). To counteract these risks, the simulation model and its parameters should as accurately as possible reflect the part of the real world that they claim to represent. The results of simulations should also be validated empirically. This may also suggest that search engines or their interfaces should be modified, or that human searchers should be informed/educated, to produce interactive behavior that the simulation model proposes as effective.

The opponents questioning utility often focus on search engine development. They state that mixing many other variables with the contribution (and quality) of the search engine may become difficult to assess. This is true—but on the other hand, if the contribution of the search engine does not show in the effectiveness of IIR, then some other factors, alone or together, dominate. As a scientific community, we should identify those factors through suitable experimental designs.

IIR THEORY DEVELOPMENT—DISCUSSION AND CONCLUSIONS

Theory development in the strict IR sense requires an experimental approach where the effects of some independent variables are tested on one or more dependent variables (see fig. 7.5). To make experimentation easier, some variables are controlled so that their variation need not be taken into account in the experiments. The dependent variables may further affect some ultimate dependent variable that remains outside the study design. The dotted lines indicate some other, unidentified, variables that may affect the ultimate dependent variable.

In information retrieval research, especially in test-collection evaluation studies, the design seen in figure 7.5 is specified so that, typically, the dependent variable is the search engine's ranking effectiveness (measured through some metric), and the independent variables consist of document representation and topic methods, as well as matching methods for comparing the former (see fig. 7.6). The test collection and its topic set are typically held constant. The ultimate

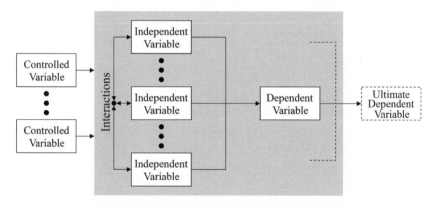

FIGURE 7.5. Experimental design generally (adapted from Järvelin 2013, p. 90)

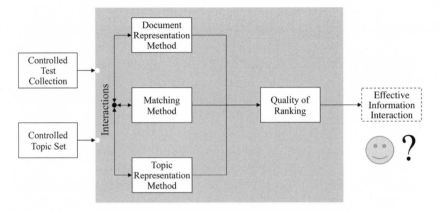

FIGURE 7.6. IR experimentation based on test collection (adapted from Järvelin 2013, p. 90)

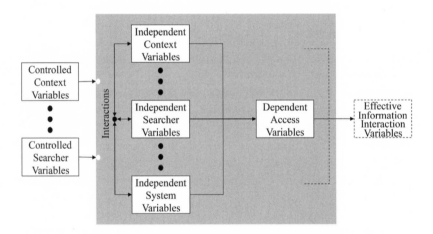

FIGURE 7.7. User-oriented, comprehensive IR experimentation (adapted from Järvelin 2013, p. 90)

dependent variable is *effective information interaction*, and it is, often, implicitly, believed that the latter is positively correlated with the ranking effectiveness. In other words, the better the ranking, the better the information interaction. From the viewpoint of IIR this is of course simplistic, since the human searcher as an active component in interaction is not taken into account.

Figure 7.7 illustrates study designs that seek to comprehensively identify context, searcher, and system factors affecting information retrieval and ultimately effective information interaction. The controlled variables may contain some context variables, searcher variables, or system variables. The independent variables may belong to the same categories. Ingwersen and Järvelin (2005; see esp. chap. 7) discuss these categories of variables.

Technology alone is insufficient in explaining effectiveness in IIR. In order to develop technology sensibly, we need to understand how technology, together with users-in-context, produces the desired outcomes and ultimate benefits in information retrieval (Järvelin 2013). Failing to take context and searchers into account in many study designs may be one reason for the views that the IR field is more pragmatic than theoretical (as discussed in the introduction to this chapter). The complexities that follow from trying to take context and searcher into account may be the reason for modest development of IIR theories.

Personally I think that in order to foster theoretical understanding and technology development, it is first necessary to do empirical groundwork like that discussed in the section "Model Development: Pretheoretical Stage." This helps ensure that the research designs contain pertinent factors. Second, it is necessary to do experimental work in order to understand the factors influencing the effectiveness of interactive information retrieval and their interactions. Due to the complexities involved, simulation as discussed in this chapter is a fruitful approach. There is a lot to do.

Pursuing these lines of research has been personally satisfying, especially the insight about task-based information interaction and the role of IIR therein. Progress is slow, however, because only a few researchers have similar interests and because the available research infrastructure much better supports document-ranking studies based on test collections and search engine log analyses.

REFERENCES

Alemayehu, N. (2003). Analyzing performance variation using query expansion. *Journal of the American Society for Information Science and Technology, 54*(5), 379–391.

Allen, T. J. (1969). Information needs and uses. In C. A. Cuadra (Ed.), *Annual review of information science and technology* (Vol. 4, pp. 3–29). Chicago: Information Today.

Alper, B. S., Stevermer, J. J., White, D. S., and Ewigman, B. G. (2001). Answering family physicians' clinical questions using electronic medical databases. *Journal of Family Practice, 50*(11), 960–965.

Azzopardi, L. (2011). The economics in interactive information retrieval. In W. Ma, J-Y. Nie, R. Baeza-Yates, T-S. Chua, and W. B. Croft (Eds.), *SIGIR '11: Proceedings of the 34th international ACM SIGIR conference on research and development in information retrieval* (pp. 15–24). New York: ACM.

Azzopardi, L., Järvelin, K., Kamps, J., and Smucker, M. D. (2010). Report on the SIGIR 2010 workshop on the simulation of interaction. *SIGIR Forum, 44*(2), 35–47.

Baskaya, F., Keskustalo, H., and Järvelin, K. (2011). Simulating simple and fallible relevance feedback. In P. Clough et al. (Eds.), *Advances in information retrieval: Proceedings of the 33th European Conference on Information Retrieval* (LNCS 6611, pp. 593–604). Heidelberg: Springer. doi:10.1007/978-3-642-20161-5_59.

Baskaya, F., Keskustalo, H., and Järvelin, K. (2012). Time drives interaction: Simulating sessions in diverse searching environments. In W. Hersh, J. Callan, Y. Maarek, and M. Sanderson (Eds.), *SIGIR '12: Proceedings of the 35th International ACM SIGIR 2012 Conference on Research and Development in Information Retrieval* (pp. 105–114). New York: ACM. doi:10.1145/2348283.2348301.

Baskaya, F., Keskustalo, H., and Järvelin, K. (2013). Modeling behavioral factors in interactive information retrieval. In O. He, A. Iyengar, W. Nejdl, J. Pei, and R. Rastogi (Eds.), *CICKM '13: Proceedings of the 22nd International Conference on Information and Knowledge Management* (pp. 2297–2302). New York: ACM. doi:10.1145/2505515.2505660.

Berger, J., Wagner, D., and Zeldith, M. (1992). A working strategy for constructing theories. In G. Ritzer (Ed.), *Metatheorizing* (pp. 107–123). Newbury Park, CA: Sage.

Borlund, P. (2000). Experimental components for the evaluation of interactive information retrieval systems. *Journal of Documentation, 56*(1), 71–90.

Bunge, M. A. (1967). *Scientific research: The search for system.* Heidelberg: Springer.

Byström, K., and Järvelin, K. (1995). Task complexity affects information seeking and use. *Information Processing and Management, 31*(2), 191–213.

Carterette B., Kanoulas E., and Yilmaz E. (2012). Incorporating variability in user behavior into systems based evaluation. In X. Chen, G. Lebanon, H. Wang, and M. J. Zaki (Eds.), *CICKM '12: Proceedings of the 21st ACM International Conference on Information and Knowledge Management* (pp. 135–144). New York: ACM.

Dervin, B. (1983). *An overview of sense-making research: Concepts, methods and results to date.* Paper presented at the International Communications Association annual meeting, Dallas, TX. Retrieved from https://www.ideals.illinois.edu/bitstream/handle/2142/2281/Dervin83a.htm.

Dupret, G., and Piwowarski, B. (2013). Model based comparison of discounted cumulative gain and average precision. *Journal of Discrete Algorithms, 18,* 49–62.

Harman, D. (2011). *Information retrieval evaluation.* San Rafael, CA: Morgan and Claypool. doi:10.2200/S00368ED1V01Y201105ICR019.

Ingwersen, P., and Järvelin, K. (2005). *The turn: Integration of information seeking and retrieval in context.* Heidelberg: Springer.

Järvelin, K. (1986). On information, information technology and the development of society: An information science perspective. In P. Ingwersen, L. Kajberg, and A. M. Pejtersen (Eds.), *Information technology and information use: Towards a unified view of information and information technology* (pp. 35–55). London: Taylor Graham.

Järvelin, K. (2007). An analysis of two approaches in information retrieval: From frameworks to study designs. *Journal of the American Society for Information Science and Technology 58*(7), 971–986.

Järvelin, K. (2011). Evaluation. In I. Ruthven and D. Kelly (Eds.), *Interactive information seeking behaviour and retrieval* (pp. 113–138.) London: Facet.

Järvelin, K. (2013). User-oriented evaluation in IR. In M. Agosti, N. Ferro, P. Forner, H. Müller, and G. Santucci (Eds.), *Proceedings of the 2012 International Conference on Information Retrieval Meets Information Visualization* (Lecture Notes in Computer Science Vol. 7757, pp. 86–91). Heidelberg: Springer. doi: 10.1007/978-3-642-36415-0_5.

Järvelin, K., and Ingwersen, P. (2010). User-oriented and cognitive models of information retrieval. In M. J. Bates and M. N. Maack (Eds.), *Encyclopedia of library and information sciences* (3rd ed, pp. 5521–5534.) London: Taylor and Francis. doi:10.1081/E-ELIS3-120043554.

Järvelin, K., and Kekäläinen, J. (2002). Cumulated gain-based evaluation of IR techniques. *ACM Transactions on Information Systems, 20*(4), 422–446.

Järvelin, K., and Wilson, T. D. (2003). On conceptual models for information seeking and retrieval research. *Information Research, 9*(1), paper 163. Retrieved from http://InformationR.net/ir/9–1/paper163.html.

Kelly, D. (2009). Methods for evaluating interactive information retrieval systems with users. *Foundations and Trends® in Information Retrieval, 3*(1–2), 1–224.

Kuhlthau, C. C. (2004). *Seeking meaning* (2nd ed.). Westport, CT: Libraries Unlimited.

Kumpulainen, S. (2013). *Task-based information access in molecular medicine: Task performance, barriers, and searching within a heterogeneous information environment* (Unpublished doctoral dissertation). Tampere University, Tampere, Finland. Retrieved from http://tampub.uta.fi/handle/10024/94595.

Kumpulainen, S., and Järvelin, K. (2010). Information interaction in molecular medicine: Integrated use of multiple channels. In N. J. Belkin and D. Kelly (Eds.), *Proceedings of the 3rd Information Interaction in Context Conference* (pp. 95–104). New York: ACM. doi:10.1145/1840784.1840800.

Kumpulainen, S., and Järvelin, K. (2012). Barriers to task-based information access in molecular medicine. *Journal of the American Society for Information Science and Technology, 63*(1), 86–97.

Paisley, W. (1968). Information needs and uses. In C. A. Cuadra (Ed.), *Annual review of information science and technology* (Vol. 3., pp. 1–30). Chicago: Information Today.

Robertson, S. E. (2000). Salton award lecture on theoretical argument in information retrieval. *ACM SIGIR Forum, 34*(1), 1–10.

Roos, A., Kumpulainen, S., Järvelin, K., and Hedlund, T. (2008). The information environment of researchers in molecular medicine. *Information Research, 13*(3), paper 353. Retrieved from http://InformationR.net/ir/13-3/paper353.html.

Sanderson, M. (2010). Test collection based evaluation of information retrieval systems. *Foundations and Trends in Information Retrieval, 4*(4), 247–375.

Smucker, M. D., and Clarke, C. (2012). Time-based calibration of effectiveness measures. In W. Song, Q. Yu, Z. Xu, T. Liu, S. Li, and J-R. Wen (Eds.), *SIGIR '12: Proceedings of the 35th International ACM SIGIR Conference on Research and Development in Information Retrieval* (pp. 95–104). New York: ACM.

Sormunen, E. (2002). Liberal relevance criteria of TREC—Counting on negligible documents? In M. Beaulieu, R. Baeza-Yates, S.-H. Myaeng, and K. Järvelin (Eds.), *SIGIR '02: Proceedings of the 25th International ACM SIGIR Conference on Research and Development in Information Retrieval* (pp. 320–330). New York: ACM.

Vakkari, P., and Sormunen, E. (2004). The influence of relevance levels on the effectiveness of interactive information retrieval. *Journal of the American Society for Information Science and Technology, 55*(11), 963–969.

Wilson, T. D. (1997). Information behaviour: An interdisciplinary perspective. *Information Processing and Management, 33*(4), 551–572.

Wilson, T. D. (1999). Models in information behavior research. *Journal of Documentation, 55*(3), 249–270.

CHAPTER 8

RELEVANCE: IN SEARCH OF A THEORETICAL FOUNDATION

TEFKO SARACEVIC

Relevance:
1: relation to the matter at hand
2: the ability (as of an information retrieval system) to retrieve
material that satisfies the needs of the user
MERRIAM-WEBSTER ONLINE

RELEVANCE IS A—IF NOT THE—KEY NOTION in the information sciences in general and information retrieval in particular. There is a striking absence of relevance theories developed in and for the information sciences. However, there have been several attempts to adapt relevance theories from other fields as theories-on-loan. This chapter seeks to address theoretical aspects of relevance in the information sciences to (a) describe differing manifestations and models of relevance that have emerged in the information sciences, treating them as potentially useful in formulating a theory of relevance, and (b) examine theories-on-loan proposed for use in the information sciences. Manifestations of relevance are synthesized, together with a brief history going back to 1950s, when concerns about relevance came about because of problems with testing of information retrieval (IR) systems. Three relevance models are reviewed: the traditional IR model, the dynamic model, and the stratified model. The chapter ends with suggestions about what should be encompassed by a relevance theory specific to the information sciences.

PROLOGUE

Shortly after I immigrated to the United States, in 1959, I started working as an electrician in a factory called Cleveland Twist Drill.

At the start of the 1960s they got a computer—the first computer I encountered. It was named RCA 501 (I remember it to this day, and hope that there's one in some museum now). It was among the first commercial computers; it was huge and clumsy, had blinking lights, and was housed in a very big room. Its memory was smaller than the memory in my wristwatch today.

Instantly, I fell in love with computers—well, long ago I fell out of love with them, but connections linger. I wanted to continue my studies, concentrating on computers.

At that time, the early 1960s, no university in Cleveland, Ohio (where I lived), had a computer-related program; computer science as a name and as an academic entity did not exist. But I discovered a place called the Center for Documentation and Communication Research (CDCR) at what is now Case Western Reserve University (a private university in Cleveland). CDCR had a computer and offered courses in machine literature searching (an activity that was later renamed information retrieval). It was a research branch of the School of Library Science, so I enrolled at the school and went right away into machine literature searching.

Upon graduation I got a job at CDCR. The center ran an information retrieval system in metallurgy, developed for and later delivered to the American Society for Metals. It was the first commercial IR system in the United States, if not the world. (A set of databases that morphed out of that original system is still in existence.) Real users paid $600 for a search—about a month's worth of my salary when I started working there. We had plenty of search requests. Searches had to be programmed, and so I learned programming and eventually conducted searches.

Programming searches was a challenge and I loved it. However, not all of the results that came out of the computer were relevant. That was not supposed to happen (after all, computers were perfect), but it did. So CDCR had what we called "little green people" (at times I was one of them) who evaluated the computer output. Only what they considered relevant was sent to users.

William Goffman (a mathematician–information scientist, at the time a senior researcher at CDCR, and later dean of the school) suggested an experiment that I carried out. (Unfortunately it was never published.) For a specific search request, or question, I gave the "non-relevant abstracts" (i.e., ones the computer did not identify as relevant) to a person from the group of little green people who had not yet seen the computer's results. This person's task was to judge the "nonrelevant abstracts" as relevant or not relevant; the person found some abstracts relevant and some not relevant. Then the remaining "nonrelevant abstracts" were resubmitted again and again to other little green people until two abstracts remained. At the end one abstract was judged to be relevant and the other nonrelevant. This experiment turned me toward asking questions about relevance: What is relevance? What factors affect it?

Thus began my lifelong involvement with the puzzle we call relevance. Soon thereafter I also began teaching searching. The rest, as they say, is history.

RETRIEVAL OF RELEVANT INFORMATION

Retrieval of relevant information, and not just any kind of information (and there are many), is a central idea in the information sciences. Information retrieval (IR), a major branch of the information sciences, is about retrieval of relevant information. Thus, the notion of relevance is fundamental to the information sciences.

Over the past several decades, numerous articles and expositions have been written about relevance in the information sciences, all starting, stated or unstated, with the basic propositions outlined above. Included are two hundred or so experiments exploring different variables involved in relevance. Systematic reviews and interpretations of this relatively voluminous literature can be found in, among other sources, Schamber, Eisenberg, and Nilan (1990); Shamber (1994); Mizzaro (1997); Borlund (2003); Ingwersen and Järvelin (2005); Hjørland (2010); and Huang and Soergel (2013). My own work on relevance (Saracevic 1975, 1996, 2007a, 2007b, 2012) is discussed in these publications, and this chapter borrows heavily from my work on relevance dating from 1975 to 2012.

In one way or another, all of the cited publications, including my own, are treatises on the basic question: what is relevance? Definitions of relevance are offered—clarifying the meaning and essential nature of relevance—but this basic question is not answered beyond generalities such as those offered in typical dictionary definitions. In all scholarship, definitions are necessary but not sufficient. Actually, nobody has to explain the notion of relevance to anybody; it is a "you know" notion. People understand relevance intuitively and similarly, no matter the culture, time, or space. They also understand that relevance involves a relation, namely, a relation "to," be it explicit or implicit. Relevance has a context—there is always "a matter at hand." Relevance is interactive.

The listed publications deal quite a bit with these relations and elaborate on elements involved in interactions. All of them propose differing (not necessarily different) conceptual frameworks for viewing, labeling, and classifying diverse types or kinds of relevance, such as topical relevance, user relevance, system relevance, and so on. That is, the frameworks depict different manifestations of relevance. Some publications also propose relevance models. Relevance models identify elements or variables involved in relevance and their interactions (while relevance frameworks specify a variety of relevance manifestations or types of relevance).

In all of this there is a striking absence of relevance theories developed in and for the information sciences. A theory provides an explanatory framework for some observation. As yet, no theories of relevance have emerged from the information sciences. In particular, no theories have emerged that address—that is, explain or predict—processes and interactions encountered in IR, or explain a rich body of experimental and pragmatic observations. Since there are no relevance theories, publications on manifestations of relevance and on relevance models are considered here as building blocks for a theory.

However, a few authors have proposed the use of theories from other fields as theories-on-loan. After all, relevance is a universal human notion. It is of scholarly interest in fields other than the information sciences, and thus relevance theories in general should be of interest.

This chapter addresses theoretical aspects of relevance in the information sciences, with the following objectives: (a) to describe differing manifestations, frameworks, and models of relevance that have emerged in the information sciences, treating them as potentially useful in formulating a theory of relevance; and (b) to examine theories-on-loan proposed for use in the information sciences.

MANIFESTATIONS OF RELEVANCE

A manifestation is one of the forms that something has when it appears or occurs. Think of energy—potential energy and kinetic energy are some of its manifestations. Like many other notions or phenomena, relevance has a number of manifestations. For some phenomena or notions, it is not that easy to identify the variety of manifestations and to distinguish among them. Think of manifestations of an illness—or information—or relevance.

Denoting various manifestations of relevance started quite early following problems with testing and explaining performance of IR systems. In 1959, Brian Vickery was the first to recognize in print that relevance has different manifestations (Vickery 1959a). His approach also precipitated a pattern of discussion about relevance manifestations that continues to this day. In one paper in the *Proceedings of the International Conference on Scientific Information* (a highly influential publication), Vickery states: The "controlling [criterion] in deciding on the optimum level of discrimination, we may call *user relevance*" (italics his; Vickery 1959a, p. 1277). In a second paper in the same proceedings, he discusses what is meant by "relevant to a particular sought subject" (Vickery 1959b, p. 863). Thus he identified a duality of relevance manifestations—user relevance and subject relevance—and he treated each separately.

User relevance on the one hand and subject (topic, system) relevance on the other represent the basic relevance manifestations. Each involves different relations. Each can be and has been further refined and interpreted. Each can be thought of as a broad class with subclasses. In IR they dance together, sometimes in intricate patterns and with various levels of success. This is the nature of any and all retrievals of information, and it is why we consider relevance to be interaction. The interplay between the two manifestations cannot be avoided; however, the effectiveness may differ greatly depending on how the interplay is accomplished. The two should be complementary, but at times they are in conflict.

IR testing is based on comparing *user relevance* (a user's or surrogate's assessment as to the relevance of retrieved answers or of any information or information objects in the system, even if not retrieved) and *system relevance* (responses to a query that were retrieved and deemed relevant by a system following some procedure). User relevance is the gold standard against which system relevance (and with it a system's performance) is measured. Thus, performance assessment of a given system (or algorithm or procedure) is based on, and follows from, human judgments regarding the relevance of information or information objects provided in response to a given query or information need.

During the many years after Vickery's pioneering identification of two major relevance manifestations, many additional manifestations were identified—some through observation and others through introspection. Some of the manifestations are referred to by a number of different names, such as *pertinent, useful, utility, germane, material, applicable, appropriate,* and the like. No matter what, they all connote relevance manifestations, but denote slightly different relations. Relevance will be relevance by any other name.

Following is a sort of consensus on the various manifestations of relevance in the information sciences, mainly following Borlund (2003), Ingwersen and Järvelin (2005), and Saracevic (2007a). Each manifestation is based on different relations and criteria:

- *System, or algorithmic, relevance*: the relation between a query and information or information objects that a system retrieved or failed to retrieve, using a given procedure or algorithm. Each system has ways and means by which given objects are represented, organized, and matched to a query. The intent is to retrieve a set of objects that the system inferred as being relevant to a query. Comparative effectiveness in inferring relevance is the criterion for system relevance.

- *Topical, or subject, relevance*: the relation between the subject, or topic, expressed in a query and the topic, or subject, covered by information or information objects that are in the system's file or database, or even in existence, whether retrieved or not. It is assumed that both queries and objects can be identified as being about a topic or subject. Aboutness is the criterion by which topicality is inferred.

- *Cognitive relevance, or pertinence*: the relation between a user's cognitive state of knowledge and information or information objects that are in the system's file or database, or even in existence, whether retrieved or not. Cognitive correspondence, informativeness, novelty, information quality, and the like are criteria by which cognitive relevance is inferred.

- *Situational relevance, or utility*: the relation between the situation, task, or problem at hand and information objects that are in the system's file or database, or even in existence, whether retrieved or not. Usefulness in decision making, appropriateness of information in resolution of a problem, reduction of uncertainty, and the like are criteria by which situational relevance is inferred.

This may be extended to involve general social and cultural factors as well.

- *Affective relevance*: the relation between the intents, goals, emotions, and motivations of a user, and information or information objects that are in the system's file or database, or even in existence, whether retrieved or not. Satisfaction, success, accomplishment, and the like are criteria for inferring motivational relevance.

Which, if any, of these manifestations is most important? For a while, topical or subject relevance was considered as primary, leading all other manifestations in importance. Not surprisingly, this was challenged with a number of examples where information or information objects might have been relevant to a given cognitive state without being topical to the question (e.g., see Harter 1992).

Hjørland argues, "The distinction between system's relevance and user's relevance is considered defunct because relevance is only meaningful in relation to goals and tasks, and machines do not have goals . . . Relevance is thus never 'a system's,' but always 'human' and therefore the dichotomy is wrong" (2010, p. 231). Clearly relevance manifestations are subject to quite a few views.

RELEVANCE MODELS

In general, models are a simplified, abstract version of a given reality from specific examples. Unlike specification of relevance manifestations, which have been vigorously pursued since the late 1950s, efforts to develop relevance models have been sporadic, even rare. Three models, the traditional, dynamic, and stratified models, are discussed below.

THE TRADITIONAL INFORMATION RETRIEVAL (IR) MODEL

Very soon after the development of the first (computerized) IR systems in the 1950s, the perennial questions asked of all systems were raised: What is the effectiveness and performance of given IR approaches? How do they compare? From the outset of IR testing in the mid-1950s to this day, relevance has served as the primary criterion for evaluating and comparing the performance of IR systems (or algorithms).

The first IR test on record was attempted in the early 1950s, as reported by Gull (1956), with human assessment of relevance used as the gold standard. However, the human assessment of relevance was done separately by groups (rather than by a single judge), and the test collapsed because of disagreement in relevance assessments between two competing groups.

Next were the IR tests collectively known as the "Cranfield tests." With the help of funding by the National Science Foundation, these were conducted for a decade starting in 1957 at the (UK) Cranfield College of Aeronautics (to become Cranfield Institute of Technology in 1969 and Cranfield University in 1993) under the leadership of Cyril Cleverdon (British librarian, 1914–1997). Reports from Cranfield tests that include not only methods and results but also numerous testing issues are assembled in the ACM SIGIR Museum.[1]

Cleverdon was very much aware of the Gull study; he discussed it, including the associated relevance problems, at some length in the 1962 Cranfield report (Cleverdon 1962). The collapse of Gull's study influenced the Cranfield tests with respect to the selection of the method for obtaining relevance judgments and the model for IR testing, as it has (if only implicitly) every IR test done since then.

The Cranfield tests were a great success—widely debated, cited, and followed. They became so influential not only because of the results they produced, but also because they constituted a method for assessing relevance in IR tests employing a single user or user surrogate (among others) for relevance judgment.

The lesson had been learned: never, ever use more than a single judge (or a single object, such as source document) for establishing the gold standard for comparison. No test ever does. The basics of the Cranfield method and model are used to this day, for example, in the Text Retrieval Conference (TREC; Voorhees and Harman 2005; see also annual TREC reports at http://trec.nist.gov). In other words, the process used today to evaluate relevance in IR tests has its roots in the collapse of an early 1950s study.

Out of the Cranfield tests also came a model generally known as the "traditional IR model." The traditional IR model, derived from the Cranfield reports, is widely discussed in the literature (see, e.g., Harter and Hert 1997, which includes a lengthy bibliography). The model is not about relevance, but rather, about performance of IR systems; however, since relevance is the absolute key and gold standard, it is worth considering it here, as depicted in figure 8.1.

The model has two streams of activities: one is the systems side,

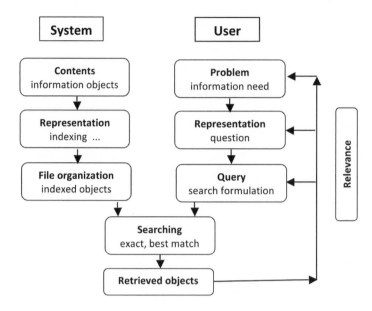

FIGURE 8.1. Traditional information retrieval model (Saracevic 1996, p. 4)

with processes performed by a system, and the other is the user side, with processes performed by users. On the system side, automatic processing is done; on the user side, human processing is done. They meet at the searching process, where the query is fed into the system and the system looks for information objects that match the query.

In practice, the system side (i.e., algorithms for representation or file organization, etc.) is used and adapted to specific circumstances encountered. On the user side, the query is used as input for searching and matching, and the rest—the problem, need, question—are taken as given and even ignored.

User relevance is the gold standard, but it is not dealt with in the model. What is relevant to a query may or may not be relevant to a question, and may be even less relevant to a problem or need at hand. Nothing on the system side is addressing possible variations on the user side, with the exception of the query, which is one way or another adjusted to the system anyhow.

But there is a positive side as well. The traditional IR model is based on a series of simplified assumptions about relevance, namely that relevance assessments are topical, binary, independent, stable, and consistent. Not surprisingly, these assumptions have been criticized.

In turn, questioning of these assumptions led to a significant amount of research on relevance. The assumptions were studied through a number of experiments; none of them hold (Saracevic 2007b). However, these simplified assumptions about relevance assessments enabled successful IR testing. Over the years, test results based on the traditional IR model have led to significant improvements in IR algorithms and procedures. IR extended from "bags of words" and texts to areas covering a variety of other expressions and media.

THE DYNAMIC MODEL

From the mid-1980s until the mid-1990s, a series of doctoral dissertations at the School of Information Studies, Syracuse University, addressed various aspects of relevance, reflecting a vigorous research environment under the guiding spirit of professors Robert Taylor and Jeffrey Katzer. These dissertations produced a number of articles, none more influential than a review by Schamber, Eisenberg, and Nilan (1990). They reexamined thinking about relevance in the information sciences, addressed the role of relevance in human information behavior and in systems evaluation, summarized major ideas and experiments, and came to the forceful conclusion that relevance should be modeled as dynamic and situational. Of course, dynamic properties of relevance had been discussed for decades before and demonstrated in experiments (which was readily acknowledged by the authors), but it was their insistence on the primacy of the dynamic and situational nature of relevance that struck a chord. While they did not build a formal model considering relevance interactions as dynamic, this became a norm ever after. Their conceptual contribution attracted wide attention and set the stage for further research. Numerous experiments followed, examining a variety of dynamic aspects and variables involved with relevance (Saracevic 2007b).

THE STRATIFIED MODEL

Relevance is a tangled affair involving interaction between and among a host of factors and variables. In philosophy, Schutz considered people in their everyday social world ("life-world"), which is not a homogeneous affair (and is really tangled!) (Schutz 1970; Schutz and Luckman 1973). Schutz suggested that the life-world is stratified into different realities, with relevance being at the root of its stratification. Models that view a complex, intertwined object (process, structure, system, phenomenon, notion) in a stratified way were suggested in a number of fields, from linguistics to medicine to meteorology to statistics and more. "Stratified" means that the object modeled is considered in terms of a set of interdependent, interacting layers; it is decomposed and composed back in terms of layers, or strata.

In 1996, after reviewing and reconsidering various relevance models, I proposed a stratified model for relevance (Saracevic 1996). It is another integrative model. Various elements in and derivations from the model were also elaborated by Cosijn and Ingwersen (2000). Later I further extended the stratified model to include IR interactions in general, encompassing a number of specific processes or notions that play a crucial role in IR interaction: relevance, user modeling, selection of search terms, and feedback (Saracevic 2007a). In the stratified model, relevance is placed within a framework of IR interaction. IR interactions are depicted as involving a number of strata; inferences about relevance are created or derived in interaction and interplay among these strata.

The stratified model starts with assumptions that users interact with IR systems in order to use information, and that the use of information is connected with cognition and then situational application; that is, it is connected with relevance. The major elements in the stratified model are user and computer, each with a host of variables of their own, having a discourse through an interface, as depicted in figure 8.2.

The user side has a number of levels. I suggest three to start with: cognitive, situational, and affective. The suggested computer levels are engineering (hardware), processing (software, algorithms), and content (information resources). It should be recognized that each level can be further delineated, and that others can be added, depending on the given set of conditions or emphasis in analysis.

A variety of interactions are instantiated on the interface, or surface, level; however, the interface is not the focus of interactions, even though it can in its own right effectively support or frustrate other interactions. We can think of interaction as a sequence of processes occurring in several connected levels. The IR interaction is then a dialogue between the participants—elements associated with the user and with the computer—through an interface, with the main purpose being to affect the cognitive state of the user for effective use of relevant information in connection with an application at hand, includ-

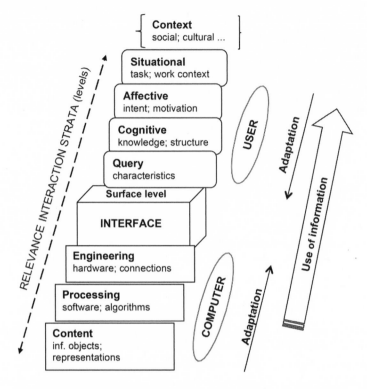

FIGURE 8.2. Stratified model of relevance interactions (Saracevic 2007a, p. 1926)

ing a context. The dialogue can be reiterative, incorporating among other things various types of feedback, and it can exhibit a number of patterns—all of which are topics for study.

Each stratum or level involves different elements or specific processes. On the human side, processes may be physiological, psychological, affective, and cognitive. On the computer side, they may be physical and symbolic. The interface provides for an interaction on the *surface* level:

1. Users carry out a dialogue by making utterances (e.g., commands) and receiving responses (computer utterances) through an interface with a computer to do searching and matching (as depicted in the traditional IR model), and also engage in a number of other processes or "things," beyond searching and matching, such as understanding and eliciting the attributes of a given computer com-

ponent or information resource; browsing; navigating within and among information resources, even distributed ones; determining the state of a given process; visualizing displays and results; obtaining and providing various types of feedback; making judgments; and so on.

2. Computers interact with users with given processes and "understandings" of their own, and provide given responses in this dialogue. In turn they also may provide elicitations or requests for responses from the user.

Let me elaborate on the nature of relevance from the stratified model point of view. I assume that the primary (but not the only) intent on both the user and computer sides of IR interaction deals with relevance. Given that we have a number of strata in interaction, and that in each of them there may be considerations or inferences as to relevance, relevance can also be considered in each stratum. In other words, in IR we have a dynamic, interdependent *system of relevances* (note the plural). This plurality is depicted by Schutz (1970), from whom I took the term "system of relevances," and by Sperber and Wilson (1986; reviewed below), who talk about principles of relevance.

While there may be differences in relevance inferences at different strata, these inferences are interdependent. The whole point of IR evaluation should be to compare relevance inferences from different levels. If we can typify relevance as it manifests itself at different levels, then we can study its behavior and effects within and between strata.

In general, models are not theories. Relevance models do not propose a relevance theory. However, they suggest which elements a relevance theory should encompass. Valid models can lead to suitable theories.

THEORIES-ON-LOAN

As mentioned, there have been several attempts to adapt relevance theories from other fields as theories-on-loan. The theories most influential in the information sciences are found in philosophy and communication. This section draws from Saracevic (2007a, pp. 1920–1924).

RELEVANCE IN PHILOSOPHY

A number of philosophers, particularly in the area of phenomenology, have been interested in relevance. Of particular interest to the information sciences are the works by Schutz (1970) and Schutz and Luckman (1973). The latter is a summary of Alfred Schutz's lifelong ideas, posthumously completed by his collaborator, Thomas Luckman.

Briefly, Schutz characterized the structure and functioning of the "life-world"—situations that people face in the reality of everyday life. These situations form layers; the life-world is stratified (as mentioned earlier). Schutz specified that relevance is the principle for stratification and dynamic interplay among strata. He believed that there is not a single relevance, but rather an interdependent system of relevances (plural). He proposed a typology of relevances with three main categories:

- *thematic relevances* (in Schutz's 1970 work called "topical"), involving perception of something problematic;
- *interpretational relevances*, involving the stock of knowledge at hand in grasping the meaning of that which is perceived; and
- *motivational relevances*, referring to the course of action to be adopted.

These categories interact. For example, the results of adopted action can motivate the process of obtaining additional interpretative material, and perceptions in thematic relevances may also be affected in this dynamic interaction.

These concepts are echoed in many later works on relevance in information science. Schutz is cited a number of times as an appropriate framework for considering relevance in information science. Even when there is not a direct citation to his work, his viewpoint is very much reflected in works on manifestations of relevance.

RELEVANCE IN COMMUNICATION

Information and communication are related, but there is also a distinction. Information is a *phenomenon*. Communication is a *process*—a process in which information is dispersed or exchanged. The process of communication encompasses a vast array of human activities and has many facets and manifestations. Similarly, the phenomenon of information encompasses many manifestations—there are many kinds of information—and the manifestations are interpreted in many senses. The concept of communication can be understood and used in numerous ways (as can the concept of information). Not surprisingly, then, the field of communication is broad and expansive. The study of communication intersects with a number of additional fields, including linguistics, semantics, psychology, cognition, philosophy, and related areas; and the study of relevance in communication also comes from an interdisciplinary tradition. Since one of the theories about relevance that emerged in the study of communication was prominently treated in information science, it is described here in some detail.

The most comprehensive and ambitious contribution to theorizing on relevance in a communication framework was made by Sperber and Wilson (1986, 1995), with the latest synthesis published by Wilson and Sperber (2004). Their relevance theory has the overarching goal of explaining what must be relevant and why to an individual with a single cognitive intention of a conceptual nature. It is based on an inferential model of communication that views communication in terms of intentions, as opposed to the more traditional and widely accepted source-message-destination model (also called the "classical code model," since messages are coded and decoded). The inferential model considers that the critical feature of most human communication—verbal or nonverbal—is the expression and recognition of intentions.

Relevance theory was originally associated with everyday speech or verbal communication, but later was extended to cover wider cognitive processes. The authors consider it a cognitive psychological theory. It has the ambitious goal of being a theory of both cognition and communication, tying them together on the basis of relevance. However, the basic problem addressed in the theory is how relevance is created in dialogs between persons.

Relevance explains "what makes an input worth picking up from the mass of competing stimuli" (Wilson and Sperber 2004, p. 252). In somewhat awkward language, these authors argue about ostensive behavior (or ostention), manifestations, and presumptions of relevance. Simply put, out of many stimuli, we pay attention only to information that seems relevant to us. Furthermore, to communicate is to claim someone's attention, and hence to imply that the information communicated is relevant. They firmly anchor relevance in a given context and talk about contextual effects—relevance is contextual. They also consider relevance assessment as comparative, not quantitative—that is, relevance is comparative.

At the center of their theory, Sperber and Wilson postulate two principles that they claim reflect universal tendencies:

- *the cognitive principle of relevance*—the claim that human cognition tends to be geared to maximization of relevance, that is, strives to maximize the relevance of inputs, and
- *the communicative principle of relevance*—the claim that every ostensive stimulus conveys a presumption of its own relevance.

In other words, human cognition is relevance oriented, and so is human communication. These two principles lead to the specification of how relevance (of an input to an individual) may be assessed in terms of two components: *cognitive effects* and *processing effort*. That is,

A. Other things being equal, the greater the positive cognitive effects achieved by processing an input, the greater the relevance of input to the individual at that time.
B. Other things being equal, the greater the processing effort expended, the lower the relevance of the input to the individual at that time. (Wilson and Sperber 2004, pp. 252–253)

Wilson and Sperber explain: "Humans do have an automatic tendency to maximise relevance, not because we have a choice in the matter—we rarely do—but because of the way our cognitive systems have evolved" (Wilson and Sperber 2004, p. 254). Treating relevance as an underlying principle in both cognition and communication evokes Schutz's (1970) explanation of what makes the life-world tick, as mentioned above; however, the life-world was not considered in Wilson and Sperber's relevance theory.

The two principles of relevance and the two components of assessment are at the heart of Wilson and Sperber's relevance theory, with the former being explanatory and the latter predictive. Thus the strength of the theory lies in proposing a number of explanations and operational, predictive principles about cognition and communication in terms of relevance. A relevance theory at last!

Two weaknesses are mentioned here. The first weakness concerns the nature of their proofs and grounds for generalization. They use hypothetical conversations between two protagonists, Peter and Mary, to provide both examples and proof. However, proof by example is no proof. The second weakness is that in the close to three decades since its first appearance, the theory has not been tested empirically or experimentally. A theory is scientific if it is refutable, that is, testable. While the authors proposed a number of possible tests and talked about possible experiments (Wilson and Sperber 2004, p. 283), such tests and experiments have not come forth as yet. Relevance theory is appealing, but it is also untested. It awaits verification and possible modification. Of course, the fact that a theory is not tested is not grounds for rejection. However, an untested theory may be untestable. In that case, it is not a scientific theory. The question is still open whether relevance theory is testable. Nevertheless, it does provide a number of insights about relevance and its behavior.

APPLICATIONS IN THE INFORMATION SCIENCES

Harter (1992) provided the first attempt to apply Wilson and Sperber's relevance theory to information sciences in general and to IR in particular. He starts with an emphatic rejection of topical relevance, that is, the notion and practice in IR where relevance is treated as topicality. As a solution, he embraces the notion of relevance as being exclusively related to cognitive states that change dynamically, calling this "psychological relevance." Relevance is what causes cognitive changes in a given context. The essence of Harter's proposal is to consider a given type, or manifestation, of relevance, as the primary or even exclusive aspect of relevance.

Harter deduces a number of excellent insights into relevance behavior. The strength of Harter's notion of psychological relevance is that he attempts to base the concept on a broader and more elaborate theoretical basis, namely Wilson and Sperber's relevance theory. The weakness is that actually he does not do that, beyond borrowing some concepts and terminology. Besides, as with Wilson and Sperber's relevance theory, Harter's construct has not been tested. He discusses, however, the difficulty of testing and applying it in practice. Unfortunately, he did not get there, but he pointed the way and opened a wide-ranging and lively discussion. Still, the value of his attempt to gain some theoretical footing for relevance in information science is in itself groundbreaking.

A second and much more comprehensive attempt to transfer Wilson and Sperber's relevance theory to an information sciences framework was made by White (2007a, 2007b). In this massive work, White confines Wilson and Sperber's relevance theory to the application of the *cognitive effects* and *processing effort*, and he does not use their two principles of relevance. In an effort to integrate relevance theory, IR, and bibliometrics, he proposes that cognitive effects and processing effort are also components in relevance assessments in IR and can be used as predictive mechanisms for the operational assessment of relevance. Briefly, White (a) translates the widely applied IR algorithm based on terms called "tf*idf" (term frequencies, inverse document frequencies) into a bibliometric retrieval algorithm based on citations; (b) uses this to create a new two-dimensional visual display of retrieved bibliometric results, called a "pennant diagram" (because it looks like a pennant); (c) interprets the dimensions of the diagram in terms of *cognitive effects* and *processing effort*; (d) derives a number of practical examples; and (e) engages in extensive interpretation of results and discussion of reasoning behind them, in a manner similar to that of Wilson and Sperber. White significantly extended the interpretation of Sperber and Wilson's relevance theory to information science circumstances and interests, with both the strength and weaknesses of the theory present.

The strength of his interpretation is that he actually applied his constructs to practical work. While the proposed bibliometric retrieval and associated pennant diagram might have been done without recourse to relevance theory, the borrowed constructs (cognitive effects and processing effort) provided the grounds for extensive abstract explanations of both processes and results. They offer insights about retrieval above and beyond the statistical nature of the process and rank-listing of results. However, the weakness of the nature of proof present in Wilson and Sperber's work is also present here. Furthermore, White's work is not a test of relevance theory, as claimed; it is structures, concepts, and terminology on loan.

Both works—Harter's and White's—are worthwhile in their efforts to adapt a theory. The field should be stimulated to think about such adaptations and think about theory, but the question remains whether the theory being adapted is worthwhile to start with.

STILL IN SEARCH OF A THEORY

As yet, authors discussing relevance in the information sciences have not developed any indigenous theory-cum-theory about the notion, nor have they successfully adapted theories from other fields, despite a few attempts. Where theories were borrowed for use, they were merely described, interpreted, and declared appropriate. They were not tested. However, and to their credit, they were conceptual and terminological borrowings used for extending our collective insight about relevance. They made us think.

We are still in search of a theory of relevance applicable to the context of the information sciences, and particularly IR. In other words, we are still in search of a conceptual basis, a set of testable principles and propositions, to explain the notion of relevance applicable to information science practice, to explain its manifestation, and to predict its behavior and effects. Of course, practice can be successfully pursued in the absence of a theory. The history of technology has a great many examples of this, IR being just one of them. But, a great many substantial advances have been achieved based on a theory; the history of modern technology has even more such examples.

The attempts to borrow and adapt theories have a positive effect on clarifying empirical knowledge and understanding about relevance in information science. Schutz's reference to systems of relevances (plural) suggests a number of manifestations of relevance that are already recognized, and his reference to "horizon" suggests the inclusion of contexts as inevitable. Wilson and Sperber's cognitive effects and processing efforts suggest dimensions used in assessing relevance, including its dynamic nature.

WHAT SHOULD A RELEVANCE THEORY ENCOMPASS?

I consider relevance as having a number of dimensions or attributes. These attributes suggest elements that an information science theory of relevance should, or even must, encompass. The attributes of relevance can be summarized as follows (Cosijn and Ingwersen 2000):

- *Relation*: Relevance arises when a relation (between objects such as a person's information need and information) is expressed along certain properties, frequently in communicative exchanges that involve people or information objects.
- *Intention*: The relation in expression of relevance involves intention(s), such as objectives, roles, and expectations. Motivation is involved.
- *Context*: The intention in expression of relevance always comes from a context and is directed toward that context. Relevance cannot be considered without a context.

- *Internal context*: Relevance involves a cognitive state. It also involves an affective state.
- *External context*: Relevance is directed toward a situation, tasks, or the problem at hand. Social and cultural components may be involved as well.
- *Inference*: Relevance involves assessment about a relation, and on that basis is created or derived.
- *Selection*: Inference may also involve a selection from competing sources geared toward maximization of results or minimization of effort in dealing with results.
- *Interaction*: Inference is accomplished as a dynamic, interacting process, where an interpretation of other attributes may change as context changes.
- *Measurement*: Relevance involves a graduated assessment of the effectiveness or degree of maximization of a given relation, such as assessment of some information sought for an intention geared toward a context.
- *Change*: Relevance may change as cognitive states change and advance, as tasks and situations progress, and as context is modified.

These conceptualizations reflect a general understanding of the meaning and practice of relevance in information science. They can be summarized as follows: relevance is a relation; follows from intentionality; has a context, external and internal; is not given; is inferred; is created or derived; involves selection; involves interaction; is a measure; and may change.

These are not the only elements that a relevance theory should encompass. Different manifestations should be addressed, as should various elements as enumerated in the various models. Most importantly, factors that play a role in how humans determine relevance of information or information objects should—indeed must—be explained.

Finally, there are some questions that should be asked in both experiments and theory. As the concept of relevance went global and became widely used, a number of questions emerged. To what extent are the results of relevance scholarship—primarily concerned with a restricted and relatively well-defined population and information—applicable to the broad public and every conceivable type of information? A great many fascinating questions worthy of research could be asked. Here are but a few:

- Are relevance clues similar or different across the broad public?
- Is relevance behavior similar or different across the broad public?
- Can the broad public be defined at all with respect to relevance effects?

It seems that the globalization of relevance also has exposed a need for additional and different agendas for—and approaches to—relevance scholarship.

EPILOGUE

I will end with the same thoughts with which I ended a large survey of relevance research: "Information technology, information systems, and information retrieval will change in ways that we cannot even imagine, not only in the long run, but even in the short term. They are changing at an accelerated pace. But no matter what, relevance is here to stay. Relevance is timeless. Concerns about relevance will always be timely" (Saracevic 2007b, p. 2142).

So is the search for a relevance theory in the information sciences.

NOTE

1. Reports from Cranfield tests and other historical documents dealing with IR can be found at the ACM SIGIR Museum website, http://www.sigir.org /museum/allcontents.html.

REFERENCES

Borlund, P. (2003). The concept of relevance in IR. *Journal of the American Society for Information Science and Technology, 54*(10), 913–925.

Cleverdon, C. W. (1962). *Report on the testing and analysis of an investigation into the comparative efficiency of indexing*. Cranfield, UK: ASLIB Cranfield Research Project. Retrieved from http://www.sigir.org/museum/allcontents .html.

Cosijn, E., and Ingwersen, P. (2000). Dimensions of relevance. *Information Processing and Management, 36*(4), 533–550.

Gull, C. D. (1956). Seven years of work on the organization of materials in the special library. *American Documentation, 7*(4), 320–329.

Harter, S. P. (1992). Psychological relevance and information science. *Journal of the American Society for Information Science, 43*(9), 602–615.

Hjørland, B. (2010). The foundation of the concept of relevance. *Journal of the American Society for Information Science and Technology, 61*(2), 217–237.

Huang, X., and Soergel, D. (2013). Relevance: An improved framework for explicating the notion. *Journal of the American Society for Information Science and Technology, 64*(1), 18–35.

Ingwersen, P., and Järvelin, K. (2005). *The turn: Integration of information seeking and retrieval in context*. Berlin: Springer.

Mizzaro, S. (1997). Relevance: The whole history. *Journal of the American Society for Information Science, 48*(9), 810–832.

Saracevic, T. (1975). Relevance: A review of and a framework for the thinking on the notion in information science. *Journal of American Society for Information Science, 26*(6), 321–343.

Saracevic, T. (1996). Relevance reconsidered '96. In P. Ingewersen and N. O. Pors (Eds.), *Information science: Integration in perspective. Proceedings of the Second International Conference on Conceptions of Library and Information Science* (pp. 201–218). Copenhagen: Royal School of Librarianship. Retrieved from http://comminfo.rutgers.edu/~tefko/articles.htm.

Saracevic, T. (2007a). Relevance: A review of the literature and a framework for thinking on the notion in information science. Part II: Nature and manifestations of relevance. *Journal of the American Society for Information Science and Technology, 58*(3), 1915–1933.

Saracevic, T. (2007b). Relevance: A review of the literature and a framework for thinking on the notion in information science. Part III: Behavior and effects of relevance. *Journal of the American Society for Information Science and Technology, 58*(13), 2126–2144.

Saracevic, T. (2012). Research on relevance in information science: A historical perspective. In T. Carbo and T. Bellardo Hahn (Eds.), *International perspectives on the history of information science and technology* (pp. 49–60). Medford, NJ: Information Today.

Schamber, L. (1994). Relevance and information behavior. *Annual Review of Information Science and Technology, 29*, 3–48.

Schamber, L., Eisenberg, M. B., and Nilan, M. S. (1990). A re-examination of relevance: Toward a dynamic, situational definition. *Information Processing and Management, 26*(6), 755–776.

Schutz, A. (1970). *Reflections on the problem of relevance*. New Haven, CT: Yale University Press.

Schutz, A., and Luckman, T. (1973). *The structures of the life-world*. Evanston, IL: Northwestern University Press.

Sperber, D., and Wilson, D. (1986). *Relevance: Communication and cognition*. Cambridge, MA: Blackwell.

Sperber, D., and Wilson, D. (1995). *Relevance: Communication and cognition* (2nd ed.). Cambridge, MA: Blackwell.

Vickery, B. C. (1959a). The structure of information retrieval systems. In *Proceedings of the International Conference on Scientific Information* (Vol. 2, pp. 1275–1290). Washington, DC: National Academy of Sciences. Retrieved from http://www.nap.edu/books/NI000518/html/1275.html.

Vickery, B. C. (1959b). Subject analysis for information retrieval. In *Proceedings of the International Conference on Scientific Information* (Vol. 2, pp. 855–866). Washington, DC: National Academy of Sciences. Retrieved from http://www.nap.edu/books/NI000518/html/855.html.

Voorhees, E. M., and Harman, D. K. (Eds.). (2005). *TREC: Experiment and evaluation in information retrieval*. Cambridge, MA: MIT Press.

White, H. D. (2007a). Combining bibliometrics, information retrieval, and relevance theory: First examples of a synthesis. *Journal of the American Society for Information Science and Technology, 58*(4), 536–559.

White, H. D. (2007b). Combining bibliometrics, information retrieval, and relevance theory: Some implications for information science. *Journal of the American Society for Information Science, 58*(4), 583–605.

Wilson, D., and Sperber, D. (2004). Relevance theory. In L. Horn and G. Ward (Eds.), *Handbook of pragmatics* (pp. 249–290). Oxford: Blackwell. Retrieved from http://people.bu.edu/bfraser/Relevance%20Theory%20Oriented/Sperber%20&%20Wilson%20-%20RT%20Revisited.pdf.

CHAPTER 9

THE STORY OF A COLONY: THEORY DEVELOPMENT IN WEBOMETRIC RESEARCH

MIKE THELWALL

THE RESEARCH FIELD OF WEBOMETRICS is primarily concerned with gathering information from the web, such as links between websites or online citations of academic documents, and analyzing it using quantitative methods. The emergence of a colony of webometricians within the information sciences was triggered by the realization that the link search facility of AltaVista in 1997 made it possible to count the number of hyperlinks to websites or between websites. AltaVista had thus made it possible to conduct a type of web-based citation analysis using hyperlinks instead of citations (Ingwersen 1998; Rodríguez i Gairín 1997). This then gave rise to a number of projects to assess whether hyperlinks behave like citations in various contexts (Rousseau 1998; Smith 1999; Vaughan and Thelwall 2002) and to investigate the tools used in many studies: web search engines (Bar-Ilan and Peritz 2004; Rousseau 1999; Vaughan and Thelwall 2004). Webometrics subsequently expanded to incorporate many new types of study, first to identify ways of extracting novel types of academic citation from the web (Kousha and Thelwall 2006, 2008, 2009; Thelwall and Kousha 2008) and then to exploit or investigate popular new websites, such as Mendeley (Bar-Ilan 2011), as well as general sites, including MySpace (Bar-Ilan 2011; Li, Thelwall, and Giustini 2012) and Flickr (Angus, Thelwall, and Stuart 2008). A more recent area to emerge as part of, or in parallel with, webometrics is altmetrics (Priem and Hemminger 2010), which is concerned with generating social web indicators to measure the impact of scholarly articles, such as counting how often a paper has been tweeted (Eysenbach 2011).

The webometrics colony largely focused on methods development and indicator evaluation, and as a result probably used relatively little theory for an information science field, and the theoretical contributions of its papers may also be somewhat unusual. For this reason it is an interesting experiment to focus on webometric theory and attempt to classify it within a scheme that may or may not be appropriate for it. Gregor's (2006) taxonomy, developed for information systems research, seems to be the most appropriate existing theory taxonomy because it is recent and developed for a similar discipline. This chapter discusses the taxonomy, gives examples of webometric research that fit each category, and describes some of the classifications in detail. It also discusses difficulties with the classification process and critically analyzes the suitability of the taxonomy for this purpose. It concludes with a more in-depth discussion of the motivations behind the creation of two webometric theories that I have developed.

GREGOR'S THEORY TAXONOMY APPLIED TO WEBOMETRIC RESEARCH

Gregor's taxonomy splits research theory into five different types. These five types are described separately below, with one section for each. The types are illustrated, when possible, with examples from webometrics. Gregor uses the term "theory" in a general sense regarding the type of contribution an article makes, so an article does not need to explicitly formulate or discuss a theory in order to qualify for the scheme (Gregor 2006).

TYPE I: THEORY FOR ANALYSIS

Type 1 represents the most basic kind of theoretical contribution. It involves describing what the research object is without seeking predictions or explanations for the results. It is appropriate for new contexts in which little is known, and can lay the basis for future studies of different types. Many webometric papers have developed type 1 theory. These papers have three primary foci: hyperlink analysis, social website analysis, and specific website analysis.

A number of papers (Bar-Ilan 2004, 2005; Wilkinson et al. 2003) have classified academic hyperlinks using content analysis. These articles have shed light on the variation in hyperlink types and their relative proportions in various contexts. They have not sought to explain why the link types exist or to predict the future occurrence of link types, although the results could aid investigations in both directions. Hyperlink analysis seems to be a common type 1 approach in the information sciences and communication science, perhaps because web objects are new and typically evolving.

To illustrate the hyperlink analysis approach, an early link analysis paper (Wilkinson et al. 2003) conducted a content analysis of hyperlinks between British university websites to describe the apparent types of motivations for creating inter-university hyperlinks. The main outcome of the study was a list of common reasons for hyperlinking and the relative frequency of these links in a sample of 414 British universities. These reasons, from most frequent to less frequent, were as follows:

1. Student learning material
2. Information for students
3. Research support
4. Research partners
5. Recreational student homepage
6. Page creator or sponsor
7. Research reference
8. Tourist information
9. Libraries and e-journals
10. Similar department

The motivation for this study was theoretically driven. Previous quantitative studies of inter-university hyperlinks had hypothesized that the research productivity of a university could be estimated by counting the number of hyperlinks pointing to its website. Checking how often such hyperlinks were research related would help to confirm or deny this hypothesis. This is made clear in the following extract from the conclusions: "Despite the informality of most links, an overwhelming majority of almost 90% appeared to be created for reasons connected to scholarly activity by researchers or students. The main conclusion is therefore that *metrics based upon link counts can be seen to be measuring an agglomeration of connections related to scholarly activities in a wide variety of ways*" (Wilkinson et al. 2003, p. 54; emphasis in original).

The conclusion also makes clear that this explicitly descriptive research is seen as relevant because of its contribution to indicator building, which is type 5 theory (see below). This was not the only webometric content analysis of hyperlinks; Bar-Ilan (2005) proposed a content analysis scheme to classify the apparent purpose of hyper-links and applied the scheme to a set of hyperlinks between Israeli universities. One of the outcomes of the paper was purely descriptive—a characterization of inter-university hyperlinks in Israel.

Thus the main outcome of the earlier paper aided future descriptive studies by providing a classification scheme. It could also aid future studies constructing other types of theory if they used the categories to hypothesize or generalize about patterns, perhaps in conjunction with other methods. Because the main goal was introducing a content analysis scheme rather than presenting the results of applying the scheme, this article has a focus on methods development, which has some overlap with type 5 theory; however, the primary goal was descriptive and so the primary outcome is type 1.

Hyperlink network analysis studies gather data on the hyperlinks among a set of websites and illustrate them in a network diagram. If the objective is to describe how the websites interlink (Ortega and Aguillo 2008; Ortega et al. 2008; Thelwall 2001, 2002; Thelwall and Smith 2002), then this is a type 1 study, although these articles also tend to introduce and justify new methods to some extent. For example, one study produced five network diagrams of the interlinking between Nordic academic websites (Ortega and Aguillo 2008). This was primarily descriptive; its aims were to "detect sub-networks within the Nordic network, the position and role of the different university web domains and to understand the structural topology of this web space" (p. 1625).

In addition to studying hyperlinks, webometricians have investigated social websites. Communication scholars have investigated why people use social websites, what they are used for, and their impact on society, often using qualitative methods such as interviews (boyd 2008) or questionnaires for specific user groups (Lampe, Ellison, and Steinfield 2008). In contrast, webometrics (and some similar computer science studies) has contributed by conducting large-scale descriptive investigations that used a computer program to download large amounts of content from a specific website and then reporting simple summary statistics extracted from that content. This is clearly a type 1 contribution. For example, an investigation of the early music-oriented general social network site MySpace downloaded a systematic sample of 22,670 profile pages and produced a number of tables and graphs using data extracted from them (Thelwall 2008). One graph reported the ages of users in the sample, showing that the median age was twenty-one years, and a table re-ported the common motivations for joining the site. This paper was purely quantitative and was explicitly cast as an attempt to provide a large-scale descriptive background as a companion contribution to communication science research into social network sites.

A more recent social website study monitored Twitter for a month. It identified the thirty world news events causing the biggest spikes of interest, and then described how the average sentiment of tweets changed during the events (Thelwall, Buckley, and Paltoglou 2011). This was partly descriptive and partly predictive in that it sought to assess whether spikes could be predicted by sentiment changes when the event started. (They couldn't.) It was also partly explana-tory in that it found that increases in negativity within a topic seem to be the cause of spikes. On balance, however, there is probably not enough evidence presented in the paper to make this a strong claim for explanatory power, and hence it is probably not reasonable to de-scribe it as type 2 (explanatory) research.

A third kind of type 1 descriptive webometric study focuses on a specific website of importance to information science research goals and describes an aspect of the site. For example, an investigation into the Technology, Education, Design (TED) website sought to de-scribe the use and impacts of TED videos (Sugimoto and Thelwall 2013). The typical TED video is a presentation by an expert on a topic of general public interest. Many of the presenters are academics, and many of the talks have academic themes. The study downloaded a range of types of usage and descriptive data about the talks from the TED website and the TED channel in YouTube, and presented the re-sults in a series of tables and graphs. This was a primarily descriptive study that sought to describe how TED was successful without try-ing to discover why it was successful. For instance, TED talks were found to be widely viewed but rarely cited, and the paper only briefly speculates about why this is the case.

TYPE 2: EXPLANATORY THEORY

Type 2 theory seeks to explain how, why, when, or where a phenome-non occurs, rather than just describing it. Although most of the web-ometric studies discussed above include at least speculations about why the described phenomena have the characteristics reported, this is not their main contribution. The speculations are typically part of a post hoc discussion of their main contribution.

It seems that relatively few webometric papers have focused on developing type 2 explanatory theory rather than predictive or descriptive theory. This is probably because much webometric research has the ultimate goal of constructing new evaluation indicators, that is, indicator design (see discussion on type 5 theory, below). Nevertheless, some studies have focused either on explaining the objects investigated in webometric research, such as link counts and search engine results, or on using webometrics to help explain phenomena that are primarily of interest outside webometrics, such as social network sites.

In order to help explain why hyperlinks are attracted by researchers' web presences, one project tested a range of factors associated with academics to identify those that were significant factors for hyperlink (inlink) counts, based upon statistical regression models (Barjak, Li, and Thelwall 2007). The authors concluded, among other things, that "contrary to expectations, the size of collaboration networks is negatively related to hyperlink counts" (p. 200). This is more than purely descriptive in that the focus is on discovering significant relationships between hyperlink counts and other factors. The explanatory nature of the paper is highlighted in its title, "Which Factors Explain the Web Impact of Scientists' Personal Homepages?" This type of research seems to be becoming more popular (Seeber et al. 2012).

One strand of webometrics has investigated aspects of the performance of commercial search engines. This topic is particularly important to webometric theory construction because commercial search engines are used in webometric indicator development. Research on this topic has included aspects of both type 1 (descriptive) and type 2 (explanatory) research. As examples of the former, some papers have described the performance of one or more search engines over time for a specific set of queries (e.g., Mettrop and Nieuwenhuysen 2001). These sought to find out how much the results varied and how frequently they varied. Other investigations have taken a similar approach but with more detail, pushing toward type 2 theory construction. For instance, an investigation into pages matching a query for the topic "informetrics" at various points in time categorized the results in a detailed way that, although descriptive, helped to explain why some types of pages disappeared permanently or temporarily from the results (Bar-Ilan and Peritz 2008). Another explanatory article used a statistical approach to test whether the omission of some websites from the indexes of commercial search engines could be explained by their country of origin (Vaughan and Thelwall 2004).

An example of a webometric paper seeking to provide explanations for phenomena outside webometrics is an analysis of homophily in MySpace (Thelwall 2009). A large collection of downloaded information from MySpace was used to identify factors in common between pairs of users that were significantly associated with their likelihood of being "friends" in the site. Friends were more likely to share a religion and many other types of affiliation than were random users, but there was no evidence of gender homophily. From this emerged the explanatory theory that homophily was quite strong in MySpace. This paper is to some extent descriptive since it measures various types of homophily, but is more explanatory since it focuses on explaining the phenomenon of social network site friendship.

Another example of an explanatory study of the social web is an investigation into MySpace that focused on dialogs between friends as expressed in comments left on profile pages (Thelwall and Wilkinson 2010). Dialogs were categorized by duration and type in order to describe their typical purposes. Although this is descriptive to some extent, the title of the paper, "Public Dialogs in Social Network Sites: What Is Their Purpose?," stakes a claim for being explanatory research. One finding was that dialogs were used for "making initial contact and keeping in touch occasionally" (p. 392).

Another explanatory paper is an investigation into the relationship between bibliometric indicators and TED talks (Sugimoto et al. 2013). This paper assessed whether giving a TED talk tended to cause an increase in citations to an academic's work (it didn't). More broadly, this paper sought to understand the impact of giving a TED talk on an academic's profile. The results suggested that the primary result of giving a TED talk was to increase general awareness of the scholar's work.

TYPE 3: PREDICTIVE THEORY

Almost no webometric study has attempted to be purely predictive in the sense of developing theory to help predict what will happen in the future. An exception is a study showing that the number of tweets of an article in the *Journal of Medical Internet Research* could be used to approximately predict the number of times that it would subsequently be cited (Eysenbach 2011). The purpose of the article was to demonstrate that tweets could be used to predict citations rather than to explain why this might be the case, perhaps because the connection appears obvious, even if unproven.

TYPE 4: EXPLANATORY AND PREDICTIVE THEORY

No webometric study has developed theory to both explain and predict events. Despite this, one of the wider goals of much webometric research has been to predict future citation counts for scholarly articles. This is because citation counts are widely used to estimate the scientific impact of papers, researchers, or groups of researchers, but citations take years to accumulate following a paper's original publication date. In contrast, web-based indicators, such as tweets, Mendeley readers, bookmarks, blog mentions, or citations in online course syllabi (see below), accumulate more quickly and so could be used to predict future citations. Nevertheless, webometric studies, despite often correlating web data with citation counts, have rarely sought to predict future citations, but have instead tended to investigate the use of web data for indicators of aspects of scholarly impact in their own right.

TYPE 5: DESIGN AND ACTION THEORY

Type 5 theory focuses on describing how to do something. Much webometric research falls into this category because it concerns how to use the web to construct indicators that can more effectively evaluate aspects of scholarly activity, including impact and quality, or to identify emerging trends.

One such indicator is the "integrated online impact" indicator for academic articles. It is constructed by counting the number of times that an article has been cited online in various different ways (Kousha, Thelwall, and Rezaie 2010). This indicator was tested by correlating it with citation counts and by invoking previous articles that provided evidence for the efficacy of different component parts of the indicator.

Other indicators are based upon mentions in online PowerPoint presentations for scholarly impact (Kousha et al. 2010), citations in books for impact in the arts and humanities (Kousha and Thelwall 2009), and mentions in online syllabi for educational impact (Kousha and Thelwall 2008).

Papers that have contributed findings toward the eventual goal of developing indicators but that have not explicitly described them are probably better classified as explanatory. In addition to the examples of type 2 papers provided earlier, this includes some studies directed toward developing research productivity indicators for universities (Thelwall and Harries 2004) and departments (Li, Musgrove, and Wilkinson 2003) based upon counting links to their websites. It also includes the new generation of altmetric (Priem, Taraborelli, Groth, and Neylon, 2011) studies, which have similar goals—to propose or evaluate new indicators for aspects of scholarly communication (Haustein and Siebenlist 2011; Li et al. 2012; Mohammadi and Thelwall 2013; Priem and Hemminger 2010; Thelwall, Haustein, et al. 2013).

Papers that describe methods to rank universities based upon web data are also essentially indicator development, even if they partially tabulate the results and hence are to some extent descriptive (Aguilo et al. 2006). In this case the primary output is not the ranked list presented in the paper but the indicator-based method used to rank the list.

Some type 5 research by webometricians overlaps with computer science or computational linguistics. This research proposes and tests new computer-based methods for various tasks. These papers are not mainstream webometrics, but draw upon webometric methods. For example, one paper developed a method to process huge amounts of blog texts to automatically identify spiking topics of interest within a broad issue (Thelwall and Prabowo 2007). Another introduced an automatic method to produce a time line of a major event with text extracted from relevant blog and news stories (Prabowo, Thelwall, and Alexandrov 2007).

Social web sentiment analysis methods also fit this category because such papers focus on developing a computer program to detect sentiment in text as the end goal (Thelwall and Buckley 2013; Thelwall, Buckley, and Paltoglou 2012; Thelwall et al. 2010; Thelwall, Buckley, et al. 2013). Still another example of type 5 research is a simple search-based method that has been proposed to get retrospective public opinion information about major events based upon blog searching (now Twitter searching), claiming to be "the first general-purpose source of retrospective public opinion in the social sciences" (Thelwall 2007, p. 277).

EVALUATION OF THE THEORY TAXONOMY

It is possible and reasonably straightforward to use Gregor's (2006) theory taxonomy to classify webometric research. Nevertheless, two of the categories, types 3 and 4, have been little used because there is a lack of prediction in webometric research. It may also be that the typology overemphasizes the importance of prediction for information sciences as a whole, unless predicting or explaining and predicting are more common in other information science areas.

Another limitation of the typology is that type 5 is perhaps not the most natural category for methods-oriented webometric research. Although methods-oriented webometric research fits within the broad type 5 category, it has a much more narrow, or specific, focus than the category in general. The type 5 category may, however, be appropriate for the information sciences as a whole because it includes information behavior theories (Fisher, Erdelez, and McKechnie 2005) and information systems design issues.

WEBOMETRIC THEORY DEVELOPMENT

Few of the articles discussed in this chapter explicitly state that they are attempting to develop theory even though they can be categorized by the type of theory that they present. However, two articles have explicitly introduced theories; both theories are type 5 because they focus on methods for research.

The first such webometric theory is information-centered research (ICR), which argues that information scientists should evaluate new web opportunities for extracting online data in order to identify the research problems that the data may help to address (Thelwall, Wouters, and Fry 2008). This is prescriptive in the sense that it advocates investigating new data for research questions rather than the more usual approach of selecting research questions first and then attempting to answer them with data.

The second is a theoretical framework for interpreting social science link analysis research (Thelwall 2006). This article attempts to delineate best practice for information science hyperlink research. It is prescriptive, with a list of actions required to perform in a link analysis.

Papers describing both of these theories were analytical rather than experimental, proposing but not evaluating a new approach. The two theories and their development are described in more detail below.

THE DEVELOPMENT OF INFORMATION-CENTERED RESEARCH (ICR)

I developed ICR as a solution to a specific academic problem: getting webometric articles published in communication science journals. Before ICR was created, I believed that webometric methods could make a significant contribution to web-related communication science, and computer-mediated communication in particular. I had written a number of webometric articles for the *Journal of Computer-Mediated Communication*. Some of these were rejected; those that were published were subject to a number of major revisions in response to the referees' comments, and I was uncomfortable with some of the requested revisions. The main problem in all cases was that the journal understandably required the articles to be underpinned by communication science theory, whereas I had written them as primarily descriptive pieces. I thought that it was useful to conduct descriptive research on new web phenomena without connecting to existing theories and so, with the help of Paul Wouters and Jenny Fry, devised ICR as a rationalized justification for this approach (Thelwall and Wouters 2005).

ICR argues that when a new phenomenon emerges on the web (e.g., blogs, social network sites, scholarly bookmarking sites, Twitter), it is reasonable to investigate it in order to identify which research problems it might help to address. This is in contrast to the traditional research approach, which would be to start with an apparently appropriate research problem and assess whether the new phenomenon is appropriate for the pre-chosen research problem. The reason given for the ICR claim is that new web phenomena are typically complex in terms of social aspects, such as how they are used in practice and how their use interacts with preexisting practices, and also in terms of the technical side: how data can be collected, and any data collection and processing practical limitations. As a result it is likely that any relevant research uses may not be immediately obvious to an outsider, and researchers from multiple fields and with multiple interests may waste time by investigating new web phenomena that turn out to be irrelevant or impractical for them. If this argument is accepted, then it would be a valid overall contribution to research to conduct descriptive (type 1) investigations into new web phenomena with the goal of identifying, or helping others to identify, relevant research problems that the web data can help address. Hence, ICR could be invoked as a rationale for publishing type 1 webometric research in communication science journals without requiring the work to connect with existing communication science theory.

A logical extension of ICR (that emerged from reflecting about it rather than from a specific external need) was that information scientists were particularly well suited to conducting ICR because this discipline deals with information. Moreover, information scientists naturally deal with the information needs of other disciplines, so the role of conducting ICR is in a way similar to the role of a specialist academic librarian in a research institution.

At the time that ICR emerged, I thought about setting up a formal ICR center to conduct and promote this type of research, but did not pursue the idea because it seemed unlikely that the UK would fund it.

The initial goal of the ICR papers was twofold: to develop a fully worked out argument for ICR to see if it made sense, and to produce refereed publications that could be cited in future articles (including articles submitted to communication science journals) as a rationale for a descriptive research approach.

The legacy of ICR is extremely disappointing compared to the early hopes. It did not take off as a new type of research and has not led to the increased publication of web-related descriptive articles in communication science journals. As evidence of this, by December 2013, according to Google Scholar, the main article had been cited only thirteen times, and only three of these citations were not by one of its authors (the exceptions included two articles co-authored by Andrea Scharnhorst, then a colleague of Paul Wouters'). Surprisingly, the earlier article had received more citations by other authors (sixteen), suggesting that the full articulation of ICR was not an improvement on the first version.

Nevertheless, Paul Wouters has used ICR in teaching web research in the Netherlands, and I have cited it in articles as a justification for the research approach used. These articles have mainly been published in journals in the information sciences rather than in communication science, however, because I believe that the information sciences are the most natural home for ICR studies. Communication science researchers can also find relevant articles through digital library keyword searches, so publication in an out-of-discipline journal did not seem like it would be a major barrier. This strategy has perhaps been successful in at least one case—a study of the social network site MySpace (Thelwall 2008) that was at one point the twelfth most frequently downloaded article in *JASIST* (Bar-Ilan 2012) despite dealing with a communication science/new media issue.

THE THEORETICAL FRAMEWORK FOR LINK ANALYSIS (TFLA)

The theoretical framework for link analysis (TFLA) arose from my concern that many (hyper)link analysis studies in webometrics that I had read as a reviewer or in journals seemed to have unconvincing results because of a number of common failures. The purpose of the TFLA was to articulate the core requirements for a link analysis in order to help ensure that future studies did not make the same mistakes, at least from my perspective.

The paper presenting the theory took the form of a summary of the TFLA and an explanation and analysis of its components. In fact most of the points made in the paper had been made in previously published link analysis papers; however, the purpose of publishing an explicit theoretical framework was to highlight the key methodological issues in a way that was not partially obscured by a specific link analysis case, as it had been in all previously published articles. The TFLA includes the following main points (Thelwall 2006):

1. Link interpretation is required in any link analysis exercise if conclusions are to be drawn about underlying reasons for link creation—for example, for all social science link analysis, including information science link analysis. An exception could be made for evaluative link analysis if it could be consistently demonstrated that inlink counts correlate with the phenomenon desired to be evaluated.
2. No single method for link interpretation is perfect. Method triangulation is required, ideally including a direct method and a correlation testing method.
3. Fundamental problems, including the rich-get-richer property of link creation and web dynamics, mean that definitive answers cannot be given to most research questions. As a result, research conclusions should always be expressed cautiously.

4. Extensive interpretation exercises are not appropriate because of the reasons given in point 3, above.

A secondary, and partly egotistical, factor motivating me to explicitly write out the TFLA was that previous webometric articles by other researchers discussing methodological issues rather than specific case studies had been very successful (Almind and Ingwersen 1997; Björneborn and Ingwersen 2001, 2004; Ingwersen 1998), and so this seemed like a good type of article to write. A final factor was that at the time, I was writing a book on link analysis (Thelwall 2004) and wanted to present a complete picture; it made sense to develop a theoretical framework as part of this effort. The paper ultimately became a chapter of the book as well as a separate published article.

The TFLA was perhaps a partial success in the sense that it had attracted one hundred citations by December 2013, according to Google Scholar. But it did not meet my initial goal—to underpin most future hyperlink analyses by providing guidelines for acceptable approaches.

CONCLUSIONS

This chapter gives an overview of the different theoretical types of research from the webometric colony from the perspective of Gregor's (2006) theory taxonomy for information systems. The taxonomy fits webometrics research surprisingly well and highlights the dominance of descriptive research and design and action research within webometrics, with the latter focused mainly on indicator construction.

The results highlight the scarcity of explicit theories within the information sciences. This perhaps contrasts with most of the social sciences, for which theory development and testing often seem to be central. Within webometrics this lack seems to be due to the heterogeneity of the object studied (everything seems to be on the web nowadays) and the wide variety of ways in which the web is used. Conceiving the web itself as an object of theory may have made sense in its early days, but this no longer seems to be reasonable. Even for the restricted area of academic-related websites, the creativity with which the web is used to support research, as well as disciplinary differences between research practices, seems to block the development of theories about how the web is used by academics or how webometric data, such as hyperlink counts, should be interpreted. Nevertheless, there is still scope for the development of methods-related theoretical contributions.

This chapter finishes with a personal reflection on the processes behind the development of two named webometric theories; this section extends my personal reflections on other webometric studies.

I have tended to focus on discovering facts and developing effective methods in my research rather than developing theory. This seems to be a natural perspective for a quantitative researcher, with the development of named theories being more appropriate for qualitative researchers, due to the greater emphasis on explanatory power in qualitative research. As a result, although my webometric articles fit within Gregor's taxonomy, I do not regard myself as developing theory in most of them (with the two exceptions noted above). Instead my focus has been on developing methods and describing important web phenomena.

The theoretical underpinnings of my articles, as articulated in the literature review sections, have probably also tended to be primarily descriptive. My literature reviews tend to serve the purposes of giving background information on the topics and discussing closely related research to inform the methods and reveal gaps in research that the paper then fills. Hence the people I cite most often are probably fellow webometricians Liwen Vaughan and Judit Bar-Ilan. I think that I rarely explicitly use named theories to underpin my research, but often call upon theoretical insights, such as Robert Merton's (1973) sociological theory of citation and, to a lesser extent, Whitley's (2000) theoretical decomposition of disciplinary differences in the organization of research. I tend to be a bit suspicious of grand, abstract theories and prefer facts and lower-level explanatory theories.

Nevertheless, I think that theory development is very important to information sciences in general. Merton's sociology of science is a particularly strong example; long after all my research has been forgotten, Merton's theory and insights will continue to guide research in the information sciences. Thus, while most of us will focus on trying to do good research and helping the incremental progress of science, striving for big theories is still a vital goal.

ACKNOWLEDGMENTS

This chapter is part of the FP7 EU-funded project ACUMEN on assessing web indicators in research evaluation.

REFERENCES

Aguillo, I. F., Granadino, B., Ortega, J. L., and Prieto, J. A. (2006). Scientific research activity and communication measured with cybermetrics indicators. *Journal of the American Society for Information Science and Technology*, 57(10), 1296–1302.

Almind, T. C., and Ingwersen, P. (1997). Informetric analyses on the world wide web: Methodological approaches to "webometrics." *Journal of Documentation*, 53(4), 404–426.

Angus, E., Thelwall, M., and Stuart, D. (2008). General patterns of tag usage amongst university groups in flickr. *Online Information Review*, 32(1), 89–101.

Bar-Ilan, J. (2004). A microscopic link analysis of academic institutions within a country—The case of Israel. *Scientometrics*, 59(3), 391–403.

Bar-Ilan, J. (2005). What do we know about links and linking? A framework for studying links in academic environments. *Information Processing and Management*, 41(3), 973–986.

Bar-Ilan, J. (2011). *Articles tagged by "bibliometrics" on mendeley and CiteU-Like*. Paper presented at the Metrics 2011 Symposium on Informetric and Scientometric Research, New Orleans.

Bar-Ilan, J. (2012). JASIST 2001–2010. *ASIST Bulletin*, 38(6), 24–28.

Bar-Ilan, J., and Peritz, B. C. (2004). Evolution, continuity, and disappearance of documents on a specific topic on the web: A longitudinal study of "informetrics." *Journal of the American Society for Information Science and Technology*, 55(11), 980–990.

Bar-Ilan, J., and Peritz, B. C. (2008). The lifespan of "informetrics" on the web: An eight year study (1998–2006). *Scientometrics*, 79(1), 7–25.

Barjak, F., Li, X., and Thelwall, M. (2007). Which factors explain the web impact of scientists' personal homepages? *Journal of the American Society for Information Science and Technology*, 58(2), 200–211.

Björneborn, L., and Ingwersen, P. (2001). Perspectives of webometrics. *Scientometrics*, 50(1), 65–82.

Björneborn, L., and Ingwersen, P. (2004). Toward a basic framework for webometrics. *Journal of the American Society for Information Science and Technology*, 55(14), 1216–1227.

boyd, d. (2008). *Taken out of context: American teen sociality in networked publics* (Unpublished doctoral dissertation). University of California, Berkeley. Retrieved from http://www.danah.org/papers/.

Eysenbach, G. (2011). Can tweets predict citations? Metrics of social impact based on Twitter and correlation with traditional metrics of scientific impact. *Journal of Medical Internet Research*, 13(4), e123.

Fisher, K. E., Erdelez, S., and McKechnie, L. (Eds.). (2005). *Theories of information behavior*. Medford, NJ: Information Today.

Gregor, S. (2006). The nature of theory in information systems. *MIS Quarterly*, 30(3), 611–642.

Haustein, S., and Siebenlist, T. (2011). Applying social bookmarking data to evaluate journal usage. *Journal of Informetrics*, 5(3), 446–457.

Ingwersen, P. (1998). The calculation of web impact factors. *Journal of Documentation*, 54(2), 236–243.

Kousha, K., and Thelwall, M. (2006). Motivations for URL citations to open access library and information science articles. *Scientometrics, 68*(3), 501–517.

Kousha, K., and Thelwall, M. (2008). Assessing the impact of disciplinary research on teaching: An automatic analysis of online syllabuses. *Journal of the American Society for Information Science and Technology, 59*(13), 2060–2069.

Kousha, K., and Thelwall, M. (2009). Google book search: Citation analysis for social science and the humanities. *Journal of the American Society for Information Science and Technology, 60*(8), 1537–1549.

Kousha, K., Thelwall, M., and Rezaie, S. (2010). Using the web for research evaluation: The integrated online impact indicator. *Journal of Informetrics, 4*(1), 124–135.

Lampe, C., Ellison, N., and Steinfield, C. (2008). Changes in use and perception of Facebook. *Proceedings of the ACM 2008 Conference on Computer Supported Cooperative Work* (pp. 721–730). San Diego, CA: ACM Press.

Li, X., Thelwall, M., and Giustini, D. (2012). Validating online reference managers for scholarly impact measurement. *Scientometrics, 91*(2), 461–471.

Li, X., Thelwall, M., Musgrove, P. B., and Wilkinson, D. (2003). The relationship between the WIFs or inlinks of computer science departments in UK and their RAE ratings or research productivities in 2001. *Scientometrics, 57*(2), 239–255.

Merton, R. K. (1973). *The sociology of science: Theoretical and empirical investigations.* Chicago: University of Chicago Press.

Mettrop, W., and Nieuwenhuysen, P. (2001). Internet search engines—Fluctuations in document accessibility. *Journal of Documentation, 57*(5), 623–651.

Mohammadi, E., and Thelwall, M. (2013). Assessing non-standard article impact using F1000 labels. *Scientometrics, 97*(2), 383–395.

Ortega, J. L., and Aguillo, I. F. (2008). Visualization of the nordic academic web: Link analysis using social network tools. *Information Processing and Management, 44*(4), 1624–1633.

Ortega, J. L., Aguillo, I. F., Cothey, V., and Scharnhorst, A. (2008). Maps of the academic web in the European higher education area: An exploration of visual web indicators. *Scientometrics, 74*(2), 295–308.

Prabowo, R., Thelwall, M., and Alexandrov, M. (2007). Generating overview timelines for major events in an RSS corpus. *Journal of Informetrics, 1*(2), 131–144.

Priem, J., and Hemminger, B. M. (2010). Scientometrics 2.0: Toward new metrics of scholarly impact on the social web. *First Monday, 15*(7). Retrieved from http://www.uic.edu/htbin/cgiwrap/bin/ojs/index.php/fm/article/viewArticle/2874/2570.

Priem, J., Taraborelli, D., Groth, P., and Neylon, C. (2011). *Altmetrics: A manifesto.* Retrieved from http://altmetrics.org/manifesto/.

Rodríguez i Gairín, J. M. (1997). Valorando el impacto de la información en internet: AltaVista, el "citation index" de la red [Evaluating the impact of Internet information: Altavista, the "citation index" of the web]. *Revista Española de Documentación Científica, 20*(2), 175–181.

Rousseau, R. (1998). Citation analysis as a theory of friction or polluted air? Comments on theories of citation. *Scientometrics, 43*(1), 63–67.

Rousseau, R. (1999). Daily time series of common single word searches in AltaVista and NorthernLight. *Cybermetrics, 2/3*, Retrieved from http://www.cindoc.csic.es/cybermetrics/articles/v2i1p2.html.

Seeber, M., Lepori, B., Lomi, A., Aguillo, I., and Barberio, V. (2012). Factors affecting web links between European higher education institutions. *Journal of Informetrics, 6*(3), 435–447.

Smith, A. G. (1999). A tale of two web spaces: Comparing sites using web impact factors. *Journal of Documentation, 55*(5), 577–592.

Sugimoto, C. R., and Thelwall, M. (2013). Scholars on soap boxes: Science communication and dissemination via TED videos. *Journal of the American Society for Information Science and Technology, 64*(4), 663–674.

Sugimoto, C. R., Thelwall, M., Larivière, V., Tsou, A., Mongeon, P., and Macaluso, B. (2013). Scientists popularizing science: Characteristics and impact of TED talk presenters. *PLOS ONE, 8*(4), e62403.

Thelwall, M. (2001). Exploring the link structure of the web with network diagrams. *Journal of Information Science, 27*(6), 393–402.

Thelwall, M. (2002). An initial exploration of the link relationship between UK university web sites. *ASLIB Proceedings, 54*(2), 118–126.

Thelwall, M. (2004). *Link analysis: An information science approach.* San Diego, CA: Academic Press.

Thelwall, M. (2006). Interpreting social science link analysis research: A theoretical framework. *Journal of the American Society for Information Science and Technology, 57*(1), 60–68.

Thelwall, M. (2007). Blog searching: The first general-purpose source of retrospective public opinion in the social sciences? *Online Information Review, 31*(3), 277–289.

Thelwall, M. (2008). Social networks, gender and friending: An analysis of MySpace member profiles. *Journal of the American Society for Information Science and Technology, 59*(8), 1321–1330.

Thelwall, M. (2009). Homophily in MySpace. *Journal of the American Society for Information Science and Technology, 60*(2), 219–231.

Thelwall, M., and Buckley, K. (2013). Topic-based sentiment analysis for the social web: The role of mood and issue-related words. *Journal of the American Society for Information Science and Technology, 64*(8), 1608–1617.

Thelwall, M., Buckley, K., and Paltoglou, G. (2011). Sentiment in Twitter events. *Journal of the American Society for Information Science and Technology, 62*(2), 406–418.

Thelwall, M., Buckley, K., and Paltoglou, G. (2012). Sentiment strength detection for the social web. *Journal of the American Society for Information Science and Technology, 63*(1), 163–173.

Thelwall, M., Buckley, K., Paltoglou, G., Cai, D., and Kappas, A. (2010). Sentiment strength detection in short informal text. *Journal of the American Society for Information Science and Technology, 61*(12), 2544–2558.

Thelwall, M., Buckley, K., Paltoglou, G., Skowron, M., Garcia, D., Gobron, S., . . . Holyst, J. A. (2013). Damping sentiment analysis in online communication: Discussions, monologs and dialogs. In A. Gelbukh (Ed.), *CICLing 2013, part II, LNCS 7817* [null] (pp. 1–12). Heidelberg: Springer.

Thelwall, M., and Harries, G. (2004). Do the web sites of higher rated scholars have significantly more online impact? *Journal of the American Society for Information Science and Technology, 55*(2), 149–159.

Thelwall, M., Haustein, S., Larivière, V., and Sugimoto, C. (2013). Do altmetrics work? Twitter and ten other candidates. *PLOS ONE, 8*(5), e64841. doi:10.1371 /journal.pone.0064841.

Thelwall, M., and Kousha, K. (2008). Online presentations as a source of scientific impact? An analysis of PowerPoint files citing academic journals. *Journal of the American Society for Information Science and Technology, 59*(5), 805–815.

Thelwall, M., and Prabowo, R. (2007). Identifying and characterizing public science-related concerns from RSS feeds. *Journal of the American Society for Information Science and Technology, 58*(3), 379–390.

Thelwall, M., and Smith, A. G. (2002). A study of interlinking between Asia-Pacific University web sites. *Scientometrics, 55*(3), 335–348.

Thelwall, M., and Wilkinson, D. (2010). Public dialogs in social network sites: What is their purpose? *Journal of the American Society for Information Science and Technology, 61*(2), 392–404.

Thelwall, M., and Wouters, P. (2005). What's the deal with the web/blogs/the next big technology: A key role for information science in e-social science research? *Lecture Notes in Computer Science, 3507*, 187–199.

Thelwall, M., Wouters, P., and Fry, J. (2008). Information-centred research for large-scale analysis of new information sources. *Journal of the American Society for Information Science and Technology, 59*(9), 1523–1527.

Vaughan, L., and Thelwall, M. (2002). Web link counts correlate with ISI impact factors: Evidence from two disciplines. *Proceedings of the Annual Meeting of the American Society for Information Science and Technology, 39.* doi:10.1002/meet.1450390148.

Vaughan, L., and Thelwall, M. (2004). Search engine coverage bias: Evidence and possible causes. *Information Processing and Management, 40*(4), 693–707.

Whitley, R. (2000). *The intellectual and social organization of the sciences* (2nd ed.). Oxford: Oxford University Press.

Wilkinson, D., Harries, G., Thelwall, M., and Price, L. (2003). Motivations for academic web site interlinking: Evidence for the web as a novel source of information on informal scholarly communication. *Journal of Information Science, 29*(1), 49–56.

PART 3

DESIGN

CHAPTER 10

THEORIZING THE UNPRECEDENTED

JOHN M. CARROLL

INFORMATION SCIENCES OFTEN ADDRESS unprecedented phenomena—designs, systems, applications, tools, data and visualizations, and human interactions and experiences—that never existed before. Examples include designs like Bush's (1945) memex, systems like Engelbart's (1962) NLS (oN Line System), applications like Bricklin and Frankston's VisiCalc (Grad 2007), tools like PageRank (Brin and Page 1998), data like Twitter's visualization of billions of tweets as a 3-D geo-texture (https://blog.twitter.com/2013/topography-tweets), and the wide range of gestural user interactions for Microsoft's Kinect (www.xbox.com/KINECT), Leap Motion (https://www.leapmotion.com/), and various smartphones. These examples are clearly, even famously, transformative contributions; all such work is judged in part by its novelty and potential to be transformative.

None of this should shock anyone familiar with information sciences and technology, but it creates a distinctive challenge with respect to method and theory. Method and theory tend to thrive, with respect to codification, validation, and institutionalization, when empirical phenomena are *highly* precedented, that is, self-similar, repeated, and replicable. Consider the scientific edifice of operant learning in animal psychology stretching from Edward Thorndike through B. F. Skinner; it includes a rich catalog of minute variations on the narrow themes of pigeons pecking keys and rats pressing levers to get bits of food (Wong 2012).

In a case like operant learning, the dimensions of a situation that matters were well understood, distinctly conceptualized, clearly operationalized, and precisely measurable. Animals make simple responses that are reinforced, punished, or extinguished, and these simple responses are tallied. It is remarkable what an elaborate body of theory was constructed for operant learning, documented in thousands of scientific papers, hundreds of books. It is a clear case of what Kuhn (1962) called normal science, a recurring pattern in the history of science. But it is a pattern that is obverse to the unprecedented phenomena of information sciences and technology.

One way that information sciences differ from operant learning, and also from the traditional science disciplines Kuhn analyzed, is that information sciences are strongly applied and thus driven by unsatisfied and newly emerging information needs and opportunities, as well as by the development and pricing of new hardware components, the adoption and deployment of new communications infrastructures, and so forth. In recent decades, these external factors have been extraordinarily powerful and dynamic, and their cycle time for creating an impact on information sciences has accelerated. Indeed, this context of rapid sociotechnical change more or less dictates that information sciences will be largely focused on the unprecedented. However, this effect is self-fulfillingly amplified by the attractiveness of information sciences to persons seeking the challenge of the unprecedented.

The title of this essay is a homage to Hermann Kahn's 1962 classic book *Thinking about the Unthinkable*. In that book Kahn reflects on the emergence of modern strategic planning in the context of the Cold War. Most vividly, he recalls how structured analysis techniques had failed to identify one of the most important threatening scenarios of the Cold War period, one he called the Accidental War. In this scenario, an incident of equipment malfunction or unauthorized behavior results in the launch of a single Soviet missile. The missile detonates in Western Europe, and this is immediately detected and disseminated throughout Western military and civilian installations. Although the incident is not interpretable as a serious attack, the level of anxiety throughout the US Strategic Air Command results in one officer's misunderstanding or disobeying orders and firing the missiles under his or her command. The counterattack is also not interpretable as an all-out first strike; however, it is an escalated military response to the original mistake and could provoke the Soviets to launch their own ready missiles and bombers. In response the United States might well order the rest of its missiles to be fired, as well as launching its bombers to protect them from the Soviet assault and to position them for a subsequent response.

Not a nice story, though it later provided the plotline for the 1950s genre of nuclear-apocalypse novels and films, culminating in Stanley Kubrick's 1964 film *Doctor Strangelove*. Indeed, Kahn's scenario became a shared nightmare for much of the world for a quarter-century. It proved to be a very useful design aid for policy. It is still shocking to know that early in the Cold War no one had considered planning to communicate with the USSR during the five to forty minutes it would take for accidentally launched missiles to reach their targets. And yet doing so could pretty literally save the world. It is fortunate, then, that this possibility was eventually identified by working through the Accidental War scenario. Kahn also developed extensions of this scenario in which the US and USSR negotiated a limited nuclear war (anticipating the novel *Red Alert* [Bryant 1958] and the novel and film *Fail-Safe* [Burdick and Wheeler 1962]) and in which the two countries unilaterally establish a world government (after surveying the first 10 million casualties of Armageddon).

The title, *Thinking about the Unthinkable*, is a double entendre because the Accidental War scenario—and the nuclear holocaust it precipitates—was something ordinary people might find both hard to fathom and uncomfortable to envision. But it was also something that Kahn and other strategic analysts in 1949 using game theoretic techniques found inconceivable. A key limitation of many analysis and decision methods is that the set of options is enumerated a priori. The key to the Accidental War is that something happens that was not enumerated a priori, something unprecedented. During the 1950s Kahn became quite well known, and to some extent disliked, for insisting that the horrifying consequences of nuclear war be concretely envisioned and planned for. He was the model for the character Dr. Strangelove in that film of the same name.

A STRANGE AID TO THOUGHT

Kahn (1962) called scenarios "a strange aid to thought" because they were not conventionally employed. He argued that scenarios nonetheless provide five critical resources to strategic planners: (1) Scenarios help analysts avoid the tempting assumption that circumstances remain largely the same. They dramatically and persuasively emphasize the dynamics of a narrative plot, and the wide range of possible consequences and side effects of plot elements. (2) Scenarios compel analysts to address contextual details and temporal dynamics in problems, which they can miss if they focus only on abstract descriptions. (3) By concretely illustrating a complex space of possibilities, and imposing a simple linear rubric of time, scenarios help analysts deal with several aspects of a problem situation simultaneously. They facilitate the comprehension and integration of many interacting threads—psychological, social, political, and, in Kahn's case, military. (4) Scenarios stimulate the imagination, helping analysts to consider contingencies they might otherwise overlook. Scenarios vividly illustrate principles or issues that might be overlooked if one only considered actual events. (5) Scenarios can be used to consider alternative outcomes to past, present, and future crises.

Kahn's analysis of scenario thinking had a huge impact across fields that need to anticipate and manage future contingencies and initiatives. It would be difficult to find any field of this sort that does not now make use of the concept of scenario. Yet, in part because scenarios are so easily assimilated into existing practices and methodologies, it is also difficult to identify clear cases where any particular scenario-based planning or decision-making innovation made a critical difference in organizational outcomes, analogous to Kahn's Accidental War scenario. In that sense they remain "a strange aid to thought." The best documented example of a scenario effect in a business context is that of Royal Dutch Shell, which used scenario planning to anticipate two major OPEC-induced oil market disruptions during the 1970s, as described in two *Harvard Business Review* articles (Wack 1985a, 1985b).

In the late 1980s, scenarios began to appear in the information sciences. They were used as an alternative or supplement to functional specifications in software development. For example, Wirfs-Brock and Wilkerson (1989) described software design as a process of identifying objects and their responsibilities in scenarios depicting the software's functionality. Jacobson and colleagues (1992) defined a schematic use-case representation for scenarios describing system interactions, later incorporated into the unified modeling language (UML; Jacobson, Booch, and Rumbaugh 1998). Carroll and Rosson (1990) argued that representing a software design with a set of typical and critical user interaction scenarios could enable usability evaluation at the earliest possible design point, and seamlessly integrate with task-oriented empirical evaluation methods in subsequent stages of software development. This approach was subsequently articulated as a comprehensive approach to human-computer interaction (HCI) design and development (Carroll 1995; Rosson and Carroll 2002).

Scenarios were also used in theory development per se (Young and Barnard 1987, 1991; Young et al. 1989). During the latter 1980s, human information processing theories were still the primary foundation for research in HCI. These theories were often embodied as cognitive architectures or user models, basically following the simulation paradigm of creating a formal system that mimicked key characteristics of human interactions with information systems (e.g., Card, Moran, and Newell 1983; Newell and Card 1985). In the latter 1980s, the approach was challenged for being promissory, impractical, narrow, and largely irrelevant to real HCI phenomena (Carroll and Campbell 1986).

Young and Barnard suggested that scenarios could help cognitive theories address such challenges by grounding the theories in concrete phenomena. They suggested that a set of scenarios could be constructed to describe recognized and important HCI situations. For example, one of their scenarios involved a text editor in which the user knows that the expression "4U" moves the cursor up four lines, and so types "4D" to move it four lines down, and is surprised that four lines of text are deleted. Young and Barnard (1987) identified this scenario in empirical studies of command-based interactions (Carroll 1982). They argued that a set of such scenarios would provide a filter on the breadth and relevance of theories, that is, provide a set of touchstones that each theory should insightfully analyze. They suggested that scenarios could supplement the laboratory experiments of the cognitive paradigm to produce a more adequate foundation of theory for HCI.

Young and Barnard were chiefly leveraging only the second of Kahn's five affordances of scenarios; their concern was to improve relatively paradigmatic theory by grounding it in real phenomena. It is notable that their scenarios were drawn from research literature and field reports. Indeed, Young and Barnard (1987, p. 294) explain that scenarios, in their sense, should not only be observationally attested but also address high-impact issues in the user experience. In addition, collections of scenarios should be representative across cognitive resources (such as short-term memory and visual perception), style of user interfaces (menus, command languages, etc.), empirical classifications of HCI phenomena (especially user errors), and types of tasks (text, drawing, database interactions, etc.). Ironically, in developing the idea of grounding theory in scenarios, Young and Barnard (1991) ultimately came to focus on fixed, minimal-contrast scenarios that highlighted key distinctions among existing models, deemphasizing considerations of face validity, concreteness, and novel challenges for theory.

Young and Barnard were not concerned with theorizing the unprecedented. They were concerned that cognitive science, as a laboratory-based theory foundation for HCI, was too slow and too paradigm bound to keep up with HCI phenomena or analyze them relevantly with respect to real-world needs. These are worthwhile objectives! Indeed, if theory cannot analyze what is already codified and in use, it will not be capable of providing guidance toward the unprecedented. And it is important to keep in mind that Young and Barnard were setting a high bar: often theory is claimed to be relevant by a kind of loose metaphor. For example, operant learning is relevant to pretty much any case of human learning in the loose sense that learning involves doing something, getting feedback from the environment, and then adjusting subsequent behavior. However, if this is all there is to operant learning, what are the thousands of scientific papers and hundreds of books *about*? Young and Barnard were concerned with engaging the technical theory of cognitive science, and not just its overall metaphors, with HCI phenomena.

DESIGN-BASED THEORY

An assumption in Young and Barnard's work is that theory is prior and exogenous to domains of application. In other words, the problem they pose is, given a massive amount of research and theory in cognitive science, how can we assess its relevance and applicability? How can we make it (more) relevant and (more) applicable to understanding HCI? This is a reasonable assumption and program that follows from the ambition of cognitive science to identify, codify, and validate universal principles of human cognition. If the principles are in fact universal, then they ought to provide insight and guidance in HCI, as in all human endeavors. The challenge is to bridge the theory-to-practice gap with linking structures, such as sets of scenarios.

Another way to construe the theory challenge, however, is to suspend Young and Barnard's assumption that relevant theory is universal, prior, and exogenous, and to ask instead what is the knowledge, the theory, that explains evident practices and products of a particular domain of human activity (like HCI). In other words, one could put the embodied reality of domains first, instead of engaging it only after the fact as a way of evaluating theories already in hand, as Young and Barnard did. For example, one could ask how and why specific artifacts of HCI emerged; how people adopted them, experienced them, appropriated them; and how they continued to evolve in use, including how and why they were succeeded by subsequent artifacts. This latter approach would seek to articulate indigenous and endogenous knowledge, and the embodied theory that animates the domain itself, rather than instantiating, specializing, and deducing from universal theories that arise outside of the domain, and often, as in the cases of operant learning and cognitive science, in laboratory models of real human behavior and experience. In an anthropological analogy, this domain-first approach is ethnographic in Malinowski's (1922) sense.

Anthropological ethnographies tend to focus on established cultural artifacts and practices. They seek to understand artifacts and practices from the inside by sharing experiences with domain actors (e.g., in HCI this might mean designers and users), by directly experiencing, and by articulating experience. Ethnographic approaches try to bring the invisible background of culture into the foreground of analysis. They specialize in bringing to light surprising observations, interpretations, and significances of what seems to be straightforward, routine, and obvious. Such a program for articulating indigenous and endogenous knowledge of HCI also emerged in the latter 1980s. Thus, Suchman (1987) analyzed quite routine human-computer interactions, in her case the use of photocopiers, as problematic "conversations" in which users tried, and frequently failed, to achieve mutual intelligibility of intentions with their computer partners. Nardi and Miller (1990) observed that single-user software—in their study, spreadsheets—often was used to coordinate collaborative work. Bentley and colleagues (1992) analyzed the coordination of air traffic control work around flight progress strips—seemingly simple paper artifacts that nonetheless were routinely used to depict and coordinate a vast amount of critical safety information among air traffic controllers.

This body of work, and the rapid emergence and widespread adoption of networking infrastructures in the late 1980s and early 1990s, helped to establish a new sub-area in HCI called computer-supported cooperative work (CSCW). But it was more than a sub-area focused on collaboration; as Nardi and Miller (1990) suggested, collaboration is the normal case for work activity. This was disruptive to the information processing theory paradigm, which had been the establishment paradigm for HCI in the early 1980s, and within which Young and Barnard were working.

In this unsettled context of the latter 1980s, Campbell and I argued that designed artifacts should be regarded as embodying designers' *theories of users and their activities*, and the theories could be held either tacitly or explicitly (Carroll and Campbell 1989). These embodied theories are not primarily intended to support scientific analysis or discourse, or to codify universal principles. However, embodied theories can nonetheless be more or less true/false (Popper 1963), as well as more or less progressive/degenerative (Lakatos 1978). Indeed, the empirical content of the theories can be and is routinely assessed by usability testing, user experience research, individual and organizational adoption and appropriation, and continued progressive evolution in use, as well as through further design. Moreover, unlike much theory in the human sciences, such as operant learning and the technical cognitive science models and architectures of concern to Young and Barnard, embodied theories do not have the problem of being narrow and paradigm bound, impractical to use, and largely irrelevant to real phenomena (Carroll and Campbell 1986). Rather, they are intrinsically bound to their contexts of use, and succeed through their demonstrated effectiveness at accurately responding to real phenomena.

No surprise, embodied theories have their own challenge. Because they are mostly tacit theories (Polanyi 1958), there is no way for purely embodied theories to support formal knowledge exchange and explanation, or systematic progressive development, as envisioned by Lakatos (1978). They can support practice, including design practice, but they typically do that through quite concrete mechanisms of knowledge use, such as demonstration, exemplification, and emulation (Carroll 1990). But these less systematic means of exchanging and developing knowledge can be misleading. Indeed, embodied theories can easily be speciously right for the wrong reasons. A designer might have a wrong idea about user activity, might create a design all the while guided by that misunderstanding, but yet still manage to create a design that is usable and evocative, and that might be adopted and productively appropriated. One way this could happen is if the designer's (tacit) intention were different from the design result. There is every reason to think this could happen (Reason 1990) and that it would be troublesome and complicated: people characteristically believe that their intentions are aligned with their actions and vice versa, even when they are not, and frequently distort their own perceptions and interpretations to maintain this spurious "consistency" (Cooper 2007).

One way to address this challenge is to construct explicit propositional analyses of embodied HCI theories. Thus, one could articulate the scenarios that describe key user interactions afforded by a designed artifact, and take that set of scenarios as a theoretical description (Carroll, Kellogg, and Rosson 1991). Consider again Young and Barnard's (1987) scenario of command-based interaction: the user knows that U means "move the pointer up" and so types 4D, deleting four lines of text, because D in fact means "delete." For Young and Barnard the issue is whether universal, prior, and exogenous cognitive models and architectures have anything relevant or applicable to say about this. Young and colleagues (1989) concluded that one well-known theory (Card, Moran, and Newell 1983) could not analyze this scenario at all, that one other might have something relevant to say, and that three others could analyze the scenario. This is fine as far as it goes, but it does not go very far.

Taking the scenario as part of a scenario theory leads to richer conclusions. The design that enabled this scenario misled the user in a specific way. The embodied theory was to that extent falsified in Popper's (1963) sense, and in need of further development (Lakatos 1978). The scenario provides specific guidance for this. The user may have assumed that the command language instantiated a consistent schema in which the semantic opposition of up/down entailed the command opposition U/D. The command language design, and the theory of users and their activities embodied in that design, could be revised to fulfill this user expectation. This simple example shows how a local generalization, a situated claim about indigenous and endogenous knowledge, can be induced from an attested scenario. Thus, instead of merely assessing whether existing theories have anything at all to say, *we build theory out of designs.*

Ethnographic analyses of domains are ipso facto relevant and applicable to understanding actual human conduct; thus, the issues that motivated Young and Barnard regarding cognitive models and architectures become nonissues. Ethnographic analyses must address things that matter in a domain, irrespective of their a priori theoretical category. Thus, it could be that redesigning the U/D command pair will make learning the system easier for new users, but also decrease the status of more experienced users who formerly were able to coach their less-skilled colleagues. Cognitive consistency and social status are not often addressed by the same theory mechanisms. For example, none of Young and colleagues' five theories address social status in the workplace at all. However, in the embodied world, cognitive and social phenomena mutually influence one another all the time. Theory embodied in a designed artifact and practices is typically a synthetic nexus of claims across levels of analysis (Carroll and Kellogg 1989).

THEORY-BASED DESIGN

Analyzing existing designs, embodied artifacts, and practices is the traditional descriptive and explanatory enterprise of theory projected into design. Typical domains for theory are the self-similar, repeated, and replicable patterns of the natural and social world, for example, chemical reactions, gravity, operant learning, and so on. In design, acts of human initiative transform the natural and social world, creating new material and social phenomena for analysis. Eventually, of course, successful designs are adopted, appropriated, and assimilated into common practice. At that stage, theorizing design can begin to look like theorizing other aspects of complex human behavior. For example, Petroski (1992) investigated the design history of the pencil; however, for contemporary people the pencil is a traditional cultural artifact, not an innovation. It is this well-socialized region of design that is often addressed by design theorists (e.g., Simon 1973), and it was this region of design that Young and Barnard (1987) addressed. But there is an important distinction between theory in the sense of understanding the already-designed world of human artifacts (including information systems) and theory in the sense of understanding and guiding the design of unprecedented artifacts. Projects pursuing the former goal understandably focus on analyzing existing designs, often on quite routine designs, such as Simon's analysis of designing a house. They do not address design innovation as a theory-based activity, or as an activity at all (Carroll 2000).

The doing of design, the innovative edge of design, is a kind of activity in which something new and original—often something unprecedented—emerges from a palette of known materials, prior creations, unmet needs, and imagination. This takes us back to Kahn. Part of Kahn's analysis of scenarios, the second of his five affordances, pertains to better understanding phenomena and patterns that have already been identified. He came to the conclusion that scenarios force analysts to consider contextual details and temporal dynamics in problems—issues they can avoid when they focus only on abstract descriptions. Young and Barnard were also oriented to this characteristic of scenarios.

Kahn's other four scenario affordances pertain more to identifying and analyzing *new* phenomena and patterns. Scenarios remind analysts that circumstances are dynamic and unpredictable; they help analysts envision possibilities by projecting multifaceted plot threads along a time line; they stimulate the imagination by vividly suggesting "what-if?" possibilities and contingencies along the time line; they allow analysts to compare and contrast alternative outcomes. These characteristics suggest how scenarios could be tools for doing design, for identifying and analyzing the unprecedented. Thus, instead of grounding scenarios in direct observation and empirical literature—and in so doing tying them to the present and the past— we could ask merely that the scenarios be *intelligible and plausible* to domain actors, with respect to what happens or could happen and what matters or could matter in domains, and to be *productive and critical* to domain analysts and designers with respect to raising intellectual and practical challenges and opportunities, and scientific hypotheses. Such scenarios embody unprecedented concepts as envisioned scenarios or demonstrations, and provide the basis for a *projective ethnography*, an ethnography that envisions possible artifacts that do not yet exist and possible activities that could be carried out with those artifacts.

Bush's (1945) description of the memex included an explicit user scenario that was intelligible and plausible enough to engage imagination of unprecedented events and experiences, and productive and critical enough to launch and focus explicit thinking about information management, techniques for displaying and interacting with information, and broader consequences of information, such as overload. The user scenario was described as follows:

> The owner of the memex, let us say, is interested in the origin and properties of the bow and arrow. Specifically he is studying why the short Turkish bow was apparently superior to the English long bow in the skirmishes of the Crusades. He has dozens of possibly pertinent books and articles in his memex. First he runs through an encyclope-

dia, finds an interesting but sketchy article, leaves it projected. Next, in a history, he finds another pertinent item, and ties the two together. Thus he goes, building a trail of many items. Occasionally he inserts a comment of his own, either linking it into the main trail or joining it by a side trail to a particular item. When it becomes evident that the elastic properties of available materials had a great deal to do with the bow, he branches off on a side trail which takes him through textbooks on elasticity and tables of physical constants. He inserts a page of longhand analysis of his own. Thus he builds a trail of his interest through the maze of materials available to him. (sec. 7, para. 4)

A generation later, Engelbart performed a live ninety-minute demo of his NLS project at a conference (Engelbart and English 1968). The demo depicted the flow of a future, or at least futuristic, workplace interaction integrating word processing, pointing with a mouse, and hypertext/hypermedia. It included live links and cross-references within a file, object addressing, dynamic file linking, video conferencing, and shared-screen remote collaboration that persuasively previewed the future experience of computing. No one before, and possibly no one since, had animated such a complete and completely unprecedented vision of the future of online work. It is now often called "the mother of all demos" (Levy 1994).

These scenarios *make vivid how circumstances are dynamic and unpredictable.* Bush emphasized opportunistic discovery interactions in his illustration of "trails." He was just reasoning from his imagination, but he anticipated the characteristic web browsing scenario of fifty years later. He also reasoned that users would need tools to annotate and summarize their information explorations—tools that are still needed today. In reading the quoted excerpt above, one sees tangibly both the unprecedented possibilities for wandering through a "maze" of information and the new challenges of monitoring and sense-making that are entailed. Engelbart's demo included an incident in which his collaborator in a shared editing session experienced insufficient feedback, and wondered aloud whether the session connection had terminated. This poignantly, and for the first time, exposed the most basic awareness challenge of computer-mediated collaboration, namely, the concern that one is interacting with a dead channel.

Bush's and Engelbart's scenarios also illustrate *envisioning new possibilities by projecting multifaceted plot threads along a time line.* In Bush's scenario it is time and the succession of hyperlinks that motivate support for annotation and summary. The Engelbart demo includes discussions at the levels of user interface interactions, what the person sees and experiences, collaborative awareness and interactions, and the underlying data structures and work products that result. Engelbart stressed the simultaneous significance of all of these levels. In one segment he and his associate, Bill Paxton, are demonstrating shared video interaction and collaborative editing while discussing approaches to keyword search. Their interaction powerfully conveys the richness and usefulness of NLS just in the course of depicting an explanation of how one function in NLS works. Engelbart emphasized the distinction between what he called the "service system," the functions and user interface interactions and displays, and the "user system," the conventions and practices that would emerge as people used the service system to do real things. This is quite prescient for 1968, and it was informed by the richness of the scenario analysis.

These scenarios also illustrate *stimulating the imagination to vividly suggest possibilities.* Thus, Bush's memex user is traversing hypertext links, but this activity entrains the recognition that he or she will need to be able to create textual summaries to keep track of the emerging information structure by manually codifying and interpreting it. Engelbart made the point that the ideas embodied in NLS had emerged from an evolutionary system development approach; he and his team (about seventeen people) used the system for everyday work in order to identify and direct further design trajectories.

Bush and Engelbart did not directly *compare and contrast alternative scenarios,* Kahn's fifth scenario affordance. However, the concreteness of their scenarios evoked alternative designs from others. For example, Engelbart used an inset window for video conferencing, but NLS did not have general functionality for multiple windows; for example, it had no way of indicating window borders. However, it concretely focused efforts for advancing a multiple-windows approach to user interface design, and over the next several years key designs and implementations appeared (Myers 1998). Bush's scenario was articulated at a far lower level of graphical and interactive detail, but it is interesting how his phrase "leaves it projected" seems to imply a multiple-windows conception of the memex display.

The scenarios introduced by Bush and Engelbart are very different from Young and Barnard's routine text editing scenario, and Simon's hierarchical decomposition of designing a house into the simpler and better-structured subproblems of designing the several subsystems that comprise the house. Bush and Engelbart were envisioning unprecedented experiences, but in ways that were transparently *intelligible and plausible* to a wide range of their contemporaries, and moreover in ways that were substantively *productive and critical* in guiding analysts and designers toward embodying and building upon their designs. Indeed, the proof of this is that their scenarios entrained a wide range of new designs, and today we live in the world enabled by these designs.

THE UNPRECEDENTED AS ROUTINE

The starting point of this chapter was the observation that unprecedented phenomena—novel designs, systems, applications, tools, data and visualizations, and human interactions and experiences—play a central role in information sciences and technology. Indeed, unprecedented innovation is key to the identity of information sciences and technology. Yet the pervasive, almost routine, role of unprecedented innovation is also challenging with respect to codifying, validating, and institutionalizing methodology and theory. This is no doubt in part why this field has always attracted such a rich variety of methodology and theory.

It is perhaps also in part why normal science methodology and theory have had only modest successes. In this discussion the use of scenarios, as pioneered by Kahn, was suggested as a radically different way to theorize the unprecedented, that is, a way to project and analyze circumstances unprecedented with respect to inherent risks, opportunities, and other affordances. Kahn's scenario analysis of tactical noise in the management of nuclear warfare helped to stabilize the Cold War world, identifying and analyzing factors that were unintelligible to normal science.

Scenarios have been appropriated subsequently for a wide variety of endeavors, including diverse purposes within information sciences and technology. With respect to Kahn and unprecedented innovation, these appropriations fall along a spectrum from normal science to what is called embodied theory, which considers artifacts and practices as embodiments of operative tacit knowledge that can inform situated understandings and guide technical innovation. Young and Barnard provided a creative normal science appropriation in which scenarios were used to classify and evaluate cognitive theories of routine user interface interactions. An important point is that this effort, itself explicitly a reaction to the failure of normal science to provide relevant guidance to user interface design, had only the mildest of useful consequences.

On the other hand, some of the most singular contributions to information sciences and technology can be traced to Kahn. Bush's memex and Engelbart's NLS demo are scenarios that vividly animated unprecedented designs and systems, respectively, that embodied and articulated key issues in ways that were intelligible and compelling to designers, scientists, and engineers, and that were productive and critical in the development of contemporary information sciences and technology.

The examples of Kahn, Bush, and Engelbart suggest that scenarios can be utilized through emulation and material refinement of embodied understanding. Indeed, the impact of this work has been huge. But one could reasonably ask how other researchers could learn to do what Kahn, Bush, and Engelbart managed to do. It is likely that identifying and studying these cases (in more detail than here) could indeed help information technologists to better theorize the unprecedented. And if even a few could manage to do this, the field would be much better for it.

However, the most apt analogy to using theory in information sciences and technology—in the realm of unprecedented phenomena—may not be that of merely applying and evaluating codified and conventional theory to standardized scenario test cases (as Young and Barnard suggested). A more apt analogy may be reconceptualizing gravity, matter, and time. That is, Kahn, Bush, and Engelbart—and the many other theorists of the unprecedented in information sciences and technology—may be better understood as mini-Einsteins than as physics majors. Not every problem in science and technology turns out to require nothing more than the application of normal science. Indeed, it stands to reason that the most important challenges will usually not have that property.

What is distinctive about information sciences and technology is that unprecedented phenomena are so pervasive and routine. This level of systemic indeterminacy will not make normal science models work any better. More likely, it could induce us to lower our expectations about what theory can be expected to contribute, perhaps returning to the program of Young and Barnard. Normal science theorists may remain frustrated, but such a return is unlikely. Another option is to consider that theorizing the unprecedented is a qualitatively different endeavor from theorizing operant learning in pigeons and rats, and that theories of the unprecedented may look and work differently.

A programmatic implication of this chapter is that information sciences and technology should take scenarios more seriously as theoretical objects. When we reflect on the past several decades, it seems that scenarios have become a lingua franca, utterly pervasive, and yet regarded as examples and illustrations, not as embodied theories. This is similar to ethnography in general, which is seen as being critical to carry out, and a source of important insights into human experience and design, but not as producing integrative knowledge.

A simple example of how a scenario program for theory development could work is Rosson's and my analysis (Carroll and Rosson 2003) of MOOsburg (a graphical/geo-spatial MOO—multiuser domain object oriented [Bartle 2003]). As emphasized earlier, Young and Barnard's normal science appropriation of scenarios adduced scenarios to cognitive theories in order to classify and evaluate the theories. Rosson and I turned this around. We adduced theories of motor behavior, perception, cognition, small groups, and organizations to scenarios, providing normal science grounding for the scenarios, which were the integrative knowledge objects in the analysis. An interesting feature of this analysis is that it explicitly (albeit loosely) integrates normal science descriptions across levels of analysis (recall, again, discussion of limitations of Young and Barnard's cognitive project). This is one proposal for how to leverage multiple normal science foundations to the embodied analysis of the routinely unprecedented phenomena of information sciences and technology. The main point is that taking embodied theory seriously has fairly obvious first steps, but has not been pushed very far or very hard (see also Carroll 2000).

As an area in which unprecedented phenomena are both routine and critically important, information sciences and technology are not less in need of theory than better codified and more paradigmatic areas like operant learning. They are in need of a different kind of theory, a kind of theory that makes the unprecedented concrete and amenable to rich analysis before it exists, allowing us to search for the future not only where the lights are already bright, but where the future actually might be.

REFERENCES

Bartle, R. A. (2003). *Designing virtual worlds*. Indianapolis, IN: New Riders.

Bentley, R., Hughes, J. A., Randall, D., Rodden, T., Sawyer, P., Shapiro, D., and Sommerville, I. (1992). Ethnographically-informed systems design for air traffic control. In M. Mantel and R. Baecker (Eds.), *CSCW '92: Proceedings of the ACM Conference on Computer-Supported Cooperative Work* (pp. 123–129). New York: ACM.

Brin, S., and Page, L. (1998). The anatomy of a large-scale hypertextual web search engine. *Computer Networks and ISDN Systems, 30*(1), 107–117.

Bryant, P. (1958). *Red alert*. Athens, GA: Black Masks.

Burdick, E., and Wheeler, H. (1962). *Fail-safe*. Hopewell, NJ: ECCO Press.

Bush, V. (1945, July 1). As we may think. *Atlantic, 176*. Retrieved from http://www.theatlantic.com/magazine/archive/1945/07/as-we-may-think/303881/.

Card, S. K., Moran, T. P., and Newell, A. (1983). *The psychology of human-computer interaction*. Hillsdale, NJ: Erlbaum.

Carroll, J. M. (1982). Learning, using and designing command paradigms. *Behaviour and Information Technology, 1*(4), 327–346.

Carroll, J. M. (1990). Infinite detail and emulation in an ontologically minimized HCI. In J. C. Chew and J. Whiteside (Eds.), *CHI '90: Proceedings of SIGCHI Conference on Human Factors in Computing Systems* (pp. 321–327). New York: ACM.

Carroll, J. M. (2000). *Making use: Scenario-based design of human-computer interactions*. Cambridge, MA: MIT Press.

Carroll, J. M. (Ed.). (1995). *Scenario-based design: Envisioning work and technology in system development*. New York: Wiley.

Carroll, J. M., and Campbell, R. L. (1986). Softening up hard science: Reply to Newell and Card. *Human-Computer Interaction, 2*(3), 227–249.

Carroll, J. M., and Campbell, R. L. (1989). Artifacts as psychological theories: The case of human-computer interaction. *Behaviour and Information Technology, 8*(4), 247–256.

Carroll, J. M., and Kellogg, W. A. (1989). Artifact as theory nexus: Hermeneutics meets theory-based design. In T. Bice and C. H. Lewis (Eds.), *Proceedings of CHI '89: Human Factors in Computing Systems* (pp. 7–14). New York: ACM.

Carroll, J. M., Kellogg, W. A., and Rosson, M. B. (1991). The task-artifact cycle. In J. M. Carroll (Ed.), *Designing interaction: Psychology at the human-computer interface* (pp. 74–102). Cambridge: Cambridge University Press.

Carroll, J. M., and Rosson, M. B. (1990). Human-computer interaction scenarios as a design representation. In *Proceedings of the 23rd Annual Hawaii International Conference on System Sciences* (Vol. 2, pp. 555–560). New York: IEEE.

Carroll, J. M., and Rosson, M. B. (2003). Design rationale as theory. In J. M. Carroll (Ed.), *HCI models, theories and frameworks* (pp. 431–461). San Francisco: Morgan Kaufman.

Cooper, J. (2007). *Cognitive dissonance: Fifty years of a classic theory*. Thousand Oaks, CA: Sage.

Engelbart, D. C. (1962, October). *Augmenting human intellect: A conceptual framework* (SRI summary report AFOSR-3223, prepared for Director of Information Sciences, Air Force Office of Scientific Research, SRI International). Retrieved from http://www.dougengelbart.org/pubs/augment-3906.html.

Engelbart, D. C., and English, W. K. (1968). A research center for augmenting human intellect. In *AFIPS Conference Proceedings of the 1968 Fall Joint Computer Conference*, (Vol. 33, pp. 395–410). Washington, DC: Thompson Books. Retrieved from http://www.dougengelbart.org/pubs/augment-3954.html.

Grad, B. (2007). The creation and the demise of VisiCalc. *Annals of the History of Computing, 29*(3), 20–31.

Jacobson, I., Booch, G., and Rumbaugh, J. (1998). *The unified software development process.* Reading, MA: Addison Wesley Longman.

Jacobson, I., Christerson, M., Jonsson, P., and Övergaard, G. (1992). *Object-oriented software engineering: A use case driven approach.* Reading, MA: Addison-Wesley.

Kahn, H. (1962). *Thinking about the unthinkable.* New York: Horizon Press.

Kuhn, T. S. (1962). *The structure of scientific revolutions.* Chicago: University of Chicago Press.

Lakatos, I. (1978). *The methodology of scientific research programmes: Philosophical papers* (Vol. 1). Cambridge: Cambridge University Press.

Levy, S. (1994). *Insanely great: The life and times of Macintosh, the computer that changed everything.* New York: Viking.

Malinowski, B. (1922). *Argonauts of the Western Pacific: An account of native enterprise and adventure in the Archipelagoes of Melanesian New Guinea.* London: Routledge and Kegan Paul.

Myers, B. A. (1998). A brief history of human-computer interaction technology. *Interactions, 5*(2), 44–54.

Nardi, B. A., and Miller, J. R. (1990). An ethnographic study of distributed problem solving in spreadsheet development. In *CSCW '90: Proceedings of ACM Conference on Computer-Supported Cooperative Work* (pp. 197–208). New York: ACM.

Newell, A., and Card, S. (1985). The prospects for psychological science in human-computer interaction. *Human-Computer Interaction, 1*(3), 209–242.

Petroski, H. (1992). *The pencil: A history of design and circumstance.* New York: Knopf.

Polanyi, M. (1958). *Personal knowledge: Towards a post-critical philosophy.* London: Routledge and Kegan Paul.

Popper, K. (1963). *Conjectures and refutations.* New York: Routledge.

Reason, J. (1990). *Human error.* Cambridge: Cambridge University Press.

Rosson, M. B., and Carroll, J. M. (2002). *Usability engineering: Scenario-based development of human-computer interaction.* San Francisco: Morgan-Kaufmann.

Simon, H. A. (1973). The structure of ill-structured problems. *Artificial Intelligence, 4*(3–4), 181–201.

Suchman, L. (1987). *Plans and situated actions: The problem of human-machine communication.* Cambridge: Cambridge University Press.

Wack, P. (1985a, September-October). Scenarios: Uncharted waters ahead. *Harvard Business Review*, pp. 73–74.

Wack, P. (1985b, November-December). Scenarios: Shooting the rapids. *Harvard Business Review*, pp. 139–150.

Wirfs-Brock, R., and Wilkerson, B. (1989). Object-oriented design: A responsibility-driven approach. In *OOPSLA '89: Proceedings of ACM Conference on Object-Oriented Programming Systems, Languages, and Applications* (pp. 71–75). New York: ACM.

Wong, S. E. (2012). Operant learning theory. In B. A. Thyer, C. N. Dulmus, and K. M. Sower (Eds.), *Human behavior in the social environment: Theories for social work practice* (pp. 83–121). Hoboken, NJ: Wiley.

Young, R. M., and Barnard, P. B. (1987). The use of scenarios in human-computer interaction research: Turbocharging the tortoise of cumulative science. In J. M. Carroll and P. P. Tanner (Eds.), *CHI '87: Proceedings of the SIGCHI/GI Conference on Human Factors in Computing Systems and Graphics Interface* (pp. 291–296). New York: ACM.

Young, R. M., and Barnard, P. B. (1991). Signature tasks and paradigm tasks: New wrinkles on the scenarios methodology. In D. Diaper and N. Hammond (Eds.), *People and computers VI: Proceedings of the HCI '91 Conference* (pp. 91–101). Cambridge: University of Cambridge.

Young, R. M., Barnard, P. B., Simon, T., and Whittington, J. (1989). How would your favorite user model cope with these scenarios? *ACM SIGCHI Bulletin, 20*(4), 51–55.

CHAPTER 11

APPROPRIATING THEORY

BONNIE NARDI

EUREKA! I HAVE FOUND IT

Many of the chapters in this volume concern the development of new theory. I want to take a slightly different tack and focus on the scholar's appropriation of existing theory. I believe that such appropriation is a critical step along the way in developing new theory and that many existing theories are underexploited. Most mature sciences, such as biology or physics, create intellectual community around a widely scoped but shared theoretical orientation, such as Darwin's theory of evolution or Newtonian physics. It is unlikely that information science will achieve such convergence, but at the same time, it is important, in my view, to aim high—striving for theories that capture the breadth of our subject matter through attention to both the intangibles of semiosis and the tangible properties of technological artifacts (see Dillon, chapter 12 of this volume). These theories exist and can be put to work, either directly or as scaffolding for new or modified or expanded theory. These theories include actor-network theory, activity theory, distributed cognition, and phenomenology (see Kaptelinin and Nardi 2012).

Activity theory has been my personal theoretical touchstone. In this chapter, I am not going to argue for activity theory or even say much about what it is, but I want to explain how I came to appropriate it for my work and how it has shaped my thinking. I will describe the rewards and struggles of my journey with activity theory and endorse a deep connection to theory as a desirable aspect of the growth of individual scholars and the growth and development of the fields in which scholars labor.

In 1993 I was working at Hewlett-Packard Labs in Palo Alto, California, conducting ethnographic studies in the human-computer interaction research group. Human-computer interaction (HCI) concerns the usability and usefulness of computational artifacts and entails a strong creative element in which new applications are a key output of research. The only other anthropologist in our building (who was in a product group) told me she had an article I would like and handed me a copy of Kari Kuutti's (1991) "Activity Theory and Its Applications to Information Systems Research and Development." I began to read the text in the ordinary desultory way one does with random articles, but I soon snapped to attention, the words jumping off the page. I was astonished to find that someone had theorized information systems as *activity systems* wherein the technical system was conceived as part of object-oriented human activity. The clarity and good sense in Kuutti's argument—that we should study what people are doing with technical systems and why!—set me off on a crash course in activity theory to determine whether my enthusiasm would withstand further exposure to the ideas.

I soon learned that activity theory is known as "cultural-historical activity theory" (sometimes "CHAT"), a significant point of common ground for me with my training in anthropology. At the time, I was experiencing some frustrations with my home discipline. The 1980s were a period of turmoil in anthropology, and certain disciplinary moves were made that I believe have continued to stymie anthropology's influence (a story for another time). I was disgruntled with anthropology's total lack of interest in digital technology, its insular jargon, and its somewhat negative attitude. During anthropology's relentless critique of issues of race-class-gender, my head was in a different space—I was energized and excited about what I perceived to be the development of rapidly changing, life-altering digital technologies. I had been aware since 1980 of the personal computers being produced by Apple Computer (when Apple was not a household name), Osborne, and Radio Shack, and I sensed the earthquake they, and their progeny, would set off. I felt happier seeking a positive disposition toward my research objects; I simply did not have the fortitude to bash away at huge, pervasive problems over which I felt I had little control. (I have since developed some of that fortitude, of which more later.) I found digital technology liberating, compelling, and so influential on global culture that I could scarcely believe it remained outside anthropology's sights.

In the mid-1980s, I left a tenure-track job in anthropology to follow my bliss and began working in the high-tech industry in Silicon Valley. My initial encounter with activity theory, in 1993, was a transformative moment of discovery revealing a whole group of scientists who, although far away in Northern Europe, thought digital technology was as interesting as I did. Even better, they were working within a mature social scientific theoretical tradition. This tradition took culture seriously but also had a set of shared, well-developed concepts with which to theorize human activity (something I felt anthropology lacked). Discovering activity theory was wickedly empowering: I was, unexpectedly, going to have my cake and eat it too!

Activity theory's origins go back to the 1920s in Soviet Russia (Vygotsky 1978). Its importation to studies of human-computer interaction occurred around 1987, when Susanne Bødker argued that activity theory could form a theoretical basis for HCI. At that time, HCI was in need of a more grounded, real-world orientation to technology that would move it beyond a narrow interest in usability toward a research practice in which useful designs that met or anticipated human needs and desires could flourish. Such disciplinary development was not going to happen by relying solely on psychological theory applied in laboratory-based experimental research, which had been HCI's focal positioning (Clemmensen 2006). In addition to Bødker, scholars such as Kari Kuutti, Victor Kaptelinin, and Liam Bannon were beginning to build on the activity theory/HCI connection.

I decided that if I was to penetrate the core activity theory circle—centered in what Don Norman once called "that hardy band of Scandinavians"—I would have to make personal contact with the illustrious natives. I e-mailed Kari Kuutti and Susanne Bødker, and they very kindly helped me build up a network of people to contribute to an edited volume on activity theory and HCI published by MIT Press (Nardi 1996). I reasoned that editing a bunch of papers written by activity theorists would be a good way to imbibe activity theory's principles and concerns. (I recommend editorial work, such as curating special issues or edited collections, as a general recipe for plunging into a field or deepening knowledge of a field in which a researcher seeks to gain more understanding.)

In the best tradition of snowball sampling, Victor Kaptelinin further aided me in reaching out to Russian activity theory scholars for the book. I ended up with a nice array of contemporary work in activity theory and digital technology, including chapters by American authors such as Rachel Bellamy and Dorothy Holland, as well as

Nordic and Russian authors. Editing the book was a rewarding labor, and some of the contributors continue to be friends and colleagues. Victor Kaptelinin, in particular, has been my collaborator for going on twenty years, and I have come to know much about Scandinavia from Ellen Christiansen. Many of the contributors to the volume, such as Susanne Bødker, Victor Kaptelinin, Yrjö Engeström, Vladimir Zinchenko, and Kari Kuutti, are key figures in activity theory. I was privileged to have the opportunity to produce their work and help bring it to more prominence in HCI. Through this editorial project, I came to understand some of the nuances of activity theory as a perspective that "deals with purposeful interactions of active subjects with the objective world," as Kaptelinin (2003, p. 355) says.

STRUGGLES

But the move to activity theory was not without challenges. I had already ventured from the familiarity of anthropology to the interdisciplinary field of HCI. Leaving the comforts of cultural anthropology— a discipline in which I never had to define ethnography or explain why anyone would read Lévi-Strauss and in which I knew interlocutors would understand the importance of the Trobriand Islanders— took some getting used to. While theory is disjointed in anthropology, disciplinary stability and identity flow from a kernel of common experience and literature shared by nearly all cultural anthropologists. Such stability was (and is) not the case in the more tumultuous, multidisciplinary HCI. Layered on top of the shifting sands of the diverse concerns and emphases of a varied group of scholars consisting of computer scientists, psychologists, artists, and some anthropologists was the destabilizing fact that HCI is a field of considerable ambivalence toward social theory. HCI has strong engineering and artistic influences, and social scientific theories seem to some to be superfluous and unnecessary.

I do not find this position unreasonable, though I disagree with it. We must take this position seriously because, from a design standpoint, it is undeniably true that the world's most popular everyday software is based not on theory but on simple reflection. Many life-altering digital applications involved no analysis beyond an ordinary person's hunch, based on personal experience or superficial observation, that an application would be useful. For example, in 1978 Dan Bricklin, the inventor of the spreadsheet for personal computers, dreamed up the idea while sitting in an MBA class. Spreadsheets advanced the personal computer from a hobbyist's toy to a powerful computational engine for small business and education. CAD systems, bulletin boards, instant messaging, blogs, computer games, Facebook, and many other ubiquitous digital artifacts were designed in exactly this way. In the case of Facebook, a few students brainstorming how to improve their social lives at Harvard spawned a service now in use by nearly a billion people. Amazon.com was founded by Jeff Bezos, who "in 1994 . . . learned about the rapid growth in Internet use [and] a then-new Supreme Court ruling [that] online retailers don't have to collect sales taxes in states where they lack a physical presence" (Martinez and Helm 2012). On the basis of nothing more than these observations, Bezos wrote a business plan on a road trip from New York to Seattle that changed global commerce.

So it is not surprising that social theory in HCI is regarded with some ambivalence. The following poem was written by Tom Erickson for a special issue of the *Journal of Computer-Supported Cooperative Work* that I co-edited with David Redmiles (Nardi and Redmiles 2002). The special issue is entitled "Activity Theory and the Practice of Design." Erickson is too compassionate and thoughtful to approach critique with graceless denunciation, but in his poem he speaks honestly of being "theory leery":

THEORY THEORY: A DESIGNER'S VIEW

Theory weary, theory leery,
why can't I be theory cheery?
I often try out little bits
wheresoever they might fit.
(Affordances are very pliable,
though what they add is quite deniable.)
The sages call this bricolage,
the promiscuous prefer menage . . .
A savage, I, my mind's pragmatic
I'll keep what's good, discard dogmatic.

Add the reference to my paper,
watch my cited colleagues caper,
I cite you, you cite me,
we've got solidarity.
(GOMS and breakdowns, social network,
use those terms, now don't you shirk!)

Clear concepts clad in fancy clothes,
bid farewell to lucid prose.
The inner circle understands
but we overlook the hinterlands

Dysfunctional we are, it's true,
but as long as we're a happy crew,
if strangers stare and outsiders goggle,
or students struggle, their minds a'boggle
(Dasein, throwness, ontology
ethnomethodology)
A pity 'bout that learning curve
but whose to blame if they lack verve?
A ludic take on structuration,
perhaps this causes consternation?

I see four roles that theories play:
They divide the world, come what may,
into nice neat categories,
enabling us to tell our stories.
(Info scent sure is evocative,
and cyborg theory's quite provocative)
Our talk in turn makes common ground,
where allies, skeptics may be found
Prediction's theory's holy grail,
most that seek it seem to fail.

The world is messy, fuzzy, sticky,
theoretically 'tis all quite tricky.
Theories keep it at a distance,
cov'ring up the awkward instance.
(Objects, agents, actor networks,
banish life with all its quirks)
But when edges grate and things don't mesh,
that is when I think my best.
So let not theory serve as blinders,
welcome disruptions as reminders!

Oddly now, I'm theory cheery
I find I have a theory theory!
Neither holy grail, nor deep disgrace,
theory's useful in its place,
(Framing, talking, predicting, bonding,

evoking discourse—Others responding)
Like goals and methods, plans and actions,
theory's situated, not pure abstraction.
So make your theory a public way,
where passersby may pause and stay.

Without doubt, it takes effort to educate oneself about theory, to set our minds a'boggle, as Erickson put it. Buckland observes that "discussion of theory . . . can appear intimidating" (chapter 6, this volume). At times it all seems a confusing kaleidoscope of shifting shapes and forms that one could well do without (certain French theorists still provoke this reaction in me). Erickson writes of his impatience with theory—it can be pretentious, obscure, simplistic, dogmatic. But he ends by proposing a truce in which theory has a place and, at its best, serves to promote dialog, create community, and light the world through conceptual richness. Those are exactly the advantages I, too, see in theory.

REWARDS

Despite struggles, for me there have been significant rewards in engaging theory. The possibility of such rewards may not be visible at the outset (e.g., to a student mired in the difficulties of trying to make sense of the kaleidoscope). These rewards consist primarily of more theory and excellent colleagues. It may seem we have a circular argument here, but let me explain.

In my early studies of anthropology I began to read theory. A somewhat dismal string of uninspired theories goes back a long way in anthropology, and undergraduates may still learn them as part of absorbing the discipline's history (Kroeber's theory of the superorganic comes to mind). But the beauty of toiling to comprehend even bad theory is that you begin to see how satisfying it would be to explain something of the "messy, fuzzy, sticky" world that is human life and how theories are sets of logical propositions that begin to do this work. Once you have managed (if not mastered) one theory, it becomes easier to move to another and grasp its essentials. And comparing theories becomes quite interesting. Seeing theories in relation to one another shows off what each reveals and each conceals. Putting theories side by side discloses the epistemology and ontology of a given theory, which may not be quite visible until seen in comparative light.

This way of interacting with theory is especially important to information sciences for the obvious but usually overlooked reason that human life is so complex, indeterminate, and historical that we have not yet achieved a theory with the coherence and elegance of, for example, Darwin's theory of evolution. Explaining the diversity of species is apparently an easier task than explaining the diversity of cultures, or how the mind works, or what really drives the economy. For the foreseeable future, we will probably be engaging multiple theories, and we will need to be conversant with more than one to continue to develop theoretically. David Bawden's point that "one of the problems of the information sciences is the plethora of 'novel' empirical methods and models, which make comparison and cumulative progress difficult" (chapter 15, this volume), also applies to theory, but we must still be multilingual in theory at this stage of our development. Buckland (chapter 6, this volume) remarks that "there are many kinds of problems, many different reasons to want to solve them, and many different ways to look at them, so we should expect theory development to come in a variety of forms." This statement seems an eminently sensible way to look at things.

How then can we work toward a cumulative science and yet recognize that theory is necessarily evolving and that part of this evolution is the continual spawning of new and often competing theories? I think there are many good answers to this question. My own answer has been to use activity theory as an anchor. I have never veered away from activity theory's key principles, to which I subscribe philosophically and as a matter of logic. But at the same time, I have learned new theories that might enrich what I know.

For example, while I do not endorse actor-network theory's tendency to collapse the human and nonhuman, I find its emphasis on the agency of technology an important part of the arsenal needed to challenge theories that ignore or downplay technology. In some instances, activity theory gets me part of the way there in an analysis, and I then need to bring in other theory as well. When I was writing about the aesthetics of video gaming (Nardi 2010), I used Dewey's ideas on "active aesthetic experience" along with activity theory to explain what I was seeing in the gaming world. Dewey and activity theory are quite compatible in spirit, and Dewey specifically addressed some issues I wanted to explore that are not well developed in activity theory. Recently I discovered the work of Laurent Thévenot and his colleagues, and I see value in their ideas about orders of worth for understanding collective activity at a larger scale than is usual with activity theory. And last but not least, rediscovering theory learned long ago that turns out to be useful in a new way is a bit like finding money in a forgotten bank account. For example, Weber's (1930) notion of the "ideal subject" is a construct helpful in my current work, and using it required only a trip down memory lane to *The Protestant Ethic and the Spirit of Capitalism*. Theory in social science is, then, a journey. It seems to me that the more we set forth on theoretical travels, the more we will eventually converge on shared waypoints, if not final destinations, that can enable the kind of cumulative progress Bawden argues for. So, then, the first reward of theory is more theory.

The second reward is colleagues. I feel humbled and privileged to know the colleagues I have encountered through my theoretical work. Their favorable points as scholars, and as human beings, are that they never stop asking good questions; they listen well because they want to learn as much from you as you do from them; and they often care deeply about society, which is why they have an interest in social theory to begin with. Whether you collaborate for twenty years or simply have a fascinating conversation over dinner at a conference, it is immensely enriching to know people who have been drawn to theory. Their words stay with you, and so does a cultivated sense of keeping the world constantly in play as an object of contemplation and reflection. For the epigraph to his chapter in this volume, Bawden uses a remark from Leonardo da Vinci: "The noblest pleasure is the joy of understanding." It is a sentiment with which I agree completely.

QUESTIONS AND CRITIQUE

But if theory in HCI does not produce good design, is it worth the trouble? Is it a matter only of personal satisfaction? This question must be asked in the broadest context possible. I can begin to formulate two answers. The first is that activity theory and related approaches have not produced the blockbuster applications that are part of our everyday lives, but they have produced sophisticated systems when there was lead time to do the needed research and a brief to systematically feed concrete research results into design. Many such systems are detailed in Kaptelinin and Nardi (2012). For example, the research program of Jacob Bardram and his colleagues in Denmark is devoted to redesigning clinical information systems in hospitals.

Bardram and his group observed that hospital work is conducted in a highly collaborative environment of multitasking in a complex technical and social context of urgency and mobility. To grasp this reality, it is necessary to design systems in which

> computational activities become first class entities that are represented explicitly in the computer system. This means that activities are seen as computational entities that can be managed by an infrastructure, an operating system, or some kind of middleware—depending on the manner in which they are implemented. Activities can be persistently saved and distributed via a computer network, and can thus migrate among networked computers. Activities are programmatically accessible through an application programmer's interface (API), which functions just like the API for an operating system. Activities are also directly accessible to users in the user interface. (Bardram 2009, p. 10)

In other words, the system is designed from first principles as an activity system, not a collection of files, data, or other computer science constructs—exactly as Kuutti argued it should be in his 1991 article. Bardram's clinical work is under continual development and has been deployed (see, e.g., Bardram et al. 2013). Many systems such as Bardram's come, not surprisingly, from the Nordic countries, with their culture of worker participation, deliberative work design, and long-term thinking and resource allocation.

The second answer, which is actually a question, springs from what Nordic countries have accomplished. What if much more design did not consist of applications a Harvard student could prototype in his dorm room (as in the case of Facebook) but instead was based on careful theoretical study? This is a hypothetical question, of course, but many of the applications we use every day, while indisputably useful, are also frustrating and poorly designed. They lack respect for users (e.g., their privacy) and entrain a set of third-rate systems in which we are becoming increasingly enmeshed and entrenched. The applications are free, so that we use them, and they do good things, such as helping us find information. But at the same time, they are primitive. They are not designed according to deep analysis of activity, and they often ossify into applications we use only because everyone else does, making the cost of moving to something better prohibitive (which is why I use Microsoft Word). The Apple desktop has retained the same functionality for years, and while it still offers the best design of which I am aware, it is stagnant. It makes enough money, and Apple has other fish to fry as it expands into more lucrative markets. Viable new designs created by competitors are not easily realizable, for reasons I discuss in the next paragraphs.

Design is partially an outcome of culture, as any activity theorist would aver, and at the moment, American capitalist culture is ascendant. The general strategy of rich companies (the most aggressive of which are in the United States) is to gain market share through unique designs and free or low-cost applications; tie people to the applications through habit and sometimes the accumulation of data, as in Facebook or cloud computing; and then squelch (through mechanisms such as patent litigation) or buy up competition. It works quite well. Apple, one of the most litigious companies in history, also has an enormous market valuation; at various moments it is the world's most valuable company. I have personally been involved in Apple's litigation from a patent I coauthored when I worked there in 1996. I testified at several depositions concerning the "'647," which journalist Dan Rowinski (2012) has called "a big bludgeon . . . to bully everyone else into subservience." Needless to say, I had no idea the patent would ever be used in such a way. (I no longer believe in software patents.)

To understand design more progressively, analyses of usability and usefulness are insufficient; the larger activity system in which we are enmeshed must become the remit. As a scholar of HCI, I cannot meaningfully contemplate today's digital designs without consideration of the sociomaterial conditions in which they are produced. These conditions bear on design outcomes and constitute an instance of what activity theory means by "cultural-historical" analysis. Over the years I have moved toward more expansively critical analysis (Ekbia et al. 2015; Kow and Nardi 2012; Nardi 2010), and it is central to my current work. Such analysis is exactly what I was less able to confront in the 1980s and 1990s. Part of the change for me is maturity, but part of it is understanding that anthropology's blistering critiques are not the only way to question and probe and that more nuanced positions can be developed. Activity theory has helped me in this quest by providing sound concepts—such as mediation—that enable us to see, for example, how a technology can be eminently useful yet yield certain undesirable consequences, such as loss of privacy, alterations in social relations, degradation of academic skills, or the constraining filter bubble. Such consequences need to be constantly assessed as we evaluate our human relation to digital technologies.

Shouldn't the free market ensure that if there is a need or desire for different or better applications, they will appear? I believe the answer is, increasingly, no. Mechanisms such as patent litigation tend toward the development of oligopolies, making it difficult for new companies to compete (Suarez-Villa 2015). There is a shrinkage of competition, which is, of course, the cornerstone of new and improved products. While innovative start-ups continue to produce wonderfully creative new offerings, getting them into our hands is not a straightforward process. Starting a company to compete with, say, Google, is almost impossible now. I use a search engine called DuckDuckGo that is a Google alternative (https://en.wikipedia.org/wiki/DuckDuckGo), but it is unlikely to replace Google. However, I use it because it does not collect personal data. It is more a proof of concept than a business. DuckDuckGo has about 1.8 million direct searches a day, while Google has about 5.9 billion (http://www.statisticbrain.com/google-searches/). DuckDuckGo survives on the capital of its rich founder, some venture capital, and limited advertising. Most young entrepreneurs do not have the capital of DuckDuckGo's founder, and the best they can hope for is to be bought by Google or Microsoft. At that point, some, or a lot, of the innovative edge is smoothed away, or the applications may even be abandoned.

But enough doom and gloom! We can imagine that at some point the world might look more like the Nordic countries or like something else altogether (Tomlinson et al. 2013). Continuing to design in generative ways using theories such as activity theory seems a means of working toward inventing the future, as Alan Kay long ago claimed we should. In the meantime, it is important to take seriously the cultural-historical imperative of activity theory and apprehend design influences as flowing from global technocapitalism and sociotechnical change, as well as continuing to conduct more conventional, locally focused studies. We must do all of this if we are to fulfill our role as researchers. Kuutti (2010, p. 717) observed, "If we focus only on practical usefulness and exclude explanation and interpretation, we do serious harm to our very nature as researchers." It is our obligation to engage deeply with theory in order "to develop better understanding of the world around us" (p. 717).

Much of my current work on issues related to political economy and the like (e.g., Ekbia and Nardi 2012) requires theorizing at scales

I am not used to as an anthropologist. Having grappled with theory for a long time makes this not exactly easy but at least slightly less scary. Activity theory, with its Marxist roots, has primed me to seek a critical component in my work and to look to the economy for analytical inspiration. The journey of theory may lead to unexpected locales.

I want to draw attention to a system that is just the sort of advance in design that could improve our everyday lives. It is based on activity theory research of typical office work and is premised on the concept of "projects," a common way we think about work, rather than "files," the canonical computer science structure with which users encounter computers (Kaptelinin 2003). Kaptelinin's experimental system "(a) makes it possible for the user to directly indicate a higher-level task, that is, a project, (b) monitors user activities and tracks resources used when carrying out the project, and (c) automatically organizes and updates these resources to make them easily available to the user when he or she resumes working on the project" (p. 360).

Although this system has never been actualized as a product, it is easy to imagine the utility it would provide. Kaptelinin reported that "first experiences with the system indicate that it addresses a real need of users for a low-overhead integration of various types of information around higher-level, meaningful goals" (Kaptelinin 2003, p. 361). Problems with desktop interfaces have been studied for a long time (Nardi, Anderson, and Erickson 1995), and while incremental improvements are made, the potential profits of changing the desktop do not seem to merit attention in the private sector (or the Apple-Microsoft oligarchy makes such attention moot). From a societal perspective, the productivity gains of improved work environments would be aesthetically and economically significant.

Several scholars have proposed good desktop designs over the years—not only Kaptelinen (2003) but also, for example, Henderson and Card (1986), Robertson et al. (2000), and Voida and Mynatt (2009). Studies seeking to determine how the desktop influences computer users have yielded results that suggest potential design enhancements, and the HCI community's continued efforts in this realm indicate an energetic, positive response to these results. Voida and Mynatt, whose "activity-based computing" approach draws from activity theory, produced a useful, original design in response to their observation that "while empirical characterizations of knowledge work [going back to 1994] have identified the importance of the spatial organization of short-term and transient artifacts in making sense of ongoing activities, in general, systems designed to support knowledge work have failed to emphasize these needs in their design" (Voida and Mynatt 2009, p. 260). They believe activity-based approaches are moving to fill gaps, noting that "it is anticipated that as activity-based systems are adopted more widely, they will provide a variety of benefits, including better task awareness, simpler multitasking, more natural organization of electronic information, and improved online collaboration" (p. 268). It may be just that activity theory's influence is moving more slowly than I would like!

THE IMPACT OF THEORY ON THE FIELD OF HCI

To reflect more broadly on the role of theory in HCI, I devised my own version of a popular HCI technique called "heuristic evaluation." Heuristic evaluation is based on the idea that a lot can be learned about usability from a quick, focused perusal of a user interface (Nielsen and Molich 1990). My repurposing of the method for assessing the impact of theory consists of analyzing the research contributions of a small number of members of the HCI community who belong to the CHI Academy, an honorary society recognizing HCI researchers. The CHI Academy (of which I am a member) is part of the ACM SIGCHI (Association for Computing Machinery Special Interest Group on Computer Human Interaction) and has members "who have contributed to the advancement of the field of human-computer interaction" (http://www.sigchi.org/about). Members are selected by a small ACM committee. I will argue that the use of theory in research has shaped the contributions of a substantial percentage of CHI Academy members, revealing theory's perceived value to the development of the field.

The CHI Academy dates to the year 2000 (human-computer interactions being a relatively young field within the information sciences) and as of 2013 has hosted eighty-four members (plus fourteen members with Lifetime Research Awards coextensive with membership in the academy). This sample of HCI researchers represents a demographic of mid- to late-career professionals within SIGCHI, and so while future academy membership could skew away from current trends, the analysis will reveal something about the foundations of the field. I did a simple binary coding of academy members whose work materially involved either social theory or computer science theory and those whose work did not. While such analysis is strictly pursuant to the limited purposes of this chapter, and I claim the coding to have validity only as an instance of a simple heuristic evaluation, I did attempt to code as carefully and conservatively as I could.

Everyone has some kind of theory informing their ideas, but I coded "+theory" only for members whose work was explicitly responsive to theory, work in which theory was acknowledged and embraced. Some members of the interdisciplinary CHI community work in essentially atheoretical modes—within artistic traditions, or with a focus on the pragmatics of usability in corporate settings, or on the basis of the design of intuitive prototypes based on inspiration taken from everyday life or a particular passion. Since I am arguing in favor of theory in this chapter, I tried to be cautious in my judgments, scoring "+theory" only if I could see that a body of work evidenced substantial, visible commitment to theory.

To cut to the chase, I found that the work of 63 percent of the academy members showed a clear theoretical orientation (fifty-three out of eighty-four). This number, which might be higher in a more traditional discipline, such as biology, is perhaps not surprising in the context of an interdisciplinary field with a strong emphasis on engineering and a smaller but important inflection from the arts. I noticed that psychological theory was predominant in the early awards but that an influential strand of theory concerned with group action entered the research stream almost from the start. This trend has continued, and it includes activity theory. I was pleased to see four authors from the Acting with Technology Series, which I coedit for MIT Press, included in the academy. I conclude from this "heuristic evaluation" of the discipline of HCI that theory has been foundational. At the same time, HCI is far from being a discipline with unquestioned allegiance to a particular theory or to theory in general. It remains to be seen whether such eclecticism is generative or instead destabilizes research by failing to accumulate critical mass.

CODA

The aim of this chapter has been to fulfill the volume editor's request to produce an account of my relation to theory that is personal and that reveals the struggles, challenges, successes, excitement, and satisfaction of developing theory. It is my sincere hope that this account will be of use to students and others making their own way with theory and that the somewhat fractious exercise of engaging theory, especially theories in rapidly mutating, interdisciplinary fields such as the information sciences, will appear as a tractable undertaking, one that will be evident not as an obstacle but as an encounter with intellectual objects that repay study many times over.

Sometimes poets should have the last word, and I end with two lines of Erickson's poem that invite us to theory: "So make your theory a public way, / where passersby may pause and stay" (Erickson 2000).

ACKNOWLEDGMENT

The poem by Thomas Erickson, "Theory Theory: A Designer's View" (Pliant.org, 2000), is used by permission of the author.

REFERENCES

Bardram, J. E. (2009). Activity-based computing for medical work in hospitals. *ACM Transactions on Computer-Human Interaction, 16*(2). doi: 10.1145/1534903.1534907.

Bardram, J. E., Frost, M., Szántó, K., Faurholt-Jepson, M., Vingerg, M., and Kessing, L. (2013). Designing mobile health technology for bipolar disorder: A field trial of the monarca system. In W. E. Mackay, S. Brewster, and S. Bødker (Eds.), *CHI '13: Proceedings of the SIGCHI Conference on Human Factors in Computing Systems* (pp. 2627–2636). New York: ACM.

Bødker, S. (1987). *Through the interface: A human activity approach to user interface design* (DAIMI PB-224). Aarhus, Denmark: University of Aarhus. Retrieved from https://pure.au.dk/portal/files/20861897/Full_text.

Clemmensen, T. (2006). Whatever happened to the psychology of human-computer interaction? *Information Technology and People, 19*(2), 121–151.

Ekbia, H., and Nardi, B. (2012). Inverse instrumentality: How technologies objectify patients and players. In P. Leonardi, B. Nardi, and J. Kallinikos (Eds.), *Materiality and organizing: Social interaction in a technological world* (pp. 157–176). Oxford: Oxford University Press.

Ekbia, H., Nardi, B., and Šabanovic, S. (2015). On the margins of the machine: Heteromation and robotics. *Proceedings iConference*. Retrieved from http://hdl.handle.net/2142/73678.

Erickson, T. (2000). Theory theory: A designer's view. Retrieved from http://www.pliant.org/personal/Tom_Erickson/theorytheory.html.

Henderson, A., and Card, S. (1986). Rooms: The use of virtual workspaces to reduce space contention in a window-based graphical user interface. *ACM Transactions on Graphics, 5*(3), 211–243.

Kaptelinin, V. (2003). UMEA: Translating interaction histories into project contexts. In G. Cockton and P. Korhonen (Eds.), *CHI '03: Proceedings of the SIG-*

CHI Conference on Human Factors in Computing Systems (pp. 353–360). New York: ACM.

Kaptelinin, V., and Nardi, B. (2012). *Activity theory in HCI research: Fundamentals and reflections.* San Rafael, CA: Morgan and Claypool.

Kow, Y. M., and Nardi, B. (2012). Mediating contradictions of digital media. *UCI Law Review, 2*(2), 675–693.

Kuutti, K. (1991). Activity theory and its application to information systems research and development. In H-E. Nissen, H. K. Klein, and R. Hirscheim (Eds.), *Information systems research: Contemporary approaches and emergent traditions* (pp. 529–549). Amsterdam: Elsevier.

Kuutti, K. (2010). Where are the Ionians of user experience research? In E. Hvanneberg and M. K. Lárusdóttir (Eds.), *NordiCHI '10: Proceedings of the 6th Nordic Conference on Human-Computer Interaction* (pp. 715–718). New York: ACM.

Martinez, A., and Helm, K. (2012). Amazon a virtual no-show in hometown philanthropy. *Seattle Times.* Retrieved from http://seattletimes.com/html/businesstechnology/2017883663_amazonmain25.html.

Nardi, B. (2010). *My life as a night elf priest: An anthropological account of World of Warcraft.* Ann Arbor: University of Michigan Press.

Nardi, B. (Ed.). (1996). *Context and consciousness: Activity theory and human-computer interaction.* Cambridge, MA: MIT Press.

Nardi, B., Anderson, K., and Erickson, T. (1995). Filing and finding computer files. In B. Blumenthal, I. M. Gornostaev, and C. Unger (Eds.), *Proceedings of EWHCI '95: Fifth East-West Conference on Human-Computer Interaction* (pp. 162–179). Moscow, Russia: International Centre for Scientific and Technical Information. Retrieved from http://www.artifex.org/~bonnie/Finding%26FilingComputerFiles.pdf.

Nardi, B., and Redmiles, D. (Eds.). (2002). Activity theory and the practice of design [Special issue]. *Journal of Computer-supported Cooperative Work, 11*(1–2).

Nielsen, J., and Molich, R. (1990). Heuristic evaluation of user interfaces. In J. C. Chew and J. Whiteside (Eds.), *CHI '90: Proceedings of the SIGCHI Conference on Human Factors in Computing Systems* (pp. 249–256). New York: ACM.

Robertson, G., van Dantzich, M., Robbins, D., Czerwinski, M., Hinckly, K., Risden, K., Thiel, D., and Gorokhovsky, V. (2000). The task gallery: A 3D window manager. In T. Turner and G. Szwillus (Eds.), *CHI '00: Proceedings of the SIGCHI Conference on Human factors in Computing Systems* (pp. 494–501). New York: ACM.

Rowinski, D. (2012). Apple's '647 Patent: What it is and why it's bad for the mobile ecosystem. Retrieved from http://readwrite.com/2012/06/13/apples-647-patent-what-it-is-and-why-its-bad-for-the-mobile-ecosystem#awesm=~oa37WBrJNq0QiA.

Suarez-Villa, L. (2015). *Corporate power, oligopolies, and the crisis of the state.* Albany: State University of New York Press.

Tomlinson, W., Blevis, E., Nardi, B., Patterson, Silberman, S., and Pan, Y. (2013). Collapse informatics and practice: Theory, method, and design. *ACM Transactions on Computer-Human Interaction, 20*(4). doi:10.1145/2493431.

Voida, S., and Mynatt, E. (2009). It feels better than filing: Everyday work experiences in an activity-based computing system. In D. Olsen and R. B. Arthur (Eds.), *CHI '09: Proceedings of the SIGCHI Conference on Human Factors in Computing Systems* (pp. 259–268). New York: ACM.

Vygotsky, L. S. (1978). *Mind in society.* Cambridge, MA: Harvard University Press.

Weber, M. (1930). *The Protestant ethic and the spirit of capitalism.* London: Routledge.

CHAPTER 12

THEORY FOR DESIGN: THE CASE OF READING

ANDREW DILLON

IN 1908, EDMUND HUEY REMARKED that the human ability to read text is akin to a miracle, and that "to completely analyze what we do when we read would almost be the acme of a psychologist's achievements" (p. 4). Though easily taken for granted, so much effort is put into teaching people to read and write, and consequently, so many human activities involve reading of some description, that an inability to read is recognized as a significant shortcoming for an adult in most of the world. It has been repeatedly documented that the majority of inmates in US prisons are functionally illiterate, and there is a sad but significant relationship between low reading skill and poverty. Major government initiatives in most countries target literacy as a critical component of education, and with good reason: adults who cannot read well find it difficult to function in even routine everyday task environments and are more likely to require welfare support throughout their lives (Kirssch et al. 2002).

More than a century after Huey's comments, we continue to struggle to understand what is happening between the visual stimuli of printed letters and the grasp of meaning in a human mind. Indeed, in a review of a later edition of Huey's seminal work, *The Psychology and Pedagogy of Reading*, some sixty years on, Samuels (1970) remarked how the problems then driving psychological research were largely the same ones Huey had originally identified, and not just in research on reading but in the broader sweep of cognitive psychology research at the time. Almost five decades on again, this remains remarkably true. We still have much to learn about this essential life skill and to recognize that the psychological processes underlying reading are complex, interactive, and learned.

Over the last century, experimental psychologists have made a consistent effort to model and explain the reading process. Much progress has been made, and research has produced robust findings on eye movements, perceptual span (number of characters perceived at a time or ahead of current fixation points), reading speed, the effects of layout and typography, and the general psychoperceptual behaviors of humans when reading. Rayner and colleagues (2012) provide an excellent summary of this work.

A key methodological approach in this work has been the measurement of eye movements. Interestingly, as the tools available to study these movements have improved in accuracy and refinement from the earliest studies, with bite bars to hold readers' heads still and cocaine to relax the eyeball, to the latest eye-tracking software, which is minimally intrusive once calibrated, many of the earliest findings have proven to be insightful. No matter the measurement tool employed, typical adults read between two hundred and four hundred words per minute, using ballistic eye movements to fixate at different points across a line of text. Educated adult readers in all languages can instantly recognize approximately thirty thousand unique words, even though these might vary in spelling, legibility, font type, size, and context. Text justification has an impact on readers, but word shape is not a major source of information. These as well as myriad other robust findings make up the knowledge base of reading scholarship, and it can prove both impressive and overwhelming to examine such work. Particularly noteworthy from an information studies perspective is that even as continual progress has been made and a solid science of reading has emerged, there remain significant difficulties in applying these results to interactive systems design, where it has become clear that a rather different kind of theoretical knowledge is required.

EARLY STRUGGLES WITH THEORY IN HUMAN-COMPUTER INTERACTION (HCI)

In the 1980s, when I was commencing my graduate studies, the impending impact of information technologies on our lives was beginning to be recognized in academia as a researchable phenomenon. The intellectual roots of understanding how to build better information tools and networks for real users run deeply back into the last century, from studies of workplace layout to experiments on how to develop appropriate commands and error messages in interactive systems (e.g., Shneiderman and Plaisant 2010). In the 1980s, it became widely recognized that many human occupations in the future would rely heavily on mobile tools and cognitive processing, not physical spaces or computational resources that required users to be heavily trained. This recognition gave rise to an increasing emphasis on "user-centered" design as a method for developing new tools and on the search for appropriate, applicable guidance from the deep library of research on human thinking and behavior. Of necessity, empirical methods of user-centered design tended to dominate the theoretical approaches mined from psychology, but the hope within the nascent field of HCI was that suitable theory would eventually emerge.

I was initially exposed to HCI by a psychology professor, Jurek Kirakowski, first through his mind-opening elective course on the philosophy of science, and later through membership in his human factors research group at University College Cork, which brought together like-minded graduate students and faculty. He helped me channel my frustration with what I was learning in my psychology studies, much of which I found too impractical to be of real-world use, into an actionable course of studies for my MA thesis. To my way of thinking, all the theoretical brilliance of cognitive psychology did not seem to amount to much by way of applicable knowledge, the type that would only be obtained by logical derivation of theoretical insights rather than common sense cast in the terminology of cognition.

I was struggling to figure out if this state of affairs reflected my own incompetence, or if the gap between the laboratory and the field was just too far to bridge. Of course, the answer was partially both. I had neither the required understanding nor the nuanced perspective on psychology to fully realize my ambitions of application, but it was true then, and remains true to this day, that the primary focus of academic psychology is not the application of science to everyday issues but more on the development and testing of fundamental theories concerning human information processing and behavior, so my disquiet was not entirely without grounds.

In 1986 I moved to the Human Sciences and Advanced Technology (HUSAT) Research Institute in Loughborough University in the United Kingdom. HUSAT offered a unique environment, being funded equally from long-term research grants and short-term consulting work within the European software industry. Its mission was to apply the social sciences to problems in the design and application of advanced technologies, and for the next eight years, while simultaneously completing doctoral studies, I worked on a range of projects that explicitly required the application of psychology to design. Here I would be required to evaluate innovative user interfaces and make recommendations for redesign based on empirical findings and theoretical principles. I also worked on-site in organizations where new technology was being rolled out or developed, and enjoyed such experiences as capturing real-time data from aerospace engineers moving through the transition from drawing boards to CAD, and participating in design meetings with software companies attempting to impose user-centered practices on their large-scale development projects. This was an apprenticeship in application like no other, and it provided a wealth of experience that would guide my future career for decades to come.

I also spent considerable time at HUSAT immersed in questions related to the user experience of dealing with documents presented on-screen compared to paper, and it was this that brought into sharp focus the question of how best to derive design guidance from the foundational theories of human activity. Quickly exhausting the limited HCI literature on this topic, I turned to the significantly larger psychological research on human reading for guidance, and soon discovered this vast and well-developed set of models and theories, and no small amount of empirical data on particular aspects of the reading process. The challenge became how to interpret and frame this work into a form that would be applicable to design decisions.

The desire for applicable theory for design has driven human factors work for generations. If one examines the classic texts on human factors, such as Sanders and McCormick (1993) or Wickens and Hollands (2000), one finds a mix of human performance analyses, often framed in terms of primary modality (e.g., sight, reach, auditory perception, etc.) coupled with tables and charts of information processing parameters under certain conditions or constraints. The emphasis of such information provision is on the education of a practitioner who can apply what might be required in context, utilizing a mix of empiricism and guided principle to shape outcomes. For decades this approach provided the basis of applying knowledge of human operators to technology interface design, and there was always the aim of developing better models, principles, and methods to further refine the application of such knowledge over time.

The standard complaint within the human factors profession at this time was about not limited theory but rather the typically late involvement of its practitioners in the design process. As the pro-

fession became recognized to the point that most major information technology manufacturers employed such experts, human factors evaluations of design were too often completed only at the end
of the design phase. Professionals complained that they often found
problems that were predictable and could have been identified earlier
in the process, when necessary changes or improvements in usability would have been far less costly to implement. The charge from
the human factors profession was to be involved "early and often," so
as to apply knowledge of what works and what is problematic for users before any important and expensive-to-revisit design decisions are
made. Interestingly, this is a challenge that many in the user experience roles within software design still face to this day.

The case for earlier involvement was given a significant boost
with the publication in 1983 of *The Psychology of Human-Computer
Interaction*, by Card, Newell, and Moran (1983). Here at last was a
book that contained a formal model, built from foundational work in
human cognition, that could be used to derive predictions of human
performance with specific user interface designs. This was an example of theoretical framing that could provide a scientific basis for earlier involvement, not just an argument over changing the design process to include earlier evaluations.

In this landmark text, the authors proposed a model human oper-
ator whose basic reaction times, decision cycles, and motor control
responses could be estimated reliably and, when applied to a structured task analysis for some interactive behavior, used to generate a
bounded estimate of the time taken to effect certain outcomes with
specific interface layouts. While there have been numerous critiques
of this formal model, not least for its limited application to discre-
tionary tasks performed by non-experts, it presented at last a view of
HCI knowledge as a codified formal system for determining best options at the earliest stage of design, even if it never, as proclaimed by
its developers, "drove out" soft scientific approaches to human factors work (Card et al. 1983). To me, this work was revolutionary, not
only in delivering a tool but also in staking out the territory in which
the authors felt only psychology could provide the relevant input.

GETTING THEORY INTO DESIGN PRACTICE

It was against this backdrop that I began to focus my efforts on the
design and evaluation of new reading technologies. The particu-

lar impetus was funded projects from the Online Computer Library Center (OCLC) in the United States, and from the British Library Research and Development Division and Taylor and Francis publishers in the United Kingdom. What these groups had in common was a concern with the emergence of electronic document presentation and its implications for their core business. In practical terms, the British Library was reportedly adding over twenty miles of shelf space on an annual basis just to house its growing collections, while Taylor and Francis wanted to understand how academics might respond to scholarly journals delivered electronically rather than on paper. Looking back, it's difficult to convey the view common then that electronic documents might prove to be a niche area of human-information interaction and that people would never give up on paper books or journals. The shifts we've experienced in the last two decades were not at all inevitable to those considering these issues at the time, and these organizations were somewhat farsighted in considering that human factors work might prove important in determining how to proceed.

As any junior scholar knows, the first step in a research project is to review the literature, and thus I began to synthesize the work on reading from non-paper sources. While experimental studies of reading text from screens had commenced in the 1970s, with some isolated comparisons of new display technologies, the first serious research effort comparing computer screens with paper was conducted by Gould and colleagues at IBM in the mid-1980s (Gould et al. 1987). Their work was a model of experimental design, systematically manipulating all the important variables people had supposed made a difference in reading experience: fonts, viewing distance from screen, ability to control the viewing angle, color of background, and so on. In more than a dozen experimental studies, Gould and his team presented findings that became labeled the "image quality hypothesis," a reference to the importance of key visual aspects of displays that must be addressed to minimize differences between the media, specifically, the interaction of display polarity, resolution, and use of anti-aliasing. With these conditions met, these authors determined that on most measures of reading speed and accuracy, electronic text could match paper for readability.

The identification of key perceptual variables seemed to offer designers some concrete targets to meet, but the results took several years to become recognized, as other researchers continued to do comparisons between improved screens and paper that added little new to Gould et al.'s analysis. Impressive as Gould et al.'s work appeared to me then (and still does today as a model of how science can approach fundamental design questions systematically and empirically to offer tractable advice), it was pretty clear that the image quality explanation, rooted as it was in the analysis of visual perception, could take us only so far in the study of the reading process. This recognition of the limits of the image quality hypothesis proved to be telling.

During the late 1980s and early 1990s, we witnessed the emergence of hypertext information systems, self-contained linked text and image spaces that predated the web. The design of information spaces to be linked together, with an ability to move through multiple documents at the click of a mouse button, launched a wave of research into questions of reading comprehension, document navigation, and the impact of alternative layouts and structures on task performance, which of necessity required analysis of human activity at the cognitive level. Even with image quality assured, here was a form of reading that was distinctly different and warranted fuller examination. Several commercial implementations of this technology vied for leadership in the market, and experimental tests of how well users could find their way around these applications emerged through the earliest ACM and British Computer Society conferences on hypertext and hypermedia (e.g., McAleese 1989).

What struck me as curious about much of the emerging work on hypertext was that it seemed to occur without recognition of the type of experimental human factors work conducted by Gould and others, and thus many problems associated with the new medium that resulted from the same image quality issues already identified as causal were overlooked as concerns with users' mental models of structure and sense of orientation within document spaces dominated the literature. As the research on various forms of information display and usability exploded, it became difficult to form a cohesive view of the emerging results, and again, the translation of these studies into design guidance remained challenging.

Since part of HUSAT's mission was to provide practical guidance on the human dimensions of technology design and implementation, my interest in finding appropriate means of representing HCI knowledge to those building new designs was inevitable. Others, too, were concerned with advancing HCI as an intellectual discipline within academia, and the view that such progress was predicated on the emergence of theoretical knowledge was commonly agreed on. Books of guidelines for usable interface design based on cognitive psychology emerged (e.g., Gardener and Christie 1987), but such packaging required significant interpretation and contextualization in order to offer guidance. For the design of new reading interfaces, I believed a distinct approach was required, one that would involve a different type of theoretical model of reading for digital document design.

THEORY BUILDING IN THE INFORMATION SCIENCES

In studying theory building in the social sciences, one is frequently reminded that such work is often viewed as the poor second cousin to the theories in the so-called natural sciences. Social sciences have sought better and stronger theories since the 1960s, but philosophers continue to view such work with skepticism (e.g., Chalmers 1982), arguing that it lacks sufficient consensus, is nonparadigmatic, or fails to produce definitive findings. Certainly there has been a conscious effort on the part of psychology and sociology to develop more formal theoretical foundations, but the nature of the social world and the complexity of human action makes theorizing in the social domain difficult, and thus more prone to commonsense critiques than might be faced by scientists attempting to explain the physical world. Nevertheless, most advanced graduate programs in the social sciences require students to conceptualize theories related to the discipline's problem space; to learn to distinguish between terms such as "hypotheses," "constructs," "models," "propositions," and so on; and to articulate research questions in terms of the theoretical perspectives any answers might inform.

Graduate students in information science are afforded little preparation for building a theory other than the tried-and-true approach of tweaking or refuting some preexisting theory handed down from above or attempting to explain research findings in terms of a plausible theory. Certainly students are exposed to theories, and in many programs they study methodologies of investigation deeply, but the conscious act of building theory to account for data is not explicitly taught in most information programs. Yet theory can take many forms, and while emphasis is placed on the importance of theoretical analysis for the cohesion, explanatory power, and comparability of studies, we often expect students to grapple with the process of building a theory on their own.

In HCI studies, this state of affairs has largely resulted in repeated efforts to refine and somewhat repurpose theories of human behavior, communication, and cognition. For example, my own graduate students learn various theoretical approaches to studying interaction, such as cognitive models of human thought processes and decision making, and social psychological theories of technology acceptance and adoption. These provide students with a basic framing of the problems as conceived by many researchers in the field and allow them to identify and manipulate key variables in their own research studies. This is, in my experience, crucial in helping students take the first steps in a new problem space, as it provides a language and set of data points they can use to think through possible relationships. Appropriate as such introductions to theory might be, there is little time spent formally demonstrating how these theories came to be derived, though over time I have started to address this directly with my own students by trying to offer historical explanations about where these theories came from, intellectually, and why they have endured, for example, in the case of the well-established technology acceptance model formulated by Davis, Bagozzi, and Warshaw (1989), which can be linked back to the theory of planned behavior (Ajzen 1985) and its precedent, the theory of reasoned action (Fishbein and Ajzen 1975).

Yet there remain several problems with this type of approach within the information discipline. Primarily, it suggests that the information sciences have no theoretical core, but derive theoretical structures from outside disciplines (for another view, see the collection of seventy-two possible theories, meta-theories, and models of information behavior collected in Fisher, Erdelez, and McKechnie 2005). How significant a problem this may be for the field is itself a fascinating question, but it seems to strike most graduate students early in their programs that our discipline is not quite like many others, and not always in a good way. A reasonable counterargument might be made that by its very nature, information is an interdisciplinary field and therefore it must draw theory from outside. This is certainly plausible, but my concern is that if we only derive our theoretical analyses from outside, it is even more difficult to demonstrate the process of theory building for students in the information sciences, since the main actors in theory generation are not directly participating in our community.

THEORY FOR DESIGN: THE NEED FOR APPLICABLE FRAMEWORKS

Beyond the direct concerns of the information sciences' intellectual development, there are further problems with the use of external theory in the application of information work, particularly in interaction design. Studies of design practices in the software industry indicate that most non-academics find the science base of psychology and sociology (from where we draw most of our theoretical insights) difficult to understand, and the literature base of scholarly research is either hidden or impenetrable to outsiders (Dillon, McKnight, and Richardson 1993). This suggests that there is scope for more applicable theory that deals with the type of problems information designers and system builders face routinely. It was this that motivated me to consider finding a new form of theoretical presentation.

Two distinctions proved important for me in working on theory for information use. First, scholars such as Carroll and Campbell (1989) introduced the idea of the artifact as theory—that the designed interface was itself the best embodiment of theory, capturing as it did the design team's thinking on what was required to deliver a usable system. This allowed us within HCI to at least point to the very systems being created at any given time as constituting best theory. Thus, by examining the existing designs in the world, one could deconstruct the artifact to infer the underlying theory of use it presented. Attractive as this was, I was never convinced that it was sufficient. It remained the case that most designs were little more than limited or poor theories generated by people with little or no explicit knowledge of our field. What this did provide, however, was an impetus to envisage a distinction between theory in design and theory for design, the latter being a form of representation that existed to predict and explain human interactive behavior so as to constrain design choices directly (Dillon 1996).

A second distinction that seemed important to me was the time-slicing of human cognition offered by Newell and Card (1985), which provided a set of time estimations over the range of human behaviors in which we typically engage, from perception to long-term planning. For these authors, the key aspects of cognition involved in HCI ran from 0.10 seconds to 10 seconds, with anything longer being the province of bounded rationality and organizational psychology rather than HCI. This type of carving up of human action for study has dominated theoretical work in our field, not always intentionally, perhaps, but certainly by proxy through the type of variables studied and the import of the distinctions this approach embodies in social and cognitive psychological theories. For me, a key insight came from recognizing that no matter how lawful such time constraints on human action might be for considering our experimental findings, any one individual manifested all of these levels within herself, and thus when thinking seriously about the human aspects of design, we needed to be aware that human reactions, thoughts, decisions, and responses were not limited to a ten-second duration for analysis.

In coming to terms with these two distinctions, I consciously started to imagine how best to represent "the user" (a term I came to dislike and avoid) in a meaningful way for design, particularly the design of new information systems aimed at supporting reading. While I did not deliberately set out to generate a theory of reading, what resulted became a theoretical framing of issues for information design evaluation, and perhaps gave rise to a different type of theory construction.

READING AS A MULTILEVEL PROCESS

Theoretical analyses of reading from psychology tend to consider reading somewhat narrowly, focusing on the stages of processing involved from the perception of visual stimuli to the recognition of a word or sentence. Indeed, there is disagreement still within this community regarding the proper place for comprehension, with some considering this a step beyond the act of reading and thus to be excluded from theoretical consideration (e.g., Crowder and Wagner 1992). For the purposes of design, it became clear to me that this view of reading was insufficient, failing to even acknowledge that the interactive aspects of human-information engagement were necessarily important since people manipulate and move through documents using a keyboard, mouse, touchscreen, and so on. Further, it seemed that while the image quality hypothesis had established basic parameters for a display that must be met to ensure optimal performance, these were necessary but not sufficient requirements. Once documents became longer than a single screen of text, it was equally important to understand how people located and structured the material they were navigating through. Clearly, any realistic representation of the human processes underlying this type of interaction could not be reduced to cognition or perception alone.

In attempting to outline the issues involved in using a digital document and thereby offering some points of consideration for design, I drew the following assumptions from the extant research and from the multiple observations I had been making of users in their interactions with documents, both paper and digital:

- Information tasks involve the user drawing on multiple sources of knowledge in context.
- Humans are goal oriented and use information to satisfy task demands.
- In so doing, humans form a model of the structure of the information space in which they are operating.
- Information tasks typically involve physical manipulations of information sources.
- At the level of word and sentence reading, performance is bound by the established parameters of cognition.

To place a boundary on what might be considered document use, I decided to focus only on scenarios where the initial documents were already in front of the user. In other words, I was interested not in users' searching behavior or information retrieval to generate a target set but in the interactions that occurred once a human proceeded to interact with a document for a given task (e.g., looking up a section of text to understand a process, reading a document for comprehension, checking a fact, scanning for relevance). This was more than convenience. Boundary definitions are necessary for placing limits on what can and cannot be reasonably explained or predicted with a model or theory, and my understanding of digital document design suggested that retrieval and long-term use of documents were driven by a different set of forces than were present at the reader-document interaction stages.

Having set boundary conditions, I started to consider the range of activities typical readers seemed to follow in our lab tests when performing similar tasks. I also explored their thinking processes through verbal protocol techniques (e.g., Dillon 2004). I found myself talking through these steps with colleagues, particularly my co-researchers, Cliff McKnight and John Richardson, trying to scope out how humans seemed to maneuver from a task goal through to an answer, combining perceptual, physical, and cognitive processes dynamically and iteratively as they proceeded. Mythical accounts of theoretical insights being gained in a flash or in a bathtub never applied to me, unfortunately. My experience was of a slow, compelling, repetitive effort to refine the representation of reading through discussion, diagrams, and careful checks against emerging data and published findings.

I proposed a representation of the primary processes to which humans must give attention during a reading task. Not only did these represent the major themes identified by existing research, but work in the usability lab at HUSAT indicated that in terms of verbal protocols and physical activities, these adequately captured what seemed to be going on when people performed routine tasks with documents. The four levels came to be called the TIME framework, based on these components:

- a task (T) that reflects the reader's needs and uses for the material;
- an information model (I) that consists of the user's mental model of the information space;
- the manipulation skills and facilities (M) that support physical use of the material; and
- the ergonomic variables (E) influencing the perceptual processing of words and images.

Human information usage is accordingly conceptualized as an interactive process involving the identification or setting of a task goal, the generation and/or application of an information model, the manipulation of the document through whatever facilities the interface affords, if needed, and the perception of text at the word and sentence levels.

When users interact with a document, they engage in multiple rapid acts involving the various elements in the TIME framework. For example, a user might start by targeting certain information, such as a label or a heading. To gain the fastest answer, it is likely that the user will apply his or her information model of the document's structure. Depending on experience, this model might be highly predictive or rather approximate, but we know readers acquire models through use over time. In terms of the framework, this activity would involve

T → I and I → T exchanges, as well as numerable I → M, and M → E → M activities as the user proceeds to scan headings; to use existing access structures in the documents, such as indexes or content listings; and to both read and move (often in both directions) through the text. Finally, when locating a particularly relevant section, the user will read the words in detail, usually serially, at which point the major human factors issue is image quality as the user reads the text. Thus a task that requires multiple searches and quick location of details will place manifestly different sequences of T → I → M → E interaction than a task involving once-off location followed by lengthy reading. In this way, we can appreciate that statements about importance of font size or screen resolution can only explain some parts of the interaction process and alone are insufficient to guide design.

According to the framework, there are twelve possible interactions between these elements. These are described in detail in Dillon (2004), the first single articulation of reading behavior with digital documents that captured this range of user activity. Consequently, the TIMEframe (as I started calling it) offered a way of examining document design that ensured direct examination of the important drivers of user performance at the interface. The framework's utility for predicting human performance on reading and scanning tasks with various information displays has also been reported in Dillon (2004) and Dillon et al. (2006). This framing of reading behavior with digital documents has proved to be useful for explaining many experimental results already in the literature and for correctly estimating the outcomes of tests involving new interfaces for digital documents. Over the last decade, the framework has been taught in graduate-level and professional courses to numerous HCI students to enable them to conceptualize and evaluate new designs for reading interfaces.

TIME AS A THEORY FOR DESIGN CLAIMS

TIME is intended to be used as means of understanding interaction in context in a manner that lends itself to appropriate design considerations. It avoids prescriptive guidelines for design and instead offers designers and implementers a systematic framework within which to think about the interfaces they are providing to users of information. It moves discussion about the differences between reading from paper and from screen away from single-variable explanations (e.g., image quality or navigation structures) to a broader consideration of four types of factors that must be addressed in order to make a meaningful statement about human performance.

For example, it is still not untypical to hear statements to the effect that "e-books are better than paper" or "reading from paper is faster than reading from screens." The TIMEframe suggests that such statements are relatively meaningless on their own. If human information usage involves all elements in the framework, then the only worthwhile statements are those that include all of these. Thus, the statement "digital is better than paper" carries little meaning since it fails to mention crucial aspects such as the context of use, tasks for which it is better, the nature of the information models required by readers to make it better or worse, the manipulation facilities involved, or the image quality of the screen. We know all these variables are crucial since we have over twenty-five years of research investigating them and trying to untangle their varying effects.

Thus, the TIMEframe suggests that statements about interaction with digital documents, to be of value, need to be complete and make explicit each of the elements in its claim. A more useful statement would be as follows: "For reading lengthy texts for comprehension, for which readers have a well-developed information model, on a scrolling window, mouse-based system, screens of more than forty lines are better than those of twenty lines, though both are likely to produce poorer or slower rates of comprehension than good-quality, easily handled paper copies."

It is imperative to appreciate that the truth content of the statement is not what is at issue here. It is the completion of the statement that is important. Incomplete statements (those not making reference to each element of the TIME framework) are frequently too vague to test, since there are unlimited sources of variance that could exist under the general headings "digital," "paper," or "is better than." A complete statement might be wrong, but it should be immediately testable or, in some cases, refutable given the existing body of empirical data the field has amassed. Thus, as a theoretical framing, TIME requires much work to determine the causal relationship between the interacting levels, but it moves consideration of interactive design for digital documents beyond simple discussions of "better" or "worse," and contextualizes individual variable effects so as to place boundaries on their application.

FINAL THOUGHTS

We are living through a remarkable time of transformation, when the means of information production, presentation, and management are radically changing our abilities to access, use, and share information efficiently and effectively. Humans have always been information creators and sharers, but the formal study of how we do this, as well as the application of such studies to shaping the infrastructure of information for all our benefit, is relatively new. Theorizing in this space is vital, especially where it is grounded in strong empirical testing of ideas (whether they take the form of statements or artifacts), as it is only then that we can move beyond chance or marketing power to produce new designs that really advance the human condition. I believe the information sciences must find a level of theoretical insight that serves its purpose, and this will inevitably require theories that are not just derived from existing disciplines. To do this requires those of us in the field to take the steps of theory production and to share those steps with others.

The opening quote from Huey (1908, p. 4) regarding the study of reading deserves to be considered in full. Not only would an understanding of reading be "the acme of the psychologist's achievement," but "it would describe very many of the most intricate workings of the human mind" and "unravel the tangled story of the most remarkable specific performance that civilization has learned." The quest continues.

REFERENCES

Ajzen, I. (1985). From intentions to actions: A theory of planned behavior. In J. Kuhl and J. Beckman (Eds.), *Action-control: From cognition to behavior* (pp. 11–39). Heidelberg: Springer.

Card, S. K., Newell, A., and Moran, T. P. (1983). *The psychology of human-computer interaction*. Hillsdale, NJ: Erlbaum.

Carroll, J., and Campbell, R. L. (1989). Artifacts as psychological theories: The case of human-computer interaction. *Behavior and Information Technology, 8*(4), 247–256.

Chalmers, A. (1982). *What is this thing called science?* Milton Keynes, UK: Open University Press.

Crowder, R., and Wagner, R. (1992). *The psychology of reading: An introduction* (2nd ed.). New York: Oxford University Press.

Davis, F. D., Bagozzi, R. P., and Warshaw, P. R. (1989). User acceptance of computer technology: A comparison of two theoretical models. *Management Science*, *35*(8), 982–1003.

Dillon, A. (1996). TIME: A framework for designing electronic text. In H. van Oostendorp and S. de Mul (Eds.), *Cognitive aspects of electronic text processing: Advances in discourse processes* (Vol. 58, pp. 99–120). Norwood, NJ: Ablex.

Dillon, A. (2004). *Designing usable electronic text* (2nd ed.). Boca Raton, FL: CRC Press.

Dillon, A., Kleinman, L., Choi, G., and Bias, R. (2006). Visual search and reading tasks using ClearType and regular displays: Two experiments. In R. Grinter, T. Rodden, P. Aoki, E. Cutrell, R. Jeffries, and G. Olson (Eds.), *CHI '06: CHI 2006 Conference on Human Factors in Computing Systems* (pp. 503–511). New York: ACM Press.

Dillon, A., McKnight, C., and Richardson, J. (1993). Space, the final chapter: Why physical representations are not semantic intentions. In C. McKnight, A. Dillon, and J. Richardson (Eds.), *Hypertext: A psychological perspective* (pp. 169–192). Chichester, UK: Ellis Horwood.

Fishbein, M., and Ajzen, I. (1975). *Belief, attitude, intention, and behavior: An introduction to theory and research*. Reading, MA: Addison-Wesley.

Fisher, K., Erdelez, S., and McKechnie, L. (2005). *Theories of information behavior*. Medford, NJ: Information Today.

Gardener, M., and Christie, B. (1987). *Applying cognitive psychology to user-interface design*. New York: Wiley.

Gould, J. D., Alfaro, L., Finn, R., Haupt, B., and Minuto, A. (1987). Reading from CRT displays can be as fast as reading from paper. *Human Factors*, *29*(5), 497–517.

Huey, E. B. (1908). *The psychology and pedagogy of reading*. New York: Macmillan.

Kirssch, I., Jungblut, A., Jenkins, L., and Kolstad, A. (2002). *Adult literacy in America* (3rd ed.). NCES 1993–275. Washington, DC: National Center for Education Statistics. Retrieved from https://nces.ed.gov/pubs93/93275.pdf.

McAleese, R. (Ed.). (1989). *Hypertext: Theory into practice*. Norwood, NJ: Ablex.

Newell, A., and Card, S. (1985). The prospects for psychological science in human-computer interaction. *Human-Computer Interaction*, *1*, 209–242.

Rayner, K., Pollatsek, A., Ashby, J., and Clifton, C. (2012). *Psychology of reading* (2nd ed.). New York: Psychology Press.

Samuels, S. (1970). Review of E. Huey's *Psychology and pedagogy of reading*. *American Education Research Journal*, *7*(2), 277–279.

Sanders, M., and McCormick, E. (1993). *Human factors in engineering and design* (7th ed.). New York: McGraw-Hill Science.

Shneiderman, B., and Plaisant, C. (2010). *Designing the user interface* (5th ed.). Reading, MA: Addison-Wesley.

Wickens, C. D., and Hollands, J. G. (2000). *Engineering psychology and human performance* (3rd ed.). Upper Saddle River, NJ: Pearson/Prentice Hall.

PART 4

CULTURAL AND SCIENTIFIC HERITAGE

CHAPTER 13

THE POVERTY OF THEORY; OR,
THE EDUCATION OF JEROME MCGANN

JEROME MCGANN

Your riches taught me poverty.
EMILY DICKINSON

The poor you always have with you.
MARK 14:7

EDUCATION FOR JEROME MCGANN, as for Henry Adams, seemed to come too late when it came at all. Would it have helped him to know—in those first twelve years of his formal instruction—what he learned later (when was it, thirty years later?), that *Am Anfang war die Tat* (Goethe 1808/2010)? Probably not. At eighteen he did not know what reflection meant because he didn't know how to do it. He could practice Ignatian Exercises but that wasn't really thinking. They were calisthenics for a young and sleeping mind and perhaps for that reason, excellent. Much later he saw, or thought he saw, that those first twelve years of rote learning—his first encounter with the crass materialism of education—taught him as a practical matter that experience always outruns conception. But then as a practical matter, he didn't understand or even understand that he didn't understand.

Perhaps it was in the desolate landscape of his next six years as a student—a complete waste of time—that he began to take his education seriously—which is to say, as that impractical man Thoreau would say, *deliberately*. He decided to spend his life studying literature, culture, and their media. He also decided that if he were to do that, he should try to understand what it meant to do that. When he asked a professor for advice, he was told he might learn something by investigating the controversy between the New Critics and the Chicago neo-Aristotelians. So in 1961 he wrote a master's thesis on the subject. At the end he was able to show what he already knew, or thought he knew, at the outset: that the New Critics won the argument. Why they did remained as mysterious as God Almighty. *Theoretically*, it seemed to him, the neo-Aristotelians had the best of it.

But in any event, his mind now seemed in motion—which is perhaps, it later occurred to him to think, all that John Henry Newman (1848) meant by "loss and gain," though he wondered even then if the terms might not be reversible. Whatever; the next milestone he passed was his doctoral dissertation. The year being 1965, McGann had become even more seriously interested in Theory. So he found himself returning to some of the unfinished business of his master's thesis. The triumphant New Critics had taught him, he remembered, about "history without footnotes,"[1] and even more interestingly, that if you wanted to understand literature and culture, you didn't want to get waylaid by a writer's biography. He understood how sensible that view was, but it troubled him nonetheless. For unbeknownst to himself at that dawning moment of theoretical self-awareness, he had been eating of the apple of fact. He had learned about Byron and his immense literary success and historical consequence, and he had learned that when critics and scholars studied Byron's work, his life and times and even his afterlife were unevadable. So he decided he would try to learn why.

He had read and believed Gerard Manley Hopkins (1885/1985) when he wrote: "O the mind, mind has mountains; cliffs of fall / Frightful, sheer, no-man-fathomed" (ll. 9–10). But traveling to England and Europe to study Byron in 1965, he found his own mind's mountains dwarfed by the mountains of learning in the documentary archives his quest had taken him to. His education was gaining weight and momentum but seemed for that very reason to be growing more dangerous and uncontrollable. And then came two chance events that drove McGann in unexpected and fateful directions.

The first rolled over him when he took up his appointment at the University of Chicago. It came in two waves. In the intellectual life of the university, and particularly in his undergraduate classes, he experienced a complete intellectual upheaval. Never before had he been involved with people who took such an intense and ethical interest in ideas. His undergraduate classes were both thrilling and terrifying for he was constantly aware that his students were often far smarter than he. Because he usually knew a little more than they did, he managed to keep his feet and some of his self-respect. If each day and each class were precarious events, they also brought a spiritual wealth that he would treasure for the rest of his life.

That intellectual life reached a special intensity in 1968–1969, when the Vietnam War brought such a crisis to American self-understanding that even he began to take serious notice. He did not join SDS, least of all the Weathermen, but he knew and worked with many and he helped when his students took over the administration building and shut down much of the university's daily life. When those events drove his closest friend to Canada, and eventual Canadian citizenship, he found he no longer knew how to separate his scholarly from his political life—or rather, how to integrate the two. Did The Advancement of Learning have any ethical point at all? Education was *for* life, as even those dead Victorian sages Ruskin and Morris understood. But they also understood how little their work and cultural interests would affect, in practical fact, the ignorance of political and economic power and the social injustice they sustained. "I spend my life ministering to the swinish luxury of the rich":[2] that dreadful comment by Morris would haunt him for his entire life. But in the fond illusion of McGann's young 1968 heart, he took it as a call to action.

The other event came in 1970 and was very different. He was invited to edit Byron's (1986) *Complete Poetical Works* for Clarendon Press's Oxford English Texts series.

Nothing he would ever experience would so decisively expose the irrational forces at work in his world, though at the time, ignorant as he was, he took these events easily, the first as a mission he had been assigned and meant to follow, the second as a kind of interesting opportunity. He took up the mission under what he imagined was an austere and self-critical move against his long-standing interest in theory—Marx's eleventh thesis on Feuerbach: "The philosophers have only interpreted the world, in various ways; the point is to change it." Was that initial move itself a grave error? He would never know. Whatever the case, the mission would never be accomplished or abandoned. As for the scholarly opportunity that had suddenly opened for him, it would come to prove, like the slowly grinding wheels of God, how wrong he was to approach the task with such an easy confidence. It would weigh him in the balance and find him sorely wanting—not only for that larger mission, but even for the tight little scholarly work that now lay before him. But all that knowledge lay in a future that would do him, when it came, little good.

He did realize, of course, that he was the least likely or appropriate person for such a serious professional commission. In 1970 he knew nothing about scholarly editing. As for his knowledge of Byron and Byron's world, it stood quite at the level one would expect for an eager young assistant professor. But as the poet said, "Fame is the spur . . ." Or perhaps another poet's thought was even more apposite: "Fools rush in . . ."

Having seen something of the power of Theory during his recent years, McGann judged he might get a grip on his editorial task if he approached it not only methodically—that seemed obvious—but also theoretically. As it happened, in 1971 Theory had overtaken even the dry-as-dust world of scholarly editions. The Greg-Bowers model of eclectic editing, seriously theorized, had gained preeminent status (Greetham 1992). Enrolling as a Greg-Bowers student as he began his edition, McGann soon discovered to his horror that Byron would not submit.

His object, he had learned, was to aim for a definitive edition of the work, that is, a text that most nearly represented "the author's final intentions." The means to his end required that he assemble and collate all the relevant textual documents—in multiple copies where necessary—in order to sort out authorial from non-authorial readings and, through that process, to produce the definitive eclectic text. The latter would be constructed by revising the baseline copytext where necessary with the latest authorial readings.

Given the extent of Byron's corpus and his own ignorance, McGann thought he might begin with an exemplary model of the editorial problems. *The Giaour* (Byron 1813) seemed as good as any— a work with multiple surviving manuscripts, proof copies (corrected and uncorrected), and editions. These "lengthened their rattles" over three years—Byron (1974, p. 100) called it his "snake of a poem"— as the work kept augmenting itself. By 1815 it had grown to more than 300 percent of its original length. McGann spent three years assembling and analyzing these materials but in the end (late 1973), like Wordsworth (1850) trying to begin the poem that would later be called *The Prelude*, he yielded up his scholar's questions in despair.

It turned out that the theory of a definitive edition, not to speak of an author's final intentions, had limited relevance for a poem like *The Giaour*. Along those lines of thought one might perhaps imagine two states of the poem—its first edition (1813) and its seventh edition (1815)—as representative moments in its existence. But they would only be properly understood as markers for observing the true character of the work's textual condition, which was a dynamic field of changes. More troubling still, multiple agents were cooperating together to produce those changes. Finally, he discovered as well that the text of *The Giaour*—its lexicon, syntax, and rhetoric—did not comprehend its existential character, let alone its meaning. The work's typography and book design—he would later call them its "bibliographical codes"—were key factors as well (see esp. McGann 1991).

These discoveries proved so catastrophic for McGann that his practical work on the edition stopped in its third year. He did not know how to proceed. A timely utterance, not from Wordsworth, brought a measure of relief. A wise friend, the great editorial scholar Cecil Lang, urged him to abandon his theoretical guides and study at random as many scholarly editions, ancient and modern, as possible. McGann's ignorance in this case proved helpful. He began to see that his problems did not lie only in the tension between his original documentary materials and the definitive edition theory with which he proposed to master them. Equally troublesome were the conventions, developed out of nineteenth-century British models, of the series of Oxford English Texts editions. Byron could certainly be accommodated to those conventions just as a definitive edition of his works could be theorized. Both would be full of contradictions and misrepresentations of the poetry. But now finally acquainted, in however limited a way, with the triumphs and tragedies of many scholarly editors far more learned and distinguished than he would ever be, McGann could see that whatever he did was doomed to fall short of the truth of Byron's work.

So he began again, a sadder and perhaps a wiser man. The edition had turned into a fascinating machine for discovering what both he and it could and could not do. Sometimes these discoveries proved shamefully personal, as when he learned that his proofreading skills were decidedly mediocre. He would spend the rest of his life working to improve himself in that regard, with limited success. He also learned that events beyond his control, sometimes beyond anyone's, could wreak havoc on the work. The most ludicrous instance of the power of "Circumstance, that unspiritual god" (Byron 1818, stanza 125, l. 6) came fairly early, as he was seeing the second volume of the edition through the press. The story of that debacle is sobering enough to be told here.

Burned by his proofreading lapses with volume one a few years before, McGann worked assiduously to ensure the accuracy of the text of volume two, his edition of *Childe Harold's Pilgrimage* (Byron 1981). The failure of this effort is mortalized in an errata slip that had to be inserted into the volume as it was going to press. The slip lists a set of corrections for the Greek texts in Byron's extensive notes to the first two cantos of the poem. The errata instruct the reader to change the reading texts, whose orthography is correctly classical in the text as it came from the printer, to Byron's original transcriptions, which not only follow modern Greek orthography but—more significantly—reflect Byron's effort to represent the modern Greek he read and heard in his famous travels in the Levant.

In preparing the edition McGann was anxious to see that those Greek transcriptions be letter-perfect. He sought the help of another friend, Diskin Clay, a scholar of both ancient and modern Greek, and they worked closely on the various original texts—Byron's manuscripts and corrected proofs in particular. He was acutely aware that Byron's transcriptions had a special historical value because they were made on the spot. As such, they gave a signal insight into modern Greek usage in the early nineteenth century as it was experienced by an English peer with a keen interest in contemporary Greek history and culture and a certain vanity about his classical learning. So as the edition was moving through press McGann was a hawk-eyed observer of these texts and, as the final proofs went off to England from his home in Baltimore, he felt immensely self-satisfied.

A few weeks later, as the final press work was proceeding, he had a brief telegram informing him that one of the press's printers, learned in Greek, noticed that these transcriptions were full of errors—that is to say, their orthography was incorrect by classical standards. Assuming McGann's ignorance—a not altogether unwarranted assumption to have made—the texts were being corrected, he was told, as the volume was being printed. McGann's panicked phone call to Oxford proved too late; the printing was complete. So an errata list was prepared calling the reader to restore the corrected texts to their original (in)correct condition.

Once again McGann saw that his education in scholarly theory and method had made a painful advance. Indeed, so many agents would be collaborating on his edition that he began to understand how inapt that personal pronoun was for the work he had chosen to undertake some dozen years before. And that realization only further exposed how limited was his view of Byron's original work and of the Textual Condition, as he would later come to call it, in general. He went on with the edition—he was obligated and bound to that wheel of fire—but he knew now that he had, all unawares, taken on other obligations. He had to make a report to the scholarly community about certain larger implications of the work, so far as he understood them, for literary studies. Most serious was his duty to explain what he saw as the inevitable shortcomings of the edition he was committed to. He had also to explain, as best he could, the reasons that lay behind these shortcomings.

The report came in two somewhat polemical pamphlets, both published in 1983 by the University of Chicago Press: *A Critique of Modern Textual Criticism* and *The Romantic Ideology*. That his thinking spilled into two so radically different studies pretty much defined the disordered state of his mind. But his troubles were sincerely felt. Besides, because the findings reported in these books were preliminary and theoretically incoherent, they succeeded to an unexpectedly useful result. Sometimes praised and often attacked, they forced McGann into a further and, he was hoping, a more adequate understanding of the problems his work kept turning up. As the Byron edition moved through its final five volumes between 1983 and 1992, McGann wrote a series of practico-theoretical investigations[3] into what he called "the historical method in literary studies." These works centered in a conviction that textual studies, and the scholarly edition in particular, set the ground for all literary interpretation and cultural work. That virtually no one seemed to take this claim seriously suggested just how preposterous his professional position had become. Perhaps equally preposterous was his own conviction, which only deepened over subsequent years, that he was right, that he was doing the Lord's work.

This period was framed by two additional fortuitous events. At one end (1982–1983) he moved from Johns Hopkins University, where Theory Studies had been a fierce preoccupation for some fifteen years, to the California Institute of Technology, where he was introduced to computer technology and UNIX programming. To gain at least a modicum of competence with this technology, he typeset those two polemical pamphlets of 1983 using an early experimental computer program developed at Caltech. Disaster ensued once again. The program turned out to be full of bugs, which made for many painful and drudging months. Worse still was his realization that he knew almost nothing about book design. The program's problems could be, and eventually were, worked through. But there was little to help on the other score. No one, certainly not McGann, could learn what he needed to learn about book design by spending four months generating printer's copy for two little scholarly books.

To his credit, however, he soldiered on. In 1987 he moved again, this time to the University of Virginia, where he intended to finish the Byron edition. But the event created fresh uncertainty, more acute than ever. For as he brought the last volumes of the edition to print, he wondered if his vocational work might in fact be complete. Had he anything further to contribute to his tight little island of scholarship? For better and for worse, the work seemed finished.

Beyond that perhaps pedantic worry, however, loomed a far deeper one. For at that moment humanist scholars and educators found themselves the storm center of the Culture Wars. The struggle was sharply defined in 1991 with the publication of James Davison Hunter's book *Culture Wars: The Struggle to Define America*. The book appeared just as McGann returned from a semester (spring 1991) at the University of California, Berkeley, as Visiting Beckman Professor.[4] As it happened, "Circumstance, that unspiritual god" (Byron 1818), had turned his academic visit into a vocational crisis.

McGann arrived at Berkeley just as Operation Desert Storm (January–February 1991) was bringing the Gulf War to its violent conclusion. Widely supported in the United States, the war was just as widely opposed across the Berkeley community. With the onset of Operation Desert Storm, the protests at Berkeley grew fierce. To McGann the scene recalled nothing so much as the events he was involved with at Chicago in the late 1960s.

That history was repeating itself as some dreadful black comedy became apparent when McGann attended a teach-in where his friend, the poet Peter Dale Scott, was scheduled to speak. A few days before, the two had had lunch together and Scott remarked that he was worried about how his comments at the teach-in would be received. He intended to ask the audience—many would be his friends from the resistance days of the sixties—"Where have we gone wrong?" For it seemed to Scott that he and his community had to bear a great responsibility for the perpetuation of American imperial violence. The situation was complicated because the Berkeley community appeared completely out of sympathy, if not completely out of touch, with the vast majority of the country. Outside of Berkeley the war, and especially the dreadful carnage of Operation Desert Storm, was viewed as a high-minded effort to roll back Iraq's invasion of its small neighbor, Kuwait.

Scott wanted to urge his community to reflect critically on its failure to educate the country on the persistent and now even more urgent danger of the Military Industrial Complex. When Scott asked McGann how he thought his criticism would be received, McGann enthusiastically supported his friend. But once again his judgment would be proved objectively mistaken, for Scott's worries were justified. When he finished his remarks at the teach-in he was denounced for having—in the words of an old friend from the audience— "betrayed everything you and I for years have worked together and stood for." Speaker after speaker at the meeting rose to say that the free speech and peace movements had done nothing wrong and bore no responsibility for Operation Desert Storm.

These events startled McGann into reflection on the course of his scholarly work as a whole and his larger goals as an educator. In his determined pursuit of his vocational purposes, worthy enough in themselves, McGann could read a secret history of civic failure more consequential than any of his scholarly failures. He thought of the Lady of Shalott weaving tapestries in a lonely tower. Had he passed through a strait gate and down a narrow way only to find perdition?

Perhaps, he thought, his work as a scholar was accomplished; perhaps both larger events were calling him to leave the rarified world of university research and education. Surely there were jobs he could fill that were less removed from the daily lives of people. And of course there were. But to his surprise he discovered they were not for him, for every inquiry he made was met with skepticism and distrust. His interviewers saw him as a strange, perhaps an estranged, person, and certainly not someone—he was fifty-five years old!—who inspired confidence. At each effort to see himself as a new person, he began to see himself more clearly. Such skills and learning as he had acquired over the previous thirty years—pitiful enough to be sure—had turned him into a kind of monster. He believed he had a vocation but he discovered that what he actually had was a profession.

Confused and uncertain, McGann temporized with a practical task. He would finish the series of books that began with his two polemical works of 1983, *The Romantic Ideology* and *A Critique of Modern Textual Criticism*. Two more books were called for, both relatively short, in order to finish the project he called at the time "a complete program for an historical method in literary and cultural studies."[5] Given what would command his attention in the years to come, that "project" would soon expose once again the naïveté that had marked his entire life. But of course the distinctive feature of his shortsighted naïveté was its persistent naïveté.

Then in 1992 Chance (or was it *Fortuna?*) descended into his world once again, this time in the form of an IBM grant of equipment offered to the University of Virginia's computer science (CS) department. Although CS did not need this equipment, a few people wondered if it might find a home among some humanist scholars. One thing led to another and McGann found himself on a small committee to decide how the IBM offer should be used. The upshot was the founding of the Institute for Advanced Technology in the Humanities (IATH; http://www.iath.virginia.edu). And so it happened that, as Gertrude Stein would say, McGann found himself beginning again again.

Twenty-two years editing Byron (1970–1992) had brought McGann, during that work's final ten years, to begin reflecting on what René Wellek and Austin Warren had called "Theory of Literature" in 1949. For Wellek and Warren and nearly everyone else working in the second half of the twentieth century, the practical outcome of theory was some form of interpretation, whether "intrinsic" or "extrinsic." Theory itself could be an independent pursuit, and in that mode, it became an epistemological horizon for literary and cultural studies. Those higher interpretive operations were to be distinguished from the small subset of what they called the "preliminary operations" in literary and cultural studies: that is to say, the editorial work to establish the texts to be interpretively examined. Wellek and Warren set all that bibliographical work aside as pretheoretical and precritical.

But McGann's editorial work had brought him to a very different view. It seemed to him that contemporary Theory of Literature and its derivatives all hung upon a seriously undertheorized concept of Text and an even more serious blindness about scholarly editing and scholarly editions. If Theory of Literature did not theorize its foundation—the documentary archive, primary and secondary, which was the unending work of a host of cooperating agents—would it not be simply a house built on sand? For years, since the mid-1970s, he had worried that it might. And he worried because it also seemed to him that the scholarly edition—any effort at scholarly editing, for that matter—was itself a theoretical move of a special and crucial kind: an act of literary interpretation carried out performatively, as an act of textual representation. The ground act of interpretation, in this view, involved being able to make a model of the object being interpreted. Nor could the model be primarily conceptual, as if its material form were purely vehicular and not intrinsic to its being, as one's body is intrinsic to one's identity as a person. He remembered that certain Medieval theologians—Duns Scotus for example—had thought along similar lines.

Fired with zeal for these new, some would say pedantic, ideas, and perhaps even forgetting what he had always understood as his educator's vocation, McGann returned to a new editorial project: *The Complete Writings and Pictures of Dante Gabriel Rossetti: A Hypermedia Research Archive* (McGann 1994). He did not, however, begin this work in a state of nearly invincible ignorance, as he had with the Byron edition. McGann was quite familiar with Rossetti and his Victorian world. He also had come to know at least something about the conventions and procedural demands of scholarly editing. Finally, his time at Caltech had introduced him to the analytic and representational resources of computerized (as opposed to bibliographical) technology. He could see that a digital organization of a discourse field, if carefully designed, offered signal new advantages for traditional scholarly editing. Most obvious was the promise it held out to synthesize the two great models of scholarly editing: critical editing and documentary editing (McGann 1997).[6] And in that view McGann thought he saw rising upon his mind, like an unfathered vapor, a newly reorganized Theory of Texts and Textuality, and perhaps even a recovery of a *Sachphilologie* as comprehensive as August Boeckh's and the other heroic figures of nineteenth-century scholarship.

"If carefully designed." Long experience had chastened McGann's sense of his intellectual powers. He had grown particularly wary of the threat to knowledge that lurked in accumulated learning. The primary object of the Byron edition had been to build the edition. The Rossetti Archive would be different (http://www.rossettiarchive .org/). In this case McGann would make the act of building the edition the primary focus of the work, both practical and theoretical. Given the level of his long-standing ignorance, McGann had learned a great deal during the years of the Byron edition, and much of it came as a revelation of things not seen. But he had not set out in quest of revelation. Byron was a task that turned unexpectedly into a wilderness adventure. He was determined not to be caught off guard again. The Rossetti Archive would be a controlled environment for laboratory experiments in the theory of textualities and media in the epoch of online communication.

He chose Rossetti—an improbable choice on the face of it—for several reasons that seemed good reasons. First of all, McGann found the Rossetti materials attractive precisely because of their perceived inconsequence for late twentieth-century criticism and scholarship. Had he thought about it at the time, which he did not, he might have been struck by the similarity between his choice of Rossetti and his earlier decision to study Byron. In the literary academy of 1965 Byron was an inconsequent cultural figure, even as he had once been perhaps the single most dominant influence on nineteenth-century European literature, culture, and philosophy. The Rossetti parallel was unmistakable. One hundred years earlier—in 1892—Rossetti was, as Whistler remarked at Rossetti's death ten years before, "a king." Indeed, if viewed in cultural terms, late Victorian England might well be called the Age of Rossetti. For McGann, that contradiction was the whole point. As he had with the Pre-Raphaelite movement he largely founded, Rossetti took the problem of historical discontinuity as the central focus for his work. Given his particular approach to historical method, McGann saw Rossetti's cultural discontinuity as a positive critical advantage. It would help him expose the cultural shape of his own scholarly and cultural world and hence promote useful educational change.

Second, Rossetti, a multimedia artist and writer, foregrounded the material character of cultural representations. As such, his work would make pressing demands on an editorial project set to build a new kind of editorial environment. Ever since his 1983 polemic for a social approach to scholarly editing, McGann had been in controversy over what editorial scholarship could or should do. The most pertinent charge argued that his textual theories required scholars to produce critical editions of books rather than texts—a demand, it was said, beyond the remit of the critical editor (see esp. Howard-Hill 1991). McGann did not deny the charge; he took it as a sign that a new remit for scholarly editing had emerged with the emergence of online communication. The charge thus became for him a practical and theoretical demand laid upon the Rossetti Archive: to model a discursive field comprising many different kinds of material and conceptual objects. Indeed, in this new kind of field, textual objects would themselves be critically handled as if they *were* both material and conceptual. Minimally that meant editing objects like books—objects that were, as signifying machines, both bibliographical and linguistic.

If McGann had learned to think more clearly during the previous thirty years he would have hesitated before moving ahead. He would have asked himself: Who in 1992 remembered or read Rossetti, or looked at his artwork, or—least of all—thought he was the king of late-Victorian culture? Virtually nobody he knew except his friend Cecil Lang. He would have asked himself: Who in 1992 in the humanities community is interested in a theory of scholarly editing, or for that matter in humanities computing (*that* actually didn't even exist in 1992)? A little band of ineffectual angels. A project like the Rossetti Archive—if McGann actually *thought* about it—would demand enormous funding and institutional resources. Where would they come from? McGann didn't even say to himself, like that famous lady, "I'll think about it tomorrow." He didn't think about it at all.

So in 1992 he set about designing a model for a new kind of scholarly edition. The design, he believed, had to be built to an unusual requirement: that a fully integrated online network of depositories was already theoretically operational and prepared to integrate with projects like the Rossetti Archive.[7] Such an internetwork, particularly for humanistic materials, did not *in fact* exist in 1992, although the hope toward it was well advanced among the small band of angels who were considering the matter. But McGann judged the imaginative conception necessary if the logical design of the Rossetti Archive was ever to be, from the archive's point of view, a practical reality within the online environment that was still emerging. The working hypothesis had to be a black box hypothesis since the design structure of an encompassing digital network and its constituent parts was still unknown in its particulars, even though its evolution could be predicted as a general condition. The Rossetti Archive was what Charles Saunders Peirce (1932)—a new interest for McGann—called an abduction.

The design hypothesis laid a functional demand on the process of building the archive. Its internal structure had to map to a globally internetworked organization that was technically and institutionally feasible. That conceptual horizon meant that McGann and his colleagues had to execute every local action in conscious relation to the imagined internetwork. Practically, they had to monitor in a regular way the global state of an unfolding and highly volatile internetwork. That internetwork was realizing itself during the years when the Rossetti Archive was being built—that is to say, between 1992, when the Internet began to project a global interface, and 2012, when entities like Europeana (http://www.europeana.eu/) and the DPLA (the Digital Public Library of America; http://dp.la/) were in full development. In turn, the evolving internetwork kept exerting critical pressure on McGann's understanding of what he was trying to do with the archive.

And so the Rossetti Archive got built while important futurities like Europeana and DPLA were not even words. McGann well understood that he and his colleagues were trying to imagine something they didn't and couldn't know.[8] Often it seemed a great adventure that kept turning up surprising discoveries. But as the effort proceeded, the adventure regularly turned out more threatening than romantic. McGann would sometimes think of La Salle's terrible seventeenth-century Mississippean quests, and Thomas Hardy's (1915, stanza 8) words about the *Titanic* came often to his recollection:

And as the smart ship grew
In stature, grace and hue,
In shadowy silent distance grew the iceberg too.

Building out the model exposed design flaws that only became visible when McGann and his colleagues had to implement the design under the horizon of the unfolding global internetwork. Initially these flaws appeared as "merely technical" problems that called for design accommodations. But that illusion did not survive the continual pressure of events. The de facto historical status of certain problems could only be managed but not removed from the design without tearing it all down and starting with a new design. The map of the emerging Internet that the Rossetti Archive had implicitly drawn was correct enough in a macro sense, but its micro features were being reshaped and continually redefined in unexpected ways by unknown but significant parties located across the globe. The dysfunctions that ensued then exposed deeper design issues that McGann had no idea how to address, much less resolve: for instance, how to design automated analytic relations between traditional materials and their digital surrogates. They could be linked and, as on a lightboard, compared, but beyond that lay the mysterium.

All this amounted to learning by doing, which is to say as well, learning by failing. At first that too was a thrilling discovery, but as McGann tried to engage it in practical terms, its thrill underwent the inevitable and trying transformation. How many times did he have to learn that his thrills were also threats in fetching disguise? But all that was part of the "importance of failure," as his guide, philosopher, and friend John Unsworth (1997) urged him to understand. Failure was the companion who could teach you to see something you would always fail to see: in this case, that the failure was not primarily a conceptual and technical problem at all. Forced to look at his work in more comprehensive ways, McGann pondered the institutional forces driving and hindering the rapid expansion of the technical capacities of the internetwork. He began to see that the most intractable problems were political, social, and administrative. "People problems," ultimately. Not the least of these were the people who had so internalized the inertia of institutions at *least* five hundred years old that they had great difficulty—difficulties he sympathized with—responding to pressures for needed change. Equally difficult were those other people who took it as their mission of Enlightenment to break the spell under which those other people were, they felt, ignorantly laboring. The internecine class war of the Luddites and the Digeraties.

Once more he set forth in quest of his Mississippi. Designing and implementing online environments for research-based education in the humanities, he saw, required more than a research laboratory like the archive or a think-tank institutional location like IATH. So he struck out in a new direction in 2002 by founding NINES (the Networked Infrastructure for Nineteenth-Century Electronic Scholarship; http://www.nines.org/), a professional organization of scholars who could work together to produce and make accessible a large corpus of peer-reviewed scholarly materials. For it now seemed to him (would he *never* learn?) that without an institutional structure connected directly to the regular programmatic work of university operations—intramural degree-granting mechanisms as well as their supporting extramural professional system—research education must be fundamentally constrained.

The sign of those constraints had been staring him in the face for years, but seeing, he did not see, and hearing, he did not understand. Now they appeared with too painful clarity in the institutional divide separating traditional from digital humanities. In 1992, even in

1999, it seemed to McGann that a virtuous necessity required digital scholarship to operate outside the programmatic structures of the traditional university. And perhaps he was right, for IATH flourished between 1992 and 2000 by *not* having to answer to regular faculty research and pedagogical expectations (McGann 2001).[9] But times change, and as even he would have to say once again, *non sum qualis eram.*

La Salle's dream of a great French empire stretching from the mouth of the St. Lawrence to the mouth of the Mississippi would eventually be realized by many others who carried on after he died. But then that briefly realized French dream would dissolve away in a mere seven years of war, after which it would fracture and mutate, twice over—once in 1763 and then again in 1783. Such a great enterprise as well as the changes it underwent put McGann's little academic undertakings in proper perspective. In 2013 he thought *"non sum qualis eram"* in 1961 *"bonae sub regno Theoriae."*[10] His theoretical passions had taken him out far and in deep—in one now obvious respect, too far and too deep. Or perhaps, he thought, just far and deep enough to think that so much had gone wrong for him—so much had been left undone or left badly done—that he would just have to begin again. Begin not from where he was in 2013, but from where he had set out some fifty years earlier on his conscious search for an education in books that might make a difference in life. He could still see the massive and obdurate structure of the administration building of the University of Chicago as it stood in 1968 and could still feel its institutional inertia as well as the winds of change it resisted. Or was that building a windmill?

His search had taken him beyond books and their textual conditions into computers and their digital conditions (see esp. McGann 1991, 2001). But by 2013 it was an easy task to reflect on how little he understood either of these technologies. Trying to get digital machines to simulate the operations of bibliographical machines—to get these machines to communicate with each other and, most important, to communicate with each other *each on its own terms*—had become what he imagined as the climactic point of his work. The failure of his pursuit, he began to suspect, lay in the dark backward and abysm of his time. His education in books had led him to seek an education in computers, but all that he came to learn from the computers was that he didn't actually know what books were or how they worked. All he knew about them was how he could use them— he learned that as he had earlier learned to use Ignatius and as he later learned to use computers. But he understood neither any more than he understood, as a boy, the Ignatian Exercises (St. Ignatius of Loyola 1914).

He had to go back and, this time, begin by actually trying to understand books (as it were) on their own terms.

As usual, he thought he should begin by theorizing the method of his investigation. So much would depend upon the salience of the starting point. He was no longer so naïve as to imagine he could make a perfect beginning, but surely some moves could improve his prospects. He thought he'd do well to begin with materials that had, with the exception of certain special interests like Edgar Poe and Emily Dickinson, never been a special focus of his scholarship. The work would supply him with what his old hero William Morris regarded as so important for any artisanal work: "resistance in the material" itself.[11] So he turned to what was for McGann *terra incognita*, American Literature ca. 1750–1860, and to make the task more demanding still, to James Fenimore Cooper, whose works he had years earlier decided were simply a terror *incorrigibilis*.

The question he initially posed for himself was: how does a book by Fenimore Cooper work? A book, not a text—an actual material artifact that had come into existence in determinate human times and spaces. McGann had come far enough from 1961 to know that such objects were functions of many agents, and that their agencies operated over a dynamic and open-ended field whose axes were production history on one hand and reception history on the other. Framed in that way, the question brought him to the next: how should one proceed so that a useful answer might emerge to the question?

Of course a cookbook is not the same kind of object as a novel, nor a novel the same as a romance, nor a romance as an encyclopedia or a textbook or a book of poetry. But McGann decided that those second-order facticities, and the abstractions they called for, would have to wait. Not that he was trying to devise a way to isolate the abstract "bookness" of a book by Cooper—the features it might be thought to hold in common with any book. What he was after was rather the *thisness* of a particular Cooper book. It seemed to him that if he could succeed there, even in a measure succeed, he would have advanced an understanding of books at large and set a model—a modifiable model—for beginning to theorize their operations in practical terms. These goals seemed to him—he admitted this—the ultimate proof and justification for all theoretical investigation.

So, skeptical though he was of succeeding, given his dismal personal history, he took the plunge. He decided to work with the first published volume of the famous Leatherstocking Tales, *The Pioneers* (1823). Even that single book was too much for the kind of detailed inquiry McGann had in mind. The focus had to be tighter, on one hand, and directed at a clearly significant point on the other. He decided he would try to investigate the quiddity of the book's title page—more particularly, the title page of the first edition, first issue of a copy of the book he could spend a lot of time with: a copy in the Special Collections Library of the University of Virginia (Cooper 1823).

For a month McGann set aside his other work to investigate the historical truth of that title page in what Blake would call its "minute particulars." He stopped after he had filled more than forty typescript pages with his annotations. And he stopped because he could see no end in sight.

But he did not stop in despair. The exercise exposed the possibility of modeling an online environment for exploring an indefinitely large archive of documents, born digital as well as the digital surrogates of material objects. The exercise showed that an investigation begun at any documentary point would, if resolutely pursued, expose an indefinitely extensible network of relations. The network had a center that was everywhere and a circumference that was nowhere. It showed as well that a dynamically ontological hierarchy of significance could be generated for those relations if the machinery kept track of the history of the investigations. And although the exercise did not set out to investigate data mining across large digital corpora, it inevitably showed the reciprocity that operated, within such an archival environment, between the study of particular documentary relations and the semantic or conceptual patterns that could be discovered in its webwork.

Building, testing, and scaling up such a philological machine would take the labor of many people and many years. That it would be accomplished McGann had no doubt. But he was beginning to doubt that accomplishment—that Advancement of Learning—would make much of a difference to his ethical interests. Clearly significant advances had been made even in his little, not to say pedantic, world of textual, media, and cultural scholarship. Indeed, to recognize the continuity between those recent studies and the great accomplishments of nineteenth-century philology was itself part of the historical enlightenment his vocation was committed to. That at least was what he had been telling himself for years, and while it still seemed the truth, it seemed a truth as disconnected from daily life as ever. If anything, national and global conditions seemed far more ominous in 2013 than they had been fifty years before. (There was Vietnam, there was the Gulf War, and there was Iraq. Was our violence without an effort to protect us from our violence within? [see Stevens 1951].)

Such thoughts reminded him of Milman Parry's 1934 lecture to the Board of Overseers of Harvard College, "The Historical Method in Literary Criticism" (Parry 1971). A succinct guide to historical method and critical theory, the lecture had been an inspiration for McGann since he first read it in the early 1970s. Reading it again forty years later, he saw its wisdom running along deeper and more worrying lines. For Parry climaxed his talk with a warning to humanists that was not unlike the warning President Eisenhower gave to Americans at large in his famous 1961 farewell address. "The critical study of the past" was for Parry a remarkable human achievement, but by 1934 master propagandists were gaining control of the resources of culture and historical memory. Their work revealed what to Parry was a shocking "lack of concern, or even [a] contempt, for what actually was so, or actually had been so" (Parry 1971, p. 412).

Excellent scholar that he was, Parry had a tender conscience about the perversion of the ground article of humanistic faith: that "there is nothing at the same time finer or more practical than the truth" (Parry 1971, p. 412). While Parry's commitment to that idea was not shaken, he doubted that many shared his commitment. For "the use of propaganda for political purposes . . . in the last fifty years" had developed intimidating levels of "intensity and technique" (Parry 1971, p. 412). Could humanists defend the truth of history and culture from exploitation by those cynical or self-interested powers?

> The chief emotional ideas to which men seem to be turning at present, as the older ones fade, are those of nationality—for which they exploit race—and class, and for these ideas they create a past by a fictitious interpretation (Parry 1971, p. 412).

That remark is very much of Parry's 1934 moment. By October 1933 Hitler had consolidated his power in Germany and repudiated Versailles, Stalin was master of the Soviet Union and his Gulag system well established, and capitalism, particularly the finance capitalism that had plunged the United States into depression, was just beginning to realize its global ambitions and political power. How *could* humane, least of all philological, truth protect itself against appropriation by such institutional forces? If a man like Parry had no good answer to that question in 1934, where would one look for answers in 2013? Here loomed an "importance of failure" that was far from what had inspirited McGann in the 1990s. It was catastrophic. Had Parry a premonitory glimpse of Walter Benjamin's beautiful and ineffectual Angel of History (Benjamin 1968; see esp. p. 257)? Was McGann seeing it again?

Or perhaps that terrified and terrifying Angel was an illusion that had imposed itself on Parry, obscuring his simpler if in certain respects more demanding truth. McGann thought he glimpsed a monstrous illusion in Parry's concluding sentences, where he made his final plea against "compromis[ing] with" the truth-commitment of historical theory and method:

> But the scholars must see that they must impose their truths before others impose their fictions. They must create their heroic legend—or rather they must make it known—for the European humanistic tradition that we of the universities follow is no inglorious thing. Otherwise they will be choosing a future in which they must see themselves confined not by choice, but by compulsion, to be forever ineffective, if they would not be untruthful. (Parry 1971, p. 413)

"Must impose"? "Heroic legend"? That is the language of those "history-men"[12] Stalin and Hitler, whose names alas are legion and who have never ceased moving about the world like roaring lions seeking whom they may devour. An individual person has every reason to fear the forces they represent. But perhaps even more: to fear being possessed by such power and purposes. Better surely, McGann thought, if we choose to see the "European humanistic tradition" as precisely an "inglorious thing" lest—he thought of Tennyson thinking of King Arthur's Round Table—"one good custom should corrupt the world" (Alfred 1833, line 242). Tennyson feared that his beloved England had grown to such a custom in the Age of Victoria. Had American democracy grown to such a custom in 2013?

McGann decided he ought not to think that way. If it was the truth, as it well might be, it was not a truth to set you free. Better to recall both the inglorious honor of Parry's scholarship and the truth he so deeply prized. If the pursuit of truth is a difficult undertaking, McGann decided that it would be fatuous, perhaps even dangerous, to imagine it a glorious one. Philological theory and method showed Parry how he could, from the scattered remnants of any distant past, "make for myself a picture of great detail" (Parry 1971, p. 411). The whole venture was about cherishing human particulars, "not merely a man who lived at another time than our own, but one who lived in a certain nation, or city, or in a certain social class, and in very certain years" (Parry 1971, pp. 409–410). Of course the venture to "become" that person or recover his particular world was impossible. Mortal beings, the living as well as the dead, may be loved but not possessed—unless they get possessed by demons. But therein, McGann decided to believe, lay the human truth of the humanities.

NOTES

1. This was the subtitle of Cleanth Brooks's (1947) exemplary New Critical essay "Keats's Sylvan Historian: History without Footnotes."

2. Morris made the remark to Sir Lowthian Bell around 1877; see Lethaby (1935, p. 94).

3. Besides *The Romantic Ideology* and *A Critique of Modern Textual Criticism*, the other volumes in the series were *The Beauty of Inflections: Literary Investigations in Historical Method and Theory* (1985) and *Social Values and Poetic Acts* (1987).

4. He delivered the Beckman Lectures at Berkeley in the spring of 1991. They would eventually be published as *Black Riders: The Visible Language of Modernism* (1993).

5. These were *Toward a Literature of Knowledge* (1989) and *The Textual Condition* (1991). McGann also understood the project to include four other books: two that he wrote—*The Beauty of Inflections: Literary Investigations in Historical Method and Theory* (1985a) and *Social Values and Poetic Acts* (1987)—and the two collections of essays McGann edited from two conferences he ran at the California Institute of Technology in 1982 and 1983—*Textual Studies and Literary Interpretation* (1985c) and *Historical Studies and Literary Criticism* (1985b).

6. "The Rationale of Hypertext" was written in 1993 and delivered as several lectures between then and 1995.

7. Some friends and collaborators at the time were severely critical of the assumption. It proved to be "correct" in the sense that it proved to be fruitful.

8. See McGann's essay, written in 1996 and delivered as a conference paper in 1997, "Imagining What You Don't Know: The Theoretical Goals of the Rossetti Archive." It was later published in McGann (2004).

9. See pp. 1–27, but especially 7–10, where the extra-programmatic character of work at IATH is discussed. What was a virtuous necessity in the 1990s had turned into something much less virtuous by 2013.

10. "I am not what I used to be," and "under the reign of Theory." See Horace, *Odes* 4.1.

11. Morris: "You can't have art without resistance in the material." Quote attributed to Morris in Halliday Sparling (1924, p. 14).

12. I borrow the phrase "history-men" from Laura Riding (1935), who used it to characterize historical figures—her chief example was Napoleon—who "rose like a plague of vampires" to ruin both actual human life and the simple stories (as opposed to the heroic stories) that reflect those lives.

REFERENCES

Benjamin, W. (1968). Theses on the philosophy of history (1940). In *Illuminations: With an introduction by Hannah Arendt* (H. Zohn, Trans.) (pp. 253–264). New York: Harcourt Brace Jovanovich.

Brooks, C. (1947). Keats's sylvan historian: History without footnotes. In *The well-wrought urn: Studies in the structure of poetry* (pp. 151–166). New York: Harcourt Brace.

Byron, G. G. (1813). *The Giaour.* London: T. Davison.

Byron, G. G. (1818). *Childe Harold's pilgrimage.* London: John Murray.

Byron, G. G. (1974). *Letters and journals, Vol. 3: Alas! The love of women.* L. A. Marchand (Ed.). London: John Murray, 1974.

Byron, G. G. (1981). *Complete poetical works of George Gordon Byron* (Vol. 2). J. J. McGann (Ed.). Oxford: Oxford University Press.

Byron, G. G. (1986). *Complete poetical works of George Gordon Byron.* J. J. McGann (Ed.). Oxford: Oxford University Press.

Cooper, J. F. (1823). *The pioneers.* New York: Wiley.

Goethe, J. W. (2010). *Faust: Der Tragödie erster Teil.* Retrieved from http://www.gutenberg.org/cache/epub/2229/pg2229.html. (Original work published 1808)

Greetham, D. (1992). *Textual scholarship: An introduction.* New York: Garland.

Hardy, T. (1915). *The convergence of the twain.* Retrieved from http://www.poetryfoundation.org/poem/176678.

Hopkins, G. M. (1985). *No worst, there is none: Pitched past pitch of grief.* Retrieved from http://www.poetryfoundation.org/poem/173663. (Original composed in 1885)

Howard-Hill, H. (1991). Theory and praxis in the social approach to editing. *TEXT, 5,* 31–46.

Hunter, J. D. (1991). *Culture wars: The struggle to define America.* New York: Basic Books.

Ignatius of Loyola, Saint. (1914). *The spiritual exercises of St. Ignatius of Loyola* (E. Mullan, Trans.). New York: P. J. Kennedy and Sons.

Lethaby, W. R. (1935). *Phillip Webb and his work.* London: Oxford University Press.

Marx, K. (1845). *Theses on Feuerbach.* Retrieved from http://www.marxists.org/archive/marx/works/1845/theses/theses.htm.

McGann, J. J. (1983a). *A critique of modern textual criticism.* Chicago: University of Chicago Press.

McGann, J. J. (1983b). *The romantic ideology.* Chicago: University of Chicago Press.

McGann, J. J. (1985a). *The beauty of inflections: Literary investigations in historical method and theory.* Oxford: Clarendon.

McGann, J. J. (Ed.). (1985b). *Historical studies and literary criticism,* with an introduction. Madison: University of Wisconsin Press.

McGann, J. J. (Ed.). (1985c). *Textual studies and literary interpretation,* with an introduction. Chicago: University of Chicago Press.

McGann, J. J. (1987). *Social values and poetic acts.* Cambridge, MA: Harvard University Press.

McGann, J. J. (1989). *Toward a literature of knowledge.* Oxford: Oxford University Press.

McGann, J. J. (1991). *The textual condition.* Princeton, NJ: Princeton University Press.

McGann, J. J. (1993). *Black riders: The visible language of modernism.* Princeton, NJ: Princeton University Press.

McGann, J. J. (1994). The complete writings and pictures of Dante Gabriel Rossetti: A hypermedia research archive. *TEXT, 7,* 95–105.

McGann, J. J. (1997). The rationale of hypertext. In K. Sutherland (Ed.), *Electronic text: Investigations in method and theory* (pp. 19–46). Oxford: Clarendon Press.

McGann, J. J. (2001). *Radiant textuality: Literature after the World Wide Web.* New York: Palgrave Macmillan.

McGann, J. J. (2004). Imagining what you don't know: The theoretical goals of the Rossetti Archive. In R. Modiano, L. Searle, and P. Shillingsburg (Eds.), *Voice, text, hypertext: Emerging practices in textual studies* (pp. 378–399). Seattle: University of Washington Press.

Newman, J. H. (1848). *Loss and gain.* London: James Burn.

Parry, M. (1971). The historical method in literary criticism. In A. Parry (Ed.), *The making of Homeric verse: The collected papers of Milman Parry* (pp. 408–413). Oxford: Clarendon.

Peirce, C. S. (1932). *Collected papers of Charles Sanders Peirce.* Cambridge, MA: Harvard University Press.

Riding, L. (1935). *Progress of stories.* London: Constable.

Sparling, H. H. (1924). *The Kelmscott press and William Morris mastercraftsman.* London: Macmillan. Retrieved from https://openlibrary.org/books/OL6673065M/The_Kelmscott_press_and_William_Morris_master-craftsman.

Stevens, W. (1951). The noble rider and the sound of words. In *The necessary angel* (pp. 1–36). New York: Alfred Knopf.

Tennyson, Alfred Lord (1833). *Morte d'Arthur.* Retrieved from http://www.poetryfoundation.org/poem/174637.

Unsworth, J. (1997). Documenting the reinvention of text: The importance of failure. *Journal of Electronic Publishing, 3*(2). doi:10.3998/3336451.0003.201.

Wellek, R., and Warren, A. (1949). *Theory of literature.* New York: Harcourt Brace.

Wordsworth, W. (1850). *The prelude.* London: Edward Moxon.

CHAPTER 14

ILLUMINATING DAUGHTER-MOTHER NARRATIVES IN YOUNG ADULT FICTION

HILARY S. CREW

RESEARCH FOR MY DISSERTATION BEGAN with questions that were raised while I was teaching young adult literature. Why were many stories about teenage daughters and their mothers so negative? Why was the mother so often absent? In this chapter, I discuss theoretical approaches that I found useful in analyzing the kinds of stories that were being told about teen girls and their mothers in young adult texts, and provide examples of how I brought together traditional and feminist theories of adolescent development, psychoanalytic and sociological theories of daughter-mother relationships, and writings on mothers and motherhood.

From my readings of the diverse literature on daughter-mother relationships, I identified constructs of the relationship and theoretical approaches that were relevant to explaining and interpreting its dynamics. Because these dynamics were interrelated with issues ranging from identity, sexuality, and body image to debates and choices regarding responsibilities of mothers, I drew from a multidisciplinary body of literature, including traditional theories of adolescent development, feminist theories, and writings on female development and mothers and mothering. More importantly, I wanted to examine the extent to which this literature informed how the relationships between teen daughters and their mothers were imagined in fictional texts.

Using poststructuralist narrative theories, I developed a model of analysis for listening to the voices of daughters and mothers in young adult texts and extended an understanding of how narrative strategies and conventions were employed in the telling of stories about their relationship. My approach to analysis was based on the premise articulated by Rachel DuPlessis (1985, p. 3) that there are no "neutral" conventions in telling story and that composing story raises questions about what is "felt to be narratable by both literary and social conventions." The process of my research is best explained as intertextual and interpretive in that the interdependence of theoretical narratives and fictional texts brings a new understanding of how and why certain stories are told about the daughter-mother relationship in young adult novels.

I chose to define the young adult novel as a specific generic form in the sense that it is most often written and marketed for teenage readers, with stories that socially construct the reality of what it is like to be an adolescent in different contexts. Since mothers flitted in and out of their daughters' lives in an inconsequential way in many stories, I developed a set of criteria for the selection of the one hundred novels plus short stories in which the daughter-mother relationship was treated with significance as a relationship. The most important factor was the presence of a degree of self-reflexivity in the sense that a daughter questioned her relationship with her mother. In the event of a mother's absence or death, her loss had to be treated as more than a plot device; it had to explore the significance of that absence to the daughter. It was also important to recognize that although young adult novels are reviewed and written about as a separate genre and shelved in special sections of bookstores and libraries, the relationship between a teenage daughter and mother formed part of a larger cultural discourse on mother-daughter relationships and mothering.

My initial reading soon revealed that a great deal had been written about the daughter-mother relationship in the years since Adrienne Rich (1976) first declared that the emotional relationship between mother and daughter was "the great unwritten story" (p. 225). Rich asserted that a relationship she perceived as so important to her own life had been socially constructed under patriarchy and was minimized in discourses of art, psychology, and sociology. However, by the early 1990s, when I began to explore this topic, this relationship was no longer an unwritten story. It had been written about in cross-disciplinary feminist studies and in feminist and literary studies, and celebrated in essays, poetry, and popular fiction. Where to begin? I first decided to go outside the concentration of courses available in the communication, information, and library studies doctorate program where I was enrolled to study critical theories, literary theories, and feminist writings in the English department. With these courses as background, I undertook my own readings, which would specifically address my area of research.

STARTING OUT: DAUGHTERS, MOTHERS, AND FREUDIAN ROMANCES

One of the first works that influenced my thinking about how I could approach my study was a book by Marianne Hirsch (1989) in which she analyzed mother-daughter narrative plots in nineteenth- and twentieth-century women's writing. Hirsch explored the extent to which these plots, "rooted as they are in oedipal forms and preoccupations," were premised on erasing and objectifying the mother (p. 46). Using Sigmund Freud's "Familienroman"—a "family romance"—in which a child or adolescent fantasizes liberating him- or herself from his or her parents, of whom he or she now has a low opinion and imagines replacing them with others, Hirsch identifies narrative plots that encode, discursively, Freud's family romances, including a "female family romance" plot in which mothers are rejected and absented so that their daughters can form mature attachments with a father (or husband) from whom they will gain access to the power that the mother lacks. Because Freudianism has been so influential in the way we imagine and talk about family relationships, I found Freud's essays "Family Romances" (1959) and "Femininity" (1965) especially useful for thinking about ways in which Freudianism informed narrative plots and cultural scripts integrated into young adult fictional texts.

The assumptions and tenets of traditional Freudian adolescent psychology as disseminated in the writings of Peter Blos (1962) and Erik Erikson (1968) perpetuated a hegemonic discourse that encoded a prescriptive ideological stance about the development of young people who achieved self-individuation by separating themselves from their parents. The statement that "one of the central tasks of adolescence is to extricate oneself from family ties, both psychologically and physically" (Gardner 1982, p. 24) is a typical example of the construction of adolescence found in self-help books in the 1980s. In regard to the daughter-mother relationship, the advice given was that teen daughters must liberate themselves from their mothers, who, regarded as obstacles to their daughters' development, must, in turn, let them go. Given that issues of independence, identity formation, and relationships with parents and peers had been identified as central to stories in young adult novels, it was not surprising that I was finding that tenets of Freudian adolescent psychology influenced the representation of relationships between teen daughters and their mothers in many young adult novels. In some texts, however, these tenets were expressly spelled out and debated for adolescent readers. A teen girl, for example, reiterates the familiar script of adolescent psychology word for word when discussing her relationship with her mother in *Letting Go*, by Lynn Hall (1987, p. 93): "Kids my age aren't supposed to get along with their parents. We're supposed to be cutting loose and learning to be independent and all that stuff."

I found undisguised Freudianism reproduced in passages in which daughters described their fear of becoming their mother (matrophobia), resisted the controlling voice of a mother, and moved from idealizing a mother to de-idealizing or devaluing her. I identified narrative plots that conformed closely to Freudian family romance plots in young adult novels published from the 1960s through to the 1990s, in which an adolescent daughter's development is typically predicated on her liberation from her mother. Two examples of this can be seen in the novels *Claudia, Where Are You?*, by Hila Colman (1969), and *A Formal Feeling*, by Zibby Oneal (1990 [first published in 1982]).

In *Claudia, Where Are You?*, sixteen-year-old Claudia's flight from home culminates in a romantic involvement with a young man. Claudia's rejection of her parents' "phony values" and her involvement with drugs is commensurate with a story set in the sixties. But a language emphasizing her emotional independence from de-idealized parents, conflict and alienation between Claudia and her mother, and a heterosexual romantic plot in which Claudia turns to Papa Steve is a plotted journey that encodes a Freudian model of female adolescence. Colman's use of the terms "turn" and "Papa" reproduces terminology analogous to that of the Freudian romance, in which a daughter is said to turn to the father.

A Formal Feeling, by Zibby Oneal, is an example of a Freudian family romance narrative plot in which a young woman's individuation is predicated on the death of her mother. Sixteen-year-old Anne has grown up in the shadow of her perfect, controlling mother. "'Anne is her mother's daughter,' people often said, meaning the hair, the height, even the same name Anne, which they shared" (p. 13). The death of her mother releases Anne from the controlling image of her mother flawlessly executing a figure on the ice while Anne "would try—ten, twelve, fifteen times—never getting it smooth enough" (p. 91). Her father's remarriage brings a replacement mother: "So different. So small. So unlike Anne's mother and Anne herself" (pp. 98–99). Oneal's novel is an example of a novel in which a conventional visual imagery of mirrors is employed to show a daughter's move from an identification with her mother through the permanent fracturing of their mirrored images. Privileged in the text is a daughter's move to establish her own identity.

In discussing examples of Freudian narrative plots, I also drew from Lacanian (1986) theory, which emphasizes how men and women are positioned in relation to the "symbolic order" (language, culture, and social structures) and posits that a daughter's acceptance into the world of her father is predicated on repressing her symbiotic relationship with her mother. In reference to Isabelle Holland's (1975) novel *Of Love and Death and Other Journeys*, I explored, for example, the significance of a narrative plot in which after the death of her mother, a daughter leaves Perugia—a city in which "skeletons and blackened bodies of saints . . . [were of] no great rarity" (p. 122)—and joins her father and his new wife in New York (the "New World").

I also found Anne Cranny-Francis's (1990) analysis of generic fiction useful for discussing Freudian narrative plots. As Cranny-Francis points out, it is through the "plotting of narrative, the arrangement of events into a meaningful pattern, that the ideological or political framework of a text becomes apparent" (p. 10). Fictional texts are multidimensional—certainly more so than the psychoanalytic narratives of adolescent psychology. I encountered stories in which teen daughters from all cultures and ethnicities were voicing the love that they felt for their mothers and their need for their mothers' ongoing care and nurturance—even as they criticized and blamed them. As will be discussed later, the daughter-mother narrative in young adult novels covers a range of issues, including the responsibility of mothering, that are highly significant to the lives of young women.

EXPLORING ALTERNATIVES: THE REVISIONING OF WOMEN'S AND GIRLS' PSYCHOLOGY

Important to my study were theories conceptualizing alternative models of human development. Women theorists interrogated ideologies of gender and power embedded in Freudian narratives. In the late 1970s and 1980s, for example, there were new understandings of women's psychological development in writings by Nancy Chodorow (1978), Jean Baker Miller (1986), and Carol Gilligan (1982). In Nancy Chodorow's model of female development, for example, the problem for daughters was conceptualized as one of differentiation, not separation, from the mother. A daughter was said not to give up her attachment to her mother, but rather was described as defining herself in a relational triangle with her mother and father. In "Remapping the Moral Domain," Gilligan (1988) challenged the view that a girl's development was problematic because of the continuity of relationships in her life. Gilligan deconstructed and realigned the binaries of separation and independence and attachment and dependence, arguing that dependence also signified connection, and that the "interdependence of attachment empowers both the self and the other, not one at the other's expense" (Gilligan 1988, p. 14).

But it was not until the early 1990s that the move was made to revision Freudian psychological theories of female adolescence based upon actual studies of teenage girls. Unmasked were the patriarchal ideology and gender bias embedded in Freudian discourse, both of which devalued girls' attachments to their mother, devalued the voices of mothers, and devalued the continued role a mother could have in her daughter's life. So just as I was engaged in reading for my dissertation, studies were being conducted in which the voices of girls and young women spoke of their own experiences of growing up female.

In one of the first of these studies, Terri Apter (1990) reported on her findings from interviews conducted with sixty-five pairs of daughters and mothers from England and the United States, including pairs from other cultures. She concluded that a Freudian model of adolescent development, emphasizing the concept that separation from parents was necessary in order to achieve individuation, was inadequate, and explained the daughter-mother relationship in terms of connection rather than liberation and separation.

Other studies conducted under the auspices of the Harvard Project on Women's Psychology and Girls' Development also contributed to new understandings of female adolescence. For example, in *Meeting at the Crosssroads*, Lyn Mikel Brown and Gilligan (1992) conceptualized female adolescence as a time when girls are at risk because "the crossroads between girls and women is marked by a series of disconnections or disassociations" (p. 6). In *Mother Daughter Revolution*, daughters and mothers were said to have been "betrayed . . .

[by] . . . a cycle of separation, loss, and betrayal, generation after generation" (Debold, Wilson, and Malave 1993, p. 30). In an alternative
rhetoric, mothers were being asked to connect with their daughters
so that "mothers' passion for daughters and daughters' passion for
mothers can burn away the lies that have caused women to lose each
other through the betrayals of separation" (p. 31). These studies, con-
tradicting the traditional narratives of adolescent development that
were so prominent in texts and writings about young adult literature,
reinforced the importance of critically examining the representations of daughter-mother relationships in young adult literature from
other perspectives. Understanding the daughter-mother relationship
through parameters of connection, for example, places value on different aspects of story.

MAKING CONNECTIONS: LOVING AND NEEDING A MOTHER

If feminist theories were emphasizing the importance of connections
in women's and girls' lives, and researchers were listening to adolescent girls voicing their relationships to their mothers in terms of connection, then to what extent was this aspect of the relationship encoded into the texts of young adult novels? If, as Molly Hite (1989)
argues, "changes in emphasis and value can articulate the 'other side'
of a culturally mandated story, exposing the limits it inscribes in the
process of affirming a dominant ideology" (p. 4), to what extent did
stories in which daughters profess attachment to their mother actually contradict Freudian accounts of daughter-mother relationships?

The extent to which Freudian discourses have been naturalized
into representations of relationships was also evident in examples in
which connections between teen daughters and mothers were mediated by prescriptive Freudian scripts. An example is the warning,
with homophobic undertones, that a daughter should not continue
to be close to her mother. Daughters were warned that they should
not be their mother's "best friend"; they were warned against letting
mothers become dependent on them. These warnings were sometimes issued by fictional psychologists whose voices were legitimized
by the acknowledgment of a psychologist on the verso of the title
page. For example, in C. S. Adler's (1983) *The Shell Lady's Daughter*,
a daughter who has begun to be scared that she is her mother's "best
friend" is told by a psychologist that her "emotional and social development . . . [could be] stunted" if she lets her mother become de-

pendent on her when she "should be out socializing with [her] peers" (p. 137). Adler's daughter-mother narrative is representative of novels that reinscribed a dominant Freudian paradigm despite a daughter's articulation of love for her mother.

In other daughter-mother narratives, I was finding an equally constraining ideological discourse that was informed by theories of bonding and instinctual mother love. John Bowlby's (1969) influential attachment theory (linked to imprinting in ethology studies in the early days of its development), for example, was used to justify social and political agendas to control and influence mothers and attitudes toward child care and mothering. The concept and ideology of bonding, writes Diane E. Eyer (1992), was responsible for a social myth that was widely disseminated in professional journals and popular culture. In her novel *Letting Go*, Hall (1987) shows her familiarity with this ideological cultural script in conversations held between sixteen-year-old Casey and her mother when they are attending a dog show. Casey's mother makes an analogy between instinctual animal behavior and human maternal love with the comment, "But the mothering instinct, there really isn't any logic behind that. It is just pure instinct. Survival of the species" (p. 128). The binding love imagined between a daughter and mother is mediated by somatic imagery and language that reproduces the construct of a symbiotic union between mother and child theorized in psychoanalytic object relations theories. "Flesh of my flesh, blood of my blood," is how Mary Leary thinks about her relationship to her mother in a novel by Susan Shreve (1982, p. 40). A flesh-and-blood imagery that essentializes the maternal body and primary bond of a daughter and mother is celebrated in the context of a story endorsing a pro-life stance.

The concurrent reading of theory and literary texts suggested how daughter-mother narratives in young adult novels encoded ideological positions on issues of motherhood and abortion in texts that, as discussed later, use specific narrative strategies to position teen readers to potentially identify with a daughter's position. The fantasy of the perfect mother, along with mother blame when perfection is not attained (Chodorow with Contratto 1989), has been a controlling archetype of motherhood from the nineteenth century. I also found this archetypal mother figure in young adult novels. Daughters have expectations of their mothers and blame them for falling short of meeting their needs in stories whose viewpoint colludes with theories of child-centered perspectives of mothering. There is a paradox here in that the convention of a dependent, de-idealized mother obviously works well to satisfy the requirement of a strong daughter protagonist in a young adult novel.

That Freudianism was informing many daughter-mother narratives was not an unexpected result of my study. My findings were reaffirmed by a study of mothers and daughters in popular culture by Suzanne Walters (1992), who found that the commonsense way of understanding the mother-daughter relationship had been mediated by Freudianism, which had delimited the representation of the relationship. Walters excluded materials and novels marketed specifically to young adults, but the psychological litany of terms that Walters found describing the relationship in her study are also integral to many young adult fictional descriptions of the relationships between teens and their mothers.

The works of feminist literary critics Hite (1989), Cranny-Francis (1990), and DuPlessis (1985) were useful for identifying and analyzing a small sample of novels that told another side to a "culturally mandated" story by employing narrative strategies that disrupt or reject Freudian family romance plots, decentering a daughter's voice in a text that recognizes the subjectivities of both daughters and mothers, and refusing representations of idealized mothers and mothering. For example, the novel *Author! Author!*, by Susan Terris (1990), subverts Freud's family romances in a self-reflexive text that draws attention to the ideological practices of fiction and to Freudian fantasies. In the novel, twelve-year-old Val Myerson, who aspires to be a writer, fantasizes that Tekla Reiss, a poet, is her biological mother and tells her family and Tekla that she has it all worked out. Reproduced on the top margins of the first pages of the novel's chapters is Val's own fictive melodrama. Based upon Freud's foundling fantasy, Val's fantasy concerns lost twin girls who, brought up by peasants, are searching for their royal mother. Val's fantasy is, thus, literally marginalized by the story of her real family relationships. Acknowledging its absurdity, Val immolates her manuscript in a "ceremonial pyre" (p. 148).

VOICES OF DAUGHTERS AND MOTHERS ACROSS CULTURES

In *Mother Daughter Revolution*, Debold and her coauthors (1993) expand upon feminist accounts of women's and girls' development by paying more attention to race, class, and ethnicity. In *Between Voice and Silence* (Taylor, Gilligan, and Sullivan 1995), the voices of a small sample of African American and Hispanic girls are heard in research interviews. Taylor, Gilligan, and Sullivan note that in research interviews there are "greater differences in the way the black, white, Portuguese, and Hispanic girls describe their relationships with their mothers than in the way they describe other aspects of their lives" (p. 70).

But I was also finding that in young adult novels, the personal dynamics of the daughter-mother relationship resonated across cultures: the dialogues of love and anger, the need for a mother's nurturance, and a daughter's criticism and blame when she felt her mother had let her down. But cultural, racial, and historical contexts are also shown to shape the theoretical lens through which the relationship is viewed. In the small sample of multicultural novels in my study, conflict between teen daughters and their mothers often centered on bicultural issues, as when, for example, a mother sought to pass values and traditions from her own culture on to her American-born daughter.

In regard to the study of African American daughter-mother relationships, Patricia Hill Collins (1991), writing from the standpoint of a black feminist, acknowledges the daughter-mother relationship as "one fundamental relationship among Black women" (p. 96). Collins is representative of scholars who argue that white feminist psychoanalytic theoretical perspectives on the daughter-mother relationship have disregarded cultural differences and black women's explanations, interpretations, and experiences. Gloria Joseph (1986), for example, has suggested that the relationship be addressed within the context of the black family network rather than the isolated dyad of mother and daughter in psychoanalytic theoretical frameworks. A social constructivist approach to the black daughter-mother relationship places emphasis on the social realities of mothering and addresses issues of race and gender, including the double jeopardy of growing up black and female. Aspects of the relationship identified by Collins include the role of mothers in protecting their daughters from racism and sexism and the concept of a community of mothering realized through "othermothers." Collins also writes that daughters need to recognize the differences between idealizations of maternal love disseminated in popular culture and actual mothers, whose "physical care and protection are acts of maternal love" (Collins 1991, p. 127).

This difference is spelled out in Jacqueline Woodson's (1993) novel

The Dear One, when Afeni's mother admonishes her, "Don't you ever let me hear you say I don't love you, because if I'm not saying it in words, I'm showing it with actions! I didn't grow up saying it, so I can't start now. But I love you in every meal you eat, every piece of clothing you wear, and every clean sheet you sleep on" (p. 84).

In selected African American novels, I found the daughter-mother narrative structured within the extended family or network of other-mothers that Collins (1993) writes is central to the concept of black motherhood and the mother-daughter relationship. However, intertextually, I was finding diversity in the representation of African American daughter-mother relationships across different socioeconomic contexts. A mother's role in teaching her daughters to be independent and self-reliant in order to survive the double jeopardy of being both black and female is an integral part of the daughter-mother narrative in Virginia Hamilton's (1993) *Plain City.* In the novel, Buhlaire's mother empowers her by inviting her to share in the power and the meaning that the blues has had for black women as a site of expression, self-definition, and resistance.

In other novels, the empowering voices of mothers are absent. For example, in Alice Childress's (1981) *Rainbow Jordan,* Rainbow's mother, one of several single mothers in African American daughter-mother narratives, voices in first person her anger and frustration at being a single mother with little support. This assumption that African American daughters grow up within networks of extended families and communities was contested in several novels. I was finding that stories of African American daughter-mother narratives in young adult novels were informed, rather, by diverse experiences of the reality of mothering in different socioeconomic contexts, along with an understanding of how daughters' mothers had also been oppressed by systems of race and sexism.

However, the same can be said for the representation of mothers and mothering across different racial, cultural, and socioeconomic contexts. Rainbow Jordan's mother's anger and frustration are similarly heard in the voices of other mothers who experience oppression, no matter the context. It should be noted that I have omitted from this chapter my study of selected young adult novels addressing narratives of African American daughter-mother relationships within the oppressive institution of slavery, which I addressed in Crew (1994) and in Crew (1996).

IDENTIFYING NARRATIVE STRATEGIES: LISTENING TO
THE VOICES OF DAUGHTERS AND MOTHERS

I also examined how stories about the daughter-mother relationship were mediated by specific narrative strategies and conventions in telling stories. Young adult novels have been frequently characterized as relying on a first-person point of view in which the main adolescent protagonist takes up an "I" position in the text and thus dominates how events are viewed. In relation to stories about teenage daughters and mothers, the first-person, character-bound narration of a teenage daughter would be dominant, for example, if she maintained the subject position of "I" throughout the text. Her mother's subjectivity and the representation of the relationship would thus be mediated through her daughter's narration. This formulaic convention of telling daughter-mother stories bears analogy to cultural and Freudian narratives in that they exclude the voice and subjectivity of the mother.

In order to answer questions regarding the extent to which a daughter-centered narrative colluded with child-centered narratives of psychoanalysis in these novels, or the extent to which a daughter's voice is decentered and a mother is granted agency to tell her own story, I drew upon concepts from Mieke Bal's (1985) *Narratology* and Steven Cohan and Linda Shires's (1988) *Telling Stories: A Theoretical Analysis of Narrative Fiction*. Bal, as well as Cohan and Shires, uses the term "focalization" to refer to the spatial relationship between the agency of narration and the perspective from which the story is told. Cohan and Shires further define focalization as a "triadic relation formed by the *narrating agent* [who narrates] and the *focalizer* [who sees], and the *focalized* [what is being seen and, thus, narrated]" (p. 95).

The shift of focalization from narrator to a character (e.g., from a daughter to a mother or to other characters) can be useful in gauging the extent to which a teenage daughter's voice, even in a first-person, character-bound text, may be decentered in a text, and a mother's voice legitimized, despite, perhaps, a daughter's criticism. This model was useful, for example, in looking at a text with a split narrative where there were chapters in which the daughter's mother is the narrated subject of an anonymous narrator and other chapters in which a daughter narrates story from the position of a first-person, character-bound narrator. It was important to identify an anonymous narrator's biases (or slant) toward a daughter or mother, and toward the relationship. It was also important to consider the position of a narrating agent in relation to other narrators and characters in novels employing plural narratives.

In line with feminist research on female adolescence, I also wanted to listen to voices of daughters and mothers in fictional texts and note how their relationship was negotiated through dialogue. In *Meeting at the Crossroads*, Brown and Gilligan (1992) developed an interview model that centered on voice and the harmonics of relationship. They found that questions "about voice attune one's ear to the harmonics of relationship" (p. 21). Some of their questions were analogous to ones that I was asking when listening to the voices of daughters and mothers in texts, including questions about who is speaking, what story is being told about relationships, and from whose perspective or from what vantage point the relationship is being seen, as well as questions about sociocultural contexts. It is a method of listening that involves noting gaps and silences in dialogues. Attention is paid to how girls and women talk about relationships, such as shifts from voices in harmony to voices no longer in affinity. Brown and Gilligan's voice-centered approach gave me a way of thinking about how this analysis of voice and relationship could be integrated with narrative theories based on focalization and questions of agency.

I also drew ideas from Susan Lanser's (1991) essay, "Toward a Feminist Narratology," in which she advocates for a poetics that goes beyond formal classifications of narrative theory. In particular, she suggests that a narrative theory that would "define and describe *tone* in narrative" (p. 617) in order to distinguish differences between voices would be particularly relevant for feminist criticism. For example, in my study, tone can be used to describe the distinction between the voice used openly by a daughter to her mother and the voice in which she expresses opinions of her mother in an internal monologue that is unheard by her mother. The following three examples illustrate how relationships are mediated by narrative strategies.

The first example is a *first-person, character-bound narrative*. It is taken from *A Star for the Latecomer*, by Bonnie and Paul Zindel (1980). Seventeen-year-old Brooke Hillary, who is the narrator and focalizer of her mother and their relationship, speaks about her mother's control and the loss of her own voice when her mother decided she should be a dancing star. She speaks in monologic passages, so that her thoughts and words are not available to her mother or to other characters. There are instances when her mother's unmediated voice breaks directly into Brooke's monologue, for example, "Brooke, you've got to lose five pounds.—Brooke, you're eating too much" (p. 56). Voiced in monologue, the voice of an adolescent daugher is heard inviting a reader to sympathize with her resistance to her mother's controlling and invasive comments: "I don't want to take another dance class. . . . What if I shouldn't become a star while my mother was here to enjoy it. Would I really want it for ME? Thump. A divider came down, closing me off from any feeling" (p. 56). Brooke's voice splits as she disassociates from self. The "divider" is analogous to Brown and Gilligan's (1992, p. 4) findings of an "inner division" when girls cannot express what they think and feel. Brooke's silencing of self is analogous to the self-silencing that has been observed in Brown and Gilligan's interviews with women and adolescent girls as a strategy to avoid conflict. After her mother dies, Brooke narrates that she can say "her first truthful words in years" (p. 182).

The second example comes from Colman's (1969) *Claudia, Where Are You?* This novel is an example of how a *split narrative strategy* works to create disassociation between the voices of a daughter and mother. Colman employs a split narrative in which the first-person, character-bound narrative of teenage Claudia alternates with chapters in which her mother is the narrated subject of an anonymous narrator. A daughter's voice is literally separated (by the text) and psychologically disassociated from the voice of her mother. Claudia's first-person narrative is characterized by the effective use of monologues and dialogues, making visible the different tones used by Claudia in what she says and does not say to her mother. This strategy privileges Claudia's voice and negates the voice of her mother. The convention of addressing the reader positions readers to potentially identify and sympathize with Claudia's viewpoint: "I'm only a kid and 'disturbed' as they say. You know, one of the statistics in *The New York Times* about teenagers who freak out" (p. 1). The chapters in which Claudia's mother's narrated thoughts and actions are focalized and mediated by the judgmental comments of an anonymous narrator also work to evoke sympathy for the daughter's voice. The disconnection of an adolescent daughter's voice from that of her mother aligns with the understanding of the daughter-mother relationship as one of separation and conflict—an underlying assumption in Colman's Freudian linear plot of female adolescence.

The third example is a novel that uses the narrative strategy of a *plural narrative*. In Colby Rodowsky's (1985) *Julie's Daughter*, voice and agency are given to a daughter; to her mother, who abandoned her as a baby; and to an elderly artist who also abandoned her child for her career. Each speaks in separate chapters, but their voices are woven into a daughter-mother narrative spanning three generations. The doubling of mothers' voices works to strengthen the maternal voice while decentering that of the daughter. It is a text that demonstrates well the difference between narrator and focalizer and the shifting of viewpoints as each character narrates and observes from different subject positions. It was one of the strongest examples in my study of how a plural narrative can create positions from which both a teenage daughter and a mother speak as narrating subjects.

The concept of the voices of daughters and mothers speaking together has thus been central to constructing a new understanding of this relationship. Hirsch (1989, p. 197) suggests that in order for there to be new stories about mothers and daughters, there has to be a move away from "notions of identity and subjectivity" to theories of psychology and psychoanalysis that begin with children as subject and mother as object. Virginia Hamilton's (1982) *Sweet Whispers, Brother Rush* was a rare example in my study of a novel in which a daughter narrates the experience of the shifting double consciousness of being both daughter and mother.

GOING FORWARD: NEW VISIONS FOR
THE DAUGHTER-MOTHER RELATIONSHIP

The theories we employ and the way we organize and present our work provide us with a particular way of knowing. The use of alternative theoretical approaches can bring new insights.

Hirsch (1989) suggests that new theories and fictions about mothers and daughters will have to lessen their dependence on psychoanalytic models of analysis; integrate social, economic, and historical perspectives; and include the differences in the socioeconomic and cultural contexts in which mothers mother. A social constructionist approach is advocated in Collins's (1991) *Black Feminist Thought*; she argues for a theory making that is developed from the standpoint of African American women, based on the view that although there are "common experiences" among women of different races and ethnicities, these experiences have been socially constructed on the basis of race and gender (p. 27). Central to Collins's approach to theory is the bringing together of "abstract thought with concrete action" (p. 29). Other scholars, for example, bell hooks (1989, p. 48), place value on a "cross-ethnic feminist scholarship."

Studies sponsored by the Harvard Project on Women's Psychology and Girls' Development made a move toward incorporating feminist revisions of psychology with social constructionist approaches by including teen girls from different ethnicities. The title *Mother Daughter Revolution: From Betrayal to Power* (Debold et al. 1993, p. 249) is representative of an alternative discourse in which the daughter-mother relationship is transformed into a locus of power using descriptors such as "resistance," "solidarity," and "revolutionary cells," thus answering Luce Irigaray's (1985, p. 143) call for a new "syntax" and "another 'grammar'" through which to articulate the relationship. Debold and her coauthors (1993, p. 249) incorporate the concept of othermothers in their call for a "revolution of mothers" that "joins all women in the political act of mothering the next generation of girls."

New stories depend on oppositional texts that make visible a resistance to dominant paradigms and a reworking of the conventions used in telling stories. Societal and cultural changes resulting in the production of new discourses on female adolescence, mothers, and mothering have the potential to contribute to a new articulation of the daughter-mother relationship in young adult novels.

FINAL REFLECTIONS

When I reflect back on the nonlinear, interpretive process of research and writing for my dissertation, I compare it to peeling a rather dense onion and finding layer under layer of writings and theoretical approaches pertaining to the study of the daughter-mother relationship. The most difficult part of the process was developing a model of analysis while remaining attentive to the problem of how analyses of the novels depended upon my choice of theoretical perspectives—the lenses through which I chose to look at the daughter-mother relationship. My choice of a feminist theoretical perspective was a reflection of the shifting paradigm in researching the lives and relationships of adolescent girls. It was interesting to see, for example, that as feminist research highlighting girls' development and their relationships was popularized in books such as Mary Pipher's (1994) *Reviving*

Ophelia, daughter-mother book clubs began springing up in public libraries.

As I read critiques of my published work, I valued suggestions for an approach that would have resulted in a more inclusive cross-cultural analysis. I am aware from reading other studies that alternative theoretical perspectives can yield further insights into the study of the daughter-mother relationship in young adult fictional texts.

ACKNOWLEDGMENT

Portions of this chapter are taken from Crew (1994), Crew (1996), and Crew (2000).

REFERENCES

Adler, C. S. (1983). *The shell lady's daughter*. New York: Coward McCann.

Apter, T. (1990). *Altered loves: Mothers and daughters during adolescence*. New York: St. Martin's Press.

Bal, M. (1985). *Narratology: Introduction to the theory of narrative*. Toronto: University of Toronto Press.

Blos, P. (1962). *On adolescence*. New York: Free Press.

Bowlby, J. (1969). *Attachment. Vol. 1 of Attachment and loss*. New York: Basic Books.

Brown, L. M., and Gilligan, C. (1992). *Meeting at the crossroads: Women's psychology and girls' development*. Cambridge, MA: Harvard University Press.

Childress, A. (1981). *Rainbow Jordan*. New York: Coward, McCann and Geoghegan.

Chodorow, N. J. (1978). *The reproduction of mothering: Psychoanalysis and the sociology of gender*. Berkeley: University of California Press.

Chodorow, N. J., with Contratto, S. (1989). The fantasy of the perfect mother. In N. J. Chodorow, *Feminism and psychoanalytic theory* (pp. 79–96). New Haven, CT: Yale University Press.

Cohan, S., and Shires, L. M. (1988). *Telling stories: A theoretical analysis of narrative fiction*. New York: Routledge.

Collins, P. H. (1991). *Black feminist thought: Knowledge, consciousness, and the politics of empowerment*. New York: Routledge.

Collins, P. H. (1993). The meaning of motherhood in Black culture and Black mother-daughter relationships. In P. Bell-Scott (Ed.), *Double stitch: Black women write about mothers and daughters* (pp. 42–60). New York: Harper Perennial.

Colman, H. (1969). *Claudia, where are you?* New York: Morrow.

Cranny-Francis, A. (1990). *Feminist fiction: Feminist uses of generic fiction*. New York: St. Martin's Press.

Crew, H. S. (1994). Feminist theories and the voices of mothers and daughters in selected African-American literature for young adults. In K. P. Smith (Ed.),

African-American voices in young adult literature: Tradition, transition, transformation (pp. 79–114). Metuchen, NJ: Scarecrow Press.

Crew, H. S. (1996). *A narrative analysis of the daughter mother relationship in selected young adult novels* (Unpublished doctoral dissertation). Rutgers University, New Brunswick, NJ.

Crew, H. S. (2000). *Is it really mommie dearest? Daughter-mother narratives in young adult fiction.* Lanham, MD: Scarecrow Press.

Debold, E., Wilson, M., and Malave, I. (1993). *Mother daughter revolution: From betrayal to power.* Reading, MA: Addison-Wesley.

DuPlessis, R. B. (1985). *Writing beyond the ending: Narrative strategies of twentieth-century women writers.* Bloomington: Indiana University Press.

Erikson, E. (1968). *Identity, youth, and crisis.* New York: Norton.

Eyer, D. E. (1992). *Mother-infant bonding: A scientific fiction.* New Haven, CT: Yale University Press.

Freud, S. (1959). Family romances (1909) [1908]. In J. Strachey (Ed.), *The standard edition of the complete psychological works of Sigmund Freud* (Vol. 9, pp. 235–241). London: Hogarth.

Freud, S. (1965). Femininity. In J. Strachey (Ed.), *Introductory lectures on psychoanalysis* (pp. 112–135). New York: Norton.

Gardner, J. E. (1982). *The turbulent teens: Understanding, helping, surviving.* San Diego, CA: Oak Tree.

Gilligan, C. (1982). *In a different voice: Psychological theory and women's development.* Cambridge, MA: Harvard University Press.

Gilligan, C. (1988). Remapping the moral domain: New images of self in relationship. In C. Gilligan, C. J. Ward, J. M. Taylor, and B. Bardige (Eds.), *Mapping the moral domain: A contribution of women's thinking to psychological theory and education* (pp. 3–20). Cambridge, MA: Harvard University Press.

Hall, L. (1987). *Letting go.* New York: Scribner.

Hamilton, V. (1982). *Sweet whispers, Brother Rush.* New York: Philomel.

Hamilton, V. (1993). *Plain city.* New York: Blue Sky Press.

Hirsch, M. (1989). *The mother/daughter plot: Narrative, psychoanalysis, feminism.* Bloomington: Indiana University Press.

Hite, M. (1989). *The other side of the story: Structures and strategies of contemporary feminist narrative.* Ithaca, NY: Cornell University Press.

Holland, I. (1975). *Of love and death and other journeys.* New York: Lippincott.

hooks, b. (1989). *Talking back: Thinking feminist, thinking black.* Boston: South End Press.

Irigaray, L. (1985). *This sex which is not one.* Ithaca, NY: Cornell University Press.

Joseph, G. I. (1986). Black mothers and daughters, their roles and function in American Society. In G. I. Joseph and J. Lewis (Eds.), *Common differences: Conflict in black and white perspectives* (pp. 75–126). Boston: South End Press.

Lacan, J. (1986). The mirror stage. In H. Adams and L. Searle (Eds.), *Critical theory since 1965* (pp. 734–738). Tallahassee: Florida State University Press.

Lanser, S. S. (1991). Toward a feminist narratology. In R. R. Warhol and D. P. Herndl (Eds.), *Feminisms: An anthology of literary theory and criticism* (pp. 610–619). New Brunswick, NJ: Rutgers University Press.

Miller, J. B. (1986). *Toward a new psychology of women* (2nd ed.) Boston: Beacon.

Oneal, Z. (1990). *A formal feeling.* New York: Puffin.

Pipher, M. B. (1994). *Reviving Ophelia: Saving the selves of adolescent girls.* New York: Putnam.

Rich, A. (1976). *Of woman born: Motherhood as experience and institution.* New York: Norton.

Rodowsky, C. F. (1985). *Julie's daughter.* New York: Farrar, Straus, and Giroux.

Shreve, S. (1982). *The revolution of Mary Leary.* New York: Knopf.

Taylor, J. M., Gilligan, C., and Sullivan, A. M. (1995). *Between voice and silence: Women and girls, race and relationship.* Cambridge, MA: Harvard University Press.

Terris, S. (1990). *Author! Author!* New York: Farrar, Straus and Giroux.

Walters, S. D. (1992). *Lives together/lives apart: Mothers and daughters in popular culture.* Berkeley: University of California Press.

Woodson, J. (1993). *The dear one.* New York: Dell.

Zindel, B., and Zindel, P. (1980). *A star for the latecomer.* New York: Harper.

CHAPTER 15

THE NOBLEST PLEASURE: THEORIES OF UNDERSTANDING IN THE INFORMATION SCIENCES

DAVID BAWDEN

The noblest pleasure is the joy of understanding.
LEONARDO DA VINCI

IN THIS CHAPTER, I SET OUT my approach to theory construction in the information science discipline, and the information sciences more broadly. The approach emphasizes a qualitative and conceptual analysis and synthesis, aiming to create a form of understanding that brings coherence to complex sets of information.

To explain my approach to theory, it is necessary to provide some background: not an autobiographical account—I have done that elsewhere (Bawden 2010)—but something about my intellectual origins. These are in the physical sciences, as with so many other of the "British school" of information science (Bawden 2008b; Robinson and Bawden 2013b), whose perspectives I have inherited to a considerable extent. These include a rather pragmatic attitude in general, and a liking for using concepts from, and analogies with, the physical sciences where this is feasible and sensible.

A SCIENTIFIC INFORMATIONIST

I came into information science from the physical sciences. My undergraduate education was in physics and chemistry, and my final degree in organic chemistry. "Theory" in this context was objective, quantitative, and empirical, and expressed as "laws" and "principles."

For my doctorate I made only a small disciplinary move, and worked on the handling of digital representations of chemical structures—what later came to be termed "chemoinformatics" (Willett 2008). This was at the University of Sheffield, in an environment supporting a remarkably multifaceted approach to the information disciplines, ranging from the humanities to the sciences (Benson and Willett 2014), with an emerging social science perspective that was later to culminate in Tom Wilson's (1999) widely adopted process models for information behavior.

My own research was firmly in the area of scientific information, and specifically chemical information. It involved the pragmatic development of systems that would be useful for practice: for retrieval of information and for the correlation of molecular properties with chemical structure. The underlying theory, though we did not usually reflect on this, was over one hundred years old and was originally proposed by Alexander Crum Brown. His insight was, first, that the nature of chemical substances could be represented by structure diagrams, and second, that the properties of chemical substances could be directly related to these structural representations (Crum Brown 1864, 1869; Ritter 2001; Rouvray 1977). Techniques for handling digital versions of these representations, clever though they may have been, added little to this basic theory. This has been the basis of much of modern chemistry, including the pharmaceutical and fine chemicals industries. This remarkable combination of theory and information representation is perhaps paralleled only by the periodic table (Hjørland 2011; Scerri 2011); perhaps this is why so many of the early generations of information scientists were trained in chemistry.

In terms of theories of information, Shannon's Mathematical Theory of Communication was the only game in town. Its limitations in application to the concerns of the less technical end of the information sciences were well recognized, but there was interest in how it might be applied more widely, stimulated by ideas such as those of Gatlin (1972).

After my doctoral studies, I took a job in a pharmaceutical research center. I still thought of myself as a scientist who happened to work with information rather than with laboratory equipment: a "scientific informationist" rather than an "information scientist," in the terms of a question asked at my recruitment interview.

Although I was working as a practitioner, it was in a scientific research environment, where research and development in all fields were encouraged, and in the pharmaceutical information environment, which has been the source of many innovations in information systems and services (Bawden and Robinson 2010). As a result of this, my interest in, and attitude toward, theories in the information sciences developed in several ways.

I extended my involvement in the use of digital data collections for the analysis of the relations between chemical structure and molecular properties, using both the structural analysis techniques developed in my doctoral studies (Bawden 1983) and methods involving theories of the relation between physical properties of substances and their biological activities (see, e.g., Bawden et al. 1983). The underlying principles of these methods were undeniably "scientific"; they were empirical or semi-empirical in nature; they worked and could account for observed properties and predict the properties of new substances—but they gave little insight into the reasons. While this is a common enough feature of many scientific theories, I came to find it limiting.

Working on the development of systems for the retrieval of information on chemical substances and their reactions (Bawden et al. 1988; Bawden and Wood 1986), I became aware that some of the concepts of organic chemistry—aromaticity, multiple interatomic bonds, atomic charges, and so on—were not as clearly defined or understood as I had been led to believe in my student days. (It is sometimes said that to ensure one understands a topic, one should give a lecture course on it. I would also recommend incorporating the topic into an information storage and retrieval system.) The severely practical task of providing better retrieval facilities was casting light on the nature of chemical concepts, which are now recognized as being distinctly "fuzzy" (Rouvray 1997).

As a developer of chemical retrieval systems, I was involved in devising systems for browsing and identifying patterns in chemical datasets (Bawden 1984, 1988), and some of these ideas were applied to bibliographic records (Wade, Willett, and Bawden 1989). This led to the first "theory," actually only a concept, which I can claim to have introduced. This is the idea of molecular dissimilarity, and the idea that focusing on the most dissimilar items in a set, rather than on the most similar (which is common in many retrieval systems) is of interest (Bawden 1993b). This is valuable for browsing ("I've seen this sort of thing; now show me something different") and for spanning information spaces efficiently. In the chemical context, it allows the greatest variety of substances to be synthesized or tested for some property, desirable or otherwise (Trabocchi 2013; Warr 1997).

Working with systems to encourage browsing, particularly within an organization whose raison d'être was innovation, led me to reflect on what information systems and services could contribute to creativity and innovation. At the time, this topic had not been examined systematically. I attempted a systematic literature analysis of the topic, and the resulting paper (Bawden 1986) has, I am told, been influential on a number of those researchers who have since developed this topic greatly. This paper did not propose a theory as such, but rather sought to bring together some rather disparate conceptions of the topic.

Finally, I was involved in a variety of evaluations of information systems and services. One exercise in particular, a collaborative project among a number of organizations to evaluate the performance of systems for providing toxicology information, led to the development of new ways of assessing system performance. These used a detailed qualitative failure analysis, and more sophisticated ideas of relevance than were then the norm (Bawden and Brock 1982). This led me to think about evaluation more generally, and I realized that those methods that were "scientific" actually told us least about *why* systems and services worked well or not. I was also disturbed by the then antagonism between the proponents of quantitative and qualitative evaluation. It seemed evident to me, based on my practical experience, that a combination of the two must be the optimum. I expressed these ideas in a book (Bawden 1990) that attempted not to produce a theory of evaluation but rather to reach an understanding of the various styles and their associated methods as they relate to one another, as well as an appreciation of their relative merits.

In short, by the time I left a practitioner role and re-entered academia, I had developed a strong interest in qualitative conceptual analysis of information-related topics. I certainly did not see this as a theoretical position; rather, I saw it as a pragmatic assessment of what was good for the development of better systems and services on a rational basis. Insofar as I espoused any theoretical perspective, it would have been that of Bertie Brookes. By then, I liked the idea of being an information scientist rather than a scientific informationist, and Brookes was giving information science a philosophical foundation, and even a fundamental equation (Brookes 1980). Furthermore, he was basing his ideas on the work of Karl Popper, a very acceptable philosophical choice for someone from a scientific background. Although these ideas did not develop as Brookes might have wished, they have, I believe, been strongly influential, and may yet have more to offer. They have certainly affected my ideas, and continue to do so (Bawden 2002, 2008b, 2011a). (I also have a personal fondness for Brookes, who was on the interview panel that gave me my first academic position, and who was the only panel member who smiled when I told what I regarded as a joke.)

My experience as a practitioner impressed me with the idea that theories in the information sciences very often began with issues stemming from practice. I am not a zealot in this regard, as it seems clear that concepts and ideas far removed from the everyday concerns of the information practitioner can sometimes play a valuable role in theories of information. Nonetheless, it seems to me that theory and practice in the information sciences will, and should, generally be intertwined, a belief that has been a strong feature of the "British school" (Robinson and Bawden 2013b). The science must have a link to vocational activities and a concern for the practitioner. It should be the conceptual discipline that emerges from, interacts with, underlies, and supports professional activity. As Brian Vickery (2004, p. 29) wrote, "The theory of [information] science should spring from deep immersion in practice."

THEORY IN INFORMATION SCIENCE

I believe that information science itself is best regarded, in the typology of Paul Hirst, as a field of study, rather than a traditional discipline. More specifically it is best regarded as a multidisciplinary field of study, with its subject being all aspects of human recorded information (Bawden 2007). More specifically still, I believe that it is helpful, in setting the boundaries of what is still a wide and diverse area, to distinguish it by its focus on the information chain of recorded information (Robinson 2009). Necessarily, this means that it will overlap with other disciplines involved with aspects of the communication chain, such as computer science, publishing, psychology, and sociology (Bawden and Robinson 2012; Robinson 2009; Robinson and Bawden 2012).

If this viewpoint is accepted, it follows that it is unreasonable to expect there to be "a theory" of information science specifically, or of the information sciences more generally. Rather, there will be a range of theories, dealing with different aspects of the subject, and very probably deriving from theories in cognate disciplines. We may also expect theories at different levels of scale and specificity, dealing with emergent properties of information in different contexts (Robinson and Bawden 2013a).

There is considerable support for this viewpoint. Hjørland (1998) comments that it is difficult to give even one good example of an explicit theory in the information sciences. What we have are theories taken from other fields, and some "unconscious attitudes" guiding research and practice. As Davis and Shaw (2011; see chap. 14) point out, not only do the information sciences draw on many other disciplines for their theories, but such theories are generally limited to one particular aspect, context, technology, or function. In support of this idea, Pettigrew and McKechnie's (2001) analysis of over a thousand information science articles found that the majority of the theories mentioned had been brought in from other disciplines. Where theories from within the information sciences themselves were present, these were typically rather specific theories, such as models of information seeking, rather than broader theoretical perspectives, and some were simply mentions of concepts. Similarly, of the seventy-two theories of information behavior identified by Fisher, Edelez, and McKechnie (2005), most originated from outside the information sciences. Although there has been an increased emphasis on theory within the information sciences over recent years, the field still remains without a convincing theoretical foundation of its own (Bawden and Robinson 2012; chap. 3).

Case (2012), discussing theories of information-seeking and information-related behavior generally, notes that Reynolds (1971) identified four forms of theory for the social sciences:

1. A set of laws, that is, well-supported empirical generalizations
2. An interrelated set of definitions, axioms, and propositions
3. Descriptions of causal processes
4. Vague concepts, untested hypotheses, and prescriptions for good behavior

The first type is what I believed to be a proper theory, from my scientific background. The third, although as Case points out we cannot expect strict causal laws in the social sciences, covers the process models of information behavior that have been very popular over the years. The fourth is what all too often has passed for theory in the information sciences. I may even have been guilty of proposing such myself on occasions, though I did not, I hope, ever imply they were theories. The second covers the kind of theory that I found most congenial, and that I have been interested in developing.

I am primarily interested in developing ways of understanding information, and concepts related to information, in all the contexts in which it may appear. This necessitates incorporating insights from numerous disciplines and forms of knowledge. This, in turn, means that the kind of theories I am interested in developing are of a kind that would probably not be recognized as theories at all by my early mentors in the physical sciences. They are examples of what Gregor (2006), in the context of information systems research, denotes as "theories for explaining," though I would prefer to regard them as "theories for understanding."

SEEKING UNDERSTANDING

The typical dictionary definition of "understand" is to "comprehend" or to "grasp with the mind," and this commonsense meaning is clear. The term is used differently in academic theorizing, however, including the information sciences. Stock and Stock (2013), for example, associate it with hermeneutics and the philosophy of Gadamer and Heidegger.

My own approach is somewhat different. I have found particularly helpful the definition of understanding developed by the philosopher Jonathan Kvanvig, in which he distinguishes understanding from information, knowledge, and truth. He suggests that "understanding requires the grasping of explanatory and other coherence-making relationships in a large and comprehensive body of information. One can know many unrelated pieces of information, but understanding is achieved only when informational items are pieced together" (2003, p. 192). The object of understanding (that which is understood) is, for Kvanvig, constituted not as a number of single propositions, but rather as an "informational chunk." He refers to the grasping of the structure within this chunk as an "internal seeing or appreciating" (p. 198). This approach is able to cope with ambiguity, contradiction, missing information, and all the other messy features present in real-world information collections.

This is not inconsistent with the typical dictionary definition, but it goes beyond it. It emphasizes that in understanding we are (1) dealing with a large and complex set of information, (2) going beyond a simple ordering and enumerating of the contents of that set, and (3) gaining some holistic "grasp" of the contents of the set.

It also draws from David Deutsch's (1997) explanation of understanding, as distinct from knowing, describing, and predicting. He states that understanding is hard to define exactly, but it encompasses the inner working of things, why things are as they are and have coherence and elegance.

Finally, understanding seems to have something in common with Luciano Floridi's (2011, p. 288) view of knowledge, as distinct from information. "Knowledge and information are members of the same conceptual family. What the former enjoys and the latter lacks . . . is the web of mutual relations that allow one part of it to account for another. Shatter that, and you are left with a . . . list of bits of information that cannot help to make sense of the reality they seek to address." There is certainly a close link between understanding and knowledge. As Winograd and Flores (1986, p. 30) put it: "What we understand is based on what we know, and what we already know comes from being able to understand."

In seeking this kind of theoretical understanding for concepts in the information sciences, my approach has been to make use of methods for gaining understanding of a topic, concept, or issue of a body of recorded information. For most interesting topics there is a great amount of material available. These methods are mainly forms of systematic qualitative analysis and synthesis of information (for a fuller explanation, see Bawden 2012). These go well beyond the conventional "literature review"—although that will almost certainly be their starting point—in setting out to find, or to create, a structure or framework for understanding; and they may therefore count as theories in the sense discussed above. "Conceptual model" would be a reasonable alternative way of describing many theories of this kind. They also draw on ideas for the ways in which qualitative research findings may be synthesized, when the meta-analysis approach to quantitative findings is not appropriate (see, e.g., Barnett-Page and Thomas 2009). It is worth saying clearly that this is not an exercise in linguistics or analytic philosophy. We are not interested in the definition of terms, but in the relations among concepts. This position also has an undeniably subjective aspect. As Byers (2007, p. 26) puts it: "Understanding is a difficult thing to talk about. For one thing, it contains a subjective element, whereas drawing logical inferences appears to be an objective task that even sophisticated machines might be capable of making."

I have come to the view that this kind of deep understanding is essential for both research and practice in the information sciences. For research, it enables us to fully comprehend and relate to the concepts with which we deal. To those who argue that this is not really a theory in itself, we may say that it is perhaps a proto-theory, an essential basis, on which "true" theories can be developed. For practice, it reflects the need, in a world in which information on almost any topic may be found readily, for a deep and reflective understanding. It might be argued that the most popular current forms of information systems do little to support this.

Where relevant, such analyses have been augmented by empirical research, using established mixed-method approaches. Mixed methods are usually needed to capture the complexity of situations. And when this involves investigating some aspect of information behavior, I always advocate using, or extending, an established model rather than creating a new one. An example of this is provided by two of my colleagues, Robson and Robinson (2013).

I believe that one of the problems of the information sciences is the plethora of "novel" empirical methods and models, which make comparison and cumulative progress difficult. For a thoughtful analysis of this issue, see Case (2012; chap. 6). Wilson's (1999) well-known information behavior models, for example, are sometimes criticized on the grounds that they are simplistic, and ignore the subtleties and details of different contexts. The residual scientist in me always wishes to argue that this is, of course, correct, but that this is the whole point of a model of this sort—that it is simple and context free. Having a plethora of models for the same phenomenon, albeit in different contexts, rather defeats this purpose. If they are truly needed, understanding is probably lacking; and I would far rather begin by trying to create a general qualitative framework for such understanding than to create a specific and detailed new model. (One could, of course, designate such a qualitative framework as a model, but I do not think this is a helpful use of the term.)

EXAMPLES

Some examples of this kind of theory development may make this general description clearer.

One instance is the development of ideas relating to information paradoxes and problems—the downside to the information society and the ready availability of information in many environments. I first dealt with this when, having published some rather limited accounts of the phenomenon of information overload, I was asked to produce a more detailed literature analysis. The analysis proposed a framework for understanding what was meant by this term, "information overload" (which was rather overused at the time), its causes, and what might be done to minimize its effects (Bawden 2001b). I then went on, largely through the hard work of a doctoral student, to examine another "negative information phenomenon"—information poverty. Through literature analysis and synthesis, and discourse analysis, it could be shown that this concept was very malleable, and changed its meaning several times over the years (Haider and Bawden 2006, 2007). Any theory for understanding, and potentially preventing, information poverty has to take this into account, or it will be devoid of explanatory power, and far from useful.

These ideas were then enfolded into a more all-encompassing attempt to understand all of these information problems—what we termed the "dark side" of information—in one fell swoop (Bawden and Robinson 2009). This has in turn led to attempts by others to develop deep understanding of the ways in which such problems may be overcome. One such attempt is the work of my colleague, Lyn Robinson, with her doctoral student, Liz Poirier, in developing an understanding-providing theory of "Slow information behavior," applying the ideas of the Slow Movement in the context of the theory and practice of information seeking. Being "Slow" in information terms means taking purposeful action to create the space and time for making appropriate information choices for the context. It can assist a person's capacity to absorb information and use it more effectively, by creating an "informational balance." The initial empirical test of this theory used a novel method that was, appropriately enough, a Slow variant of the Delphi technique, unimaginatively termed "Slow Delphi" (Poirier and Robinson 2013).

Another topic that began quite separately, but ultimately linked with the former, is that of digital literacy. This began when I was personally perplexed by the multiplicity of "literacies" appearing in the library/information literature—information literacy, digital literacy, media literacy, computer literacy, Internet literacy, network literacy, library literacy, and so on. This led me to produce a literature-based analysis of the concepts (Bawden 2001a). Somewhat to my surprise, this remains one of the most frequently downloaded articles from the journal in which it was published. Subsequently, feeling that information literacy, as prescribed within the academic library community in particular, was a rather restrictive model, I developed Paul Gilster's concept of digital literacy into a very general model for understanding all information-related literacies at several levels (Bawden 2008a). This model was then related to the ideas developed for the "dark side" phenomena to try to provide an overall conceptual model that links cause with effect and with potential solution (Bawden and Robinson 2011a).

It is my experience that such links occur with regularity with theories of this kind. Perhaps this is not surprising; as we saw above, the whole nature of understanding in this sense involves the making of links.

As a third example, I wish to mention an analysis of the "Open Society" philosophy in the specific context of library and information services. The idea of the Open Society was advanced by Karl Popper (1966) in his best-known work of political philosophy, and was developed by the financier and philanthropist George Soros (2000) into an active program of supporting the development of civil society in former dictatorships and other closed societies. This program had, and still has, an important element of support for libraries, media, and information provision.

The theory development in this example involved the translation of Popper's principles of Open Society into the library/information context (Robinson and Bawden 2001a, 2001b). Although Popper's political philosophy seems far removed from his better-known work in the philosophy of science, both are based on his epistemology of objective knowledge, which Brookes—as noted above—regarded as a philosophical foundation for information science (Notturno 2000).

Further examples, mentioned without detailed comment, are the development of a conceptual framework for understanding the idea and scope of a digital library, at a time when the term was being used in varying and potentially misleading ways (Bawden and Rowlands 1999a, 1999b; Rowlands and Bawden 1999); a synthesis of ideas on "information styles," including a wide spectrum of findings and perspectives relating to individual differences and personality factors involved in information-related behavior (Bawden and Robinson 2011b); and further analyses of the topic of my first attempt at such theory development—information and creativity, the concept of browsing (1993a), and linking the ideas of serendipitous encountering of information with the browsing process (Bawden 2011b).

Recently, I have been interested in the idea of the "gaps" between conceptions of information in different domains, most particularly, what, if anything, the idea of information as an objective component of the physical world has to do with recorded human information (Bawden 2007; Bawden and Robinson 2013; Robinson and Bawden 2013b). The need for this kind of theory does not, as with the examples discussed above, arise directly from the concerns of practice, but success in this respect could have interesting and largely unanticipatable consequences for practice. It is a particularly challenging kind of problem, as it involves attempting to make connections between theories of many different kinds, from the mathematical explanatory and predictive theories of the physical sciences to those from philosophy and the human sciences. Whether such understanding will best be reached by "grand designs," linking concepts of information at various levels, as in Tom Stonier's (1990, 1992, 1997) conceptions of the linking of physical, biological, and social concepts of information, or as in Luciano Floridi's (2011) more recent philosophy of information, or by a series of smaller-scale integrative connections, each dealing with information at similar levels, remains to be seen.

CONCLUSIONS

Leonardo's well-known aphorism, rendered in English as "the noblest pleasure is the joy of understanding," suggests that understanding has a special virtue. It is a particularly good place to start in developing theory for a discipline like information science, which has long been recognized to be a meta-discipline, or a borrowing and integrating science (Bawden 2008b) (as has been shown by numerous bibliometric studies, most recently by Tsay [2013]). Such a science must necessarily draw many of its concepts from other disciplines and either take its theories from them or adapt from others. A deep understanding of the nature and interrelations of this mass of material, giving coherence and clarity, is the necessary beginning to other forms of theory, as well as valuable in its own right. In the longer term, we might hope that it could catalyze the reverse process—the generation of concepts and theories from the information sciences that would contribute to the theory base of other disciplines.

POSTSCRIPT

After the first draft of this chapter was completed, I read an article analyzing, from a historical and philosophical viewpoint, the aspect of theoretical organic chemistry that was the subject area for my undergraduate dissertation—and my only hands-on experience with research in the true scientific sense, with white coats, laboratory equipment, and chemicals. This article describes the controversy, lasting for several decades, over the existence of "non-classical ions," a concept derived as part of the theoretical study of reaction mechanisms (Goodwin 2013). It was somewhat chastening to find that something in which one was personally involved is now officially historical. But beyond this, Goodwin writes in an intriguing way of the kind of "soft theory" involved in this kind of physical organic chemistry:

> Theoretical explanations in this field are often produced after the fact to rationalize results, and . . . those explanations that are produced are frequently qualitative. . . . organic chemists have made a trade-off: they have de-emphasized quantitative prediction and unambiguous explanation for something much more useful, given their pragmatic goals—a theory that helps them make plausible . . . assessments of the chemical behavior of novel, complex compounds. (pp. 807, 809)

The similarity to the kind of research in the information sciences that I have advocated here seems striking. Perhaps there is, in fact, not so much difference between the nature of the different fields as I had supposed; complex situations and emergent properties need similar treatment in both cases. And perhaps I was more influenced by this first exposure to research than I realized; first influences are surprisingly long-lasting.

REFERENCES

Barnett-Page, E., and Thomas, J. (2009). Methods for the synthesis of qualitative research: A critical review. *BMC Medical Research Methodology*, 9(59). Retrieved from http://www.webcitation.org/5shAOY1P7.

Bawden, D. (1983). Computerized chemical structure handling techniques in structure-activity studies and molecular property prediction. *Journal of Chemical Information and Computer Sciences*, 23(1), 14–22.

Bawden, D. (1984). DISCLOSE—An integrated set of multivariate display procedures for chemical and pharmaceutical data. *Analytica Chimica Acta*, 158(2), 363–368.

Bawden, D. (1986). Information systems and the stimulation of creativity. *Journal of Information Science*, 12(5), 203–216. [Reprinted in R. L. Ruggles (Ed.), *Knowledge management tools* (pp. 79–101). Boston: Butterworth-Heinemann.]

Bawden, D. (1988). Browsing and clustering of chemical structures. In W. A. Warr (Ed.), *Chemical structures: The international language of chemistry* (pp. 145–150). Berlin: Springer.

Bawden, D. (1990). *User-oriented evaluation of information systems and services.* Aldershot, UK: Gower.

Bawden, D. (1993a). Browsing: Theory and practice. *Perspectives in Information Management,* 3(1), 71–85.

Bawden, D. (1993b). Molecular dissimilarity in chemical information systems. In W. A. Warr (Ed.), *Chemical structures 2* (pp. 383–388). Berlin: Springer.

Bawden, D. (2001a). Information and digital literacies: A review of concepts. *Journal of Documentation,* 57(2), 218–259.

Bawden, D. (2001b). *Information overload* (Library and Information Briefing Series). London: South Bank University, Library Information Technology Centre.

Bawden, D. (2002). The three worlds of health information. *Journal of Information Science,* 28(1), 51–62.

Bawden, D. (2007). Organised complexity, meaning and understanding: An approach to a unified view of information for information science. *Aslib Proceedings,* 59(4/5), 307–327.

Bawden, D. (2008a). Origins and concepts of digital literacy. In C. Lankshear and M. Knobel (Eds.), *Digital literacies: Concepts, policies and paradoxes* (pp. 17–32). New York: Peter Lang.

Bawden, D. (2008b). Smoother pebbles and the shoulders of giants: The developing foundations of information science. *Journal of Information Science,* 34(4), 415–426. [Reprinted with amendments in 2009 in A. Gilchrist (Ed.), *Information science in transition* (pp. 23–43). London: Facet.]

Bawden, D. (2010). Portrait of the author as a young information scientist [blog post]. *The Occasional Informationist.* Retrieved from http://theoccasional informationist.com/2010/04/07/portrait-of-the-author-as-a-young-information -scientist/.

Bawden, D. (2011a). Brookes equation: The basis for a qualitative characterisation of information behaviours. *Journal of Information Science,* 37(1), 101–108.

Bawden, D. (2011b). Encountering on the road to Serendip? Browsing in new information environments. In A. Foster and P. Rafferty (Eds.), *Innovations in IR: Perspectives for theory and practice* (pp. 1–22). London: Facet.

Bawden, D. (2012). On the gaining of understanding: Syntheses, themes and information analysis. *Library and Information Research,* 36(112), 147–162. Retrieved from http://www.lirgjournal.org.uk/lir/ojs/index.php/lir/article/view /483.

Bawden, D., and Brock, A. M. (1982). Chemical toxicology searching: A collaborative evaluation, comparing information resources and searching techniques. *Journal of Information Science,* 5(1), 3–18.

Bawden, D., Devon, T. K., Faulkner, D. T., Fisher, J. D., Leach, J. M., Reeves, R. J., and Woodward, F. E. (1988). Development of the Pfizer integrated research data system SOCRATES. In W. A. Warr (Ed.), *Chemical structures: The international language of chemistry* (pp. 61–75). Berlin: Springer.

Bawden, D., Gymer, G. E., Marriott, M. S., and Tute, M. S. (1983). Quantitative structure activity relationships in a group of imidazole anti-mycotic agents. *European Journal of Medicinal Chemistry,* 18(1), 91–96.

Bawden, D., and Robinson, L. (2009). The dark side of information: Overload, anxiety and other paradoxes and pathologies. *Journal of Information Science, 35*(2), 180–191.

Bawden, D., and Robinson, L. (2010). Pharmaceutical information: A 30-year perspective on the literature. *Annual Review of Information Science and Technology, 45*(1), 63–119.

Bawden, D., and Robinson, L. (2011a). Digital literacy and the dark side of information: Enlightening the paradox. In L. H. Stergioulas and H. Drenoyianni (Eds.), *Pursuing digital literacy in compulsory education* (pp. 47–58). New York: Peter Lang.

Bawden, D., and Robinson, L. (2011b). Individual differences in information-related behaviour: What do we know about information styles. In A. Spink and J. Heinström (Eds.), *New directions in information behavior* (pp. 282–300). Bingley, UK: Emerald.

Bawden, D., and Robinson, L. (2012). *Introduction to information science.* London: Facet.

Bawden, D., and Robinson, L. (2013). "Deep down things": In what ways is information physical, and why does it matter for LIS? *Information Research, 18*(3). Retrieved from http://www.informationr.net/ir/18-3/colis/paperC03.html#.Ur wrq_RDtXE.

Bawden, D., and Rowlands, I. (1999a). Digital libraries: Assumptions and concepts. *Libri, 49*(4), 181–191.

Bawden, D., and Rowlands, I. (1999b). Digital libraries: developing a conceptual framework. *New Review of Information Networking, 5,* 71–90.

Bawden, D., and Wood, S. (1986). Design, implementation and evaluation of the CONTRAST reaction retrieval system. In P. Willett (Ed.), *Modern approaches to chemical reaction searching* (pp. 78–86). Aldershot, UK: Gower.

Benson, M. T., and Willett, P. (2014). The Information School at the University of Sheffield, 1963–2013. *Journal of Documentation, 70*(6), 1141–1158.

Brookes, B. C. (1980). The foundations of information science, Part 1: Philosophical aspects. *Journal of Information Science, 2*(3–4), 125–133.

Byers, W. (2007). *How mathematicians think: Using ambiguity, contradiction and paradox to create mathematics.* Princeton, NJ: Princeton University Press.

Case, D. O. (2012). *Looking for information: A survey of research on information seeking, needs and behavior* (3rd ed.). Bingley, UK: Emerald.

Crum Brown, A. (1864). On the theory of isomeric compounds. *Transactions of the Royal Society of Edinburgh, 23,* 707–719. [Also published in 1865 as XXXVII—On the theory of isomeric compounds, *Journal of the Chemical Society, 18*(1), 230–245.]

Crum Brown, A. (1869). On chemical constitution and its relation to physical and physiological properties. *Philosophical Magazine, 37,* 395–400.

Davis, C. H., and Shaw, D. (Eds.). (2011). *Introduction to information science and technology.* Medford, NJ: Information Today.

Deutsch, D. (1997). *The fabric of reality.* London: Penguin.

Fisher, K. E., Erdelez, S., and McKechnie, L. (Eds.) (2005). *Theories of information behavior.* Medford, NJ: Information Today.

Floridi, L. (2011). *The philosophy of information.* Oxford: Oxford University Press.

Gatlin, L. L. (1972). *Information theory and the living system.* New York: Columbia University Press.

Goodwin, W. (2013). Sustaining a controversy: The non-classical ion debate. *British Journal for the Philosophy of Science, 64*(4), 787–816.

Gregor, S. (2006). The nature of theory in information systems. *MIS Quarterly, 30*(3), 611–624.

Haider, J., and Bawden, D. (2006). Pairing information with poverty: Traces of development discourse in LIS. *New Library World, 107*(1228–1229), 371–385.

Haider, J., and Bawden, D. (2007). Conceptions of "information poverty" in library and information science: A discourse analysis. *Journal of Documentation, 63*(4), 534–557.

Hjørland, B. (1998). Theory and metatheory of information science: A new interpretation. *Journal of Documentation, 54*(5), 606–621.

Hjørland, B. (2011). The periodic table and the philosophy of classification. *Knowledge Organization, 38*(1), 9–21.

Kvanvig, J. L. (2003). *The value of knowledge and the pursuit of understanding.* Cambridge: Cambridge University Press.

Notturno, M. A. (2000). *Science and the open society.* Budapest: Central European University Press.

Pettigrew, K. E., and McKechnie, L. (2001). The use of theory in information science research. *Journal of the American Society for Information Science and Technology, 52*(1), 62–74.

Poirier, E., and Robinson, L. (2013). Slow Delphi: An investigation into information behaviour and the Slow Movement. *Journal of Information Science.* doi: 10.1177/0165551513502417.

Popper, K. R. (1966). *The open society and its enemies* (5th ed.). London: Routlege and Kegan Paul.

Reynolds, P. D. (1971). *A primer in theory construction.* New York: Bobbs-Merrill.

Ritter, C. (2001). An early history of Alexander Crum Brown's graphical formulas. In U. Klein (Ed.), *Tools and modes of representation in the laboratory sciences* (pp. 35–46). Dordrecht: Kluwer.

Robinson, L. (2009). Information science: Communication chain and domain analysis. *Journal of Documentation, 65*(4), 578–591.

Robinson, L., and Bawden, D. (2001a). Libraries and open society: Popper, Soros and digital information. *Aslib Proceedings, 53*(5), 167–178.

Robinson, L., and Bawden, D. (2001b). Libraries, information and knowledge in open societies. *Nordinfonytt, 2,* 21–30.

Robinson, L., and Bawden, D. (2012). Brian Vickery and the foundations of information science. In A. Gilchrist and J. Vernau (Eds.), *Facets of knowledge organization* (pp. 282–300). Bingley, UK: Emerald.

Robinson, L., and Bawden, D. (2013a). Mind the gap: Transitions between concepts of information in varied domains. In F. Ibekwe-SanJuan and T. Dousa (Eds.), *Theories of information, communication and knowledge* (pp. 121–142). Berlin: Springer.

Robinson, L., and Bawden, D. (2013b). "So wide and varied": The origins and character of British information science. *Journal of Information Science, 39*(6), 754–763.

Robson, A., and Robinson, L. (2013). Building on models of information behaviour: Linking information seeking and communication. *Journal of Documentation, 69*(2), 169–193.

Rouvray, D. H. (1977). The changing role of the symbol in the evolution of chemical notation. *Endeavour, 1*(1), 23–31.

Rouvray, D. H. (Ed.). (1997). *Concepts in chemistry: A contemporary challenge.* Taunton, UK: Research Studies Press.

Rowlands, I., and Bawden, D. (1999). Digital libraries: A conceptual framework. *Libri, 49*(4), 192–202.

Scerri, E. R. (2011). *The periodic table: A very short introduction.* Oxford: Oxford University Press.

Soros, G. (2000). *Open society.* London: Little, Brown.

Stock, W. G., and Stock, M. (2013). *Handbook of information science.* Berlin: de Gruyter.

Stonier, T. (1990). *Information and the internal structure of the universe.* Berlin: Springer.

Stonier, T. (1992). *Beyond information: The natural history of intelligence.* Berlin: Springer.

Stonier, T. (1997). *Information and meaning: An evolutionary perspective.* Berlin: Springer.

Trabocchi, A. (Ed.) (2013). *Diversity-oriented synthesis: Basics and applications in organic synthesis, drug discovery, and chemical biology.* New York: Wiley.

Tsay, M. (2013). Knowledge input for the domain of information science: A bibliometrics citation analysis study. *Aslib Proceedings, 65*(2), 203–220.

Vickery, B. C. (2004). A long search for information. Occasional Papers, No. 213, University of Illinois at Urbana-Champaign, Graduate School of Library and Information Science. [Reprinted in 2012 in A. Gilchrist and J. Vernau (Eds.), *Facets of knowledge organization* (pp. 145–174). Bingley, UK: Emerald.]

Wade, S. J., Willett, P., and Bawden, D. (1989). SIBRIS: The sandwich interactive browsing and ranking information system. *Journal of Information Science, 15*(4/5), 249–260.

Warr, W. A. (1997). Combinatorial chemistry and molecular diversity: An overview. *Journal of Chemical Information and Computer Sciences, 37*(1), 134–140.

Willett, P. (2008). From chemical documentation to chemoinformatics: Fifty years of chemical information science. *Journal of Information Science, 34*(4), 477–499.

Wilson, T. D. (1999). Models in information behaviour research. *Journal of Documentation, 55*(3), 249–270.

Winograd, T., and Flores, F. (1986). *Understanding computers and cognition: A new foundation for design.* Norwood, NJ: Ablex.

CHAPTER 16

APOLOGIA PRO THEORIA SUA

JACK MEADOWS

IN THE FIRST PART OF MY CAREER, I was in charge of an astronomy department, and then of a history of science department. The contrast between their research activities led me to explore not only the role and nature of theory in the two, but also the differences in the methodologies they adopted. It was obvious from the start that practitioners in either department might well look at the other and say—their ways are not our ways. Having worked out—to some extent—the difference between the mind-sets of researchers in the sciences and those in the humanities, I then took charge of a department of information science and library studies, and had to start all over again. Library studies, though certainly overlapping with the information sciences, seemed to me to require a separate investigation. Since my own concerns related more to information, I concentrated primarily on this. An immediately obvious problem was that the information sciences are heterogeneous in terms of both subject matter and approach. At one extreme, some practitioners work within a science-like picture; at the other, they work within a humanities-like picture. The majority, however, operate within some kind of social science environment. Consequently, I was forced to think about theory and methodology in the social sciences, and especially in sociology and psychology. This chapter recounts what I found useful for my own research activities from these forays.

THE BACKGROUND

NAVIGATING DIFFERENT THEORETICAL TRADITIONS

Astronomy and history of science have contrasting theoretical frameworks. Postgraduate students usually learn how their subject works by osmosis: it forms an integral part of their environment. As Rudyard Kipling said in another context: "Obliquely and by inference, illumination comes" (1994, p. 557). But experiencing two different environments—one science based, the other humanities based—naturally led me to look more closely at the theoretical frameworks within which each of these fields operated. Consequently, my interest in theory has always had a comparative element. The basic questions that interested me have been as follows: What is meant by "theory" in each subject field? How are theories applied in these different fields?

When I moved into the information sciences, the obvious thing to do was to ask these questions about my new research activity. As a background to this, let me outline briefly how I saw my original research fields of astronomy and the history of science.

There is a proviso here. As I soon learned via contacts with colleagues on the European continent, we in the English-speaking world draw firmer boundaries between the natural sciences, the social sciences, and the humanities than is customary there. I remember, for example, from the dim and distant past that what was originally called the Social Science Research Council in the United Kingdom had to change its name to the Economic and Social Research Council. The reason was that an influential politician of the day decreed that subjects such as sociology were not scientific. These stronger demarcation lines may, in turn, have influenced how I look at theoretical frameworks in the different disciplines. In any case, I think it may be best to start with the ideas I had relating to theory before I entered the information sciences.

I shall begin here, as I did in my career, with the natural sciences. In science, the word "theory" is usually applied to a set of principles that satisfactorily explain some particular aspect of the universe. Thus Einstein's gravitational theory provides a satisfactory explanation of how the various objects making up the universe move. Such a theory is expected not only to explain existing knowledge, but also to make predictions that will reveal new knowledge. In addition, the theory has to be progressive in the sense that a new theory must be able to explain all that the previous theory explained, plus some more. For example, Einstein's theory of gravitation can explain everything that its predecessor—Newton's theory—could explain, plus some extra. Indeed, science itself is expected to be progressive in the sense that theory should lead on to new observations that should then lead on to new theory, and so on. One further point—scientists are particularly concerned with quantitative data, which means that they typically employ mathematics in their work. They might not say, as Galileo did, that "mathematics is the language with which God has written the universe," but most would agree with that sentiment.

So much for the view of the average scientist down the years. But there is a stage beyond talking about specific scientific theories, and that is exploring metatheory. *What can be theorized about the scientific theories themselves?*

In my early days, the big debate about scientific theories centered on Karl Popper's (1959) concept of falsifiability. His idea was that you can never prove a theory totally because new observations can always arise to cast doubt on it. You can, however, disprove a theory totally by finding evidence that it fails to explain. A truly scientific theory is therefore one that is capable of being disproved. For him, a field such as psychoanalysis was not scientific because the basic principles on which its practitioners worked could not be disproved. I found this analysis useful, as did colleagues who were interested in the nature of theory. (Most of my science colleagues, however, were not interested in the philosophy of science—they were too busy doing science. As a contributor to one conference remarked: "Philosophers think and don't get anywhere; natural scientists don't think and get somewhere" [Machlup 1980, p. 74].)

I mentioned "the early days": for me, this means the 1960s and 1970s. The English translation of Popper's work—*The Logic of Scientific Discovery*—was published in 1959. Another work that influenced me appeared in 1962—Thomas Kuhn's *The Structure of Scientific Revolutions*. Kuhn suggested that, for most of their time, scientists were involved in "normal science": that is, they had an agreed theoretical framework within which they operated as they tried to solve problems. He referred to this as their paradigm. He argued that any such framework would ultimately prove inadequate, and researchers would then have to make a "paradigm shift" to a new paradigm. Having been trained as a physicist, Kuhn naturally cited the move from the worldview of Newton to the worldview of Einstein as a classic example of what he was talking about. Kuhn's ideas were greeted eagerly by some and came in for massive criticism from others.

For me, more parochially, both his work and Popper's underlined the point that I was especially interested in—the differences between different disciplines. Popper explicitly used his approach to distinguish science from nonscience, but the distinction was also there in Kuhn's work. The idea of one paradigm sweeping away another really works only in the sciences. In the humanities, introducing a new paradigm rarely extinguishes an existing paradigm completely. Instead it may nudge it sideways, so that the two coexist.

This led me to the question of the role of theory in the humanities—more specifically, in history (of which the history of science is a small subsection). The debate about this goes back a very long way, but, by the 1960s, three strands could be distinguished (Goldstein 1967). The first strand supposed that generalizations could be made that were applicable to a range of historical happenings. The second was that no such generalizations could be found: each historical event was sui generis. The third strand—a minority view, but one pressed by Popper—was that generalizations existed, but were too trivial to be useful in practice.

A further question concerned the level at which generalizations could be made. For example, economic and social historians often look at the same historical events, but formulate their explanations of these events in different terms. Is there a higher-level generalization that covers both their viewpoints? The discussion of such high-level generalizations was especially lively at the time because of Arnold Toynbee's *A Study of History*, the final volume of which was published in 1961. His aim was to set out a comprehensive model capable of explaining the growth and decay of all the major world civilizations. Needless to say, this generated considerable debate.

ELABORATING A THEORETICAL APPROACH FOR MY RESEARCH ON THE HISTORY OF SCIENCE

I first became involved in the history of science in the mid-1960s. (I started my research career in astronomy at the end of the 1950s.) The 1960s proved to be a particularly interesting time in the history of science, for it was then that discussions of the appropriate theoretical framework for research into the history of science really heated up. This was primarily a debate between two opposing viewpoints— the "internalists" and the "externalists." Internalists believed that the development of scientific ideas depended on the internal logic of the subject. Science was the same everywhere, regardless of the research environment in which it found itself. Externalists believed that the way science developed depended on the social, political, and economic environment in which it appeared. In essence, both sides adhered to the first strand I mentioned above: they both believed that valid historical generalizations could be made.

The internalist approach was much more common up to the 1960s. It tied in with the way that scientists themselves saw their discipline. The externalist approach was stimulated originally by Marxist thinking. J. D. Bernal, a leading scientist and Marxist of the time, was particularly widely quoted. In the 1950s, he published *Science in History*, a four-volume work written from a Marxist viewpoint (Bernal 1954). (I should, perhaps, add that I have been lucky enough to meet, or at least correspond with, many of the people I mention in this chapter—but not always in connection with information science. In Bernal's case, our meeting was due to a mutual interest in the study of meteorites.) Bernal's (1967) best-known book, *The Social Function of Science*, was not primarily concerned with history. It appeared first before the Second World War, but was reprinted as a paperback in the 1960s, and so became a part of the general debate in that decade. The important thing for me was that Bernal used the book to put forward a range of innovative—if not always practical—ideas about the communication of science, which was one of my growing interests. I was not the only person who was interested in Bernal's ideas. Both Derek Price and Gene Garfield were influenced by the book. (Gene Garfield started publishing the *Science Citation Index* at the beginning of the 1960s.)

At the same time that I was learning about Bernal's ideas, I also encountered Robert Merton's (1938) early work on the history of science. Like Bernal's book, Merton's article was published just before the Second World War. The early 1930s had seen the appearance of an influential Marxist analysis of science in seventeenth-century England that asserted the prime importance of economic factors. Merton opposed this as oversimplified. He demonstrated that the popularity of science in England during the seventeenth century could be explained just as well in terms of a correlation between scientific values and Protestantism.

My reaction to this debate was one shared by a number of colleagues. I believed that historians of science could learn something from both approaches, with the exact mixture depending on which scientific event or activity was under the microscope. Such mixing together of theoretical frameworks does not normally occur in science, though there are occasional exceptions. For example, Sir Lawrence Bragg once commented: "God runs electromagnetics on Monday, Wednesday, and Friday by the wave theory, and the devil runs it by quantum theory on Tuesday, Thursday, and Saturday" (quoted in Kevles 1978, p. 159).

Predictably—since we are talking about science—the two approaches were subsequently recognized as being different formulations of the same basic theory. This sort of reconciliation is obviously different from the selective use of two different historical frameworks. In the latter case, the mixture is contingent on the circumstances of the particular events being investigated. More to the point, this attitude effectively denies that either an internalist or an externalist approach can actually provide a comprehensive theory.

So I found myself in a midway position: dubious about universal theories, but believing that theory did have a part to play in historical research. When in later years I came to write about the history of libraries and information work in the UK, it proved natural to couch this primarily in terms of the institutions involved. Their role could best be seen as resulting from the interplay between the activities of information professionals (which might be termed the internalist side) and external pressures. This was my background when I started to investigate the information sciences.

AND SO TO THE INFORMATION SCIENCES

ELABORATING THE ROLE OF THEORY IN THE INFORMATION SCIENCES

When I embarked on research in the information sciences, the first thing that struck me was how broad this field of research was. At one extreme, the foundational theories were science related; at the other extreme, they were humanities related. But the bulk of the information sciences seemed to fall within the scope of the social sciences. (There has been an interesting, if rather sad, illustration of this in my own university, which recently reorganized itself, a process that included breaking up the Department of Information Science. Some staff members have gone to schools in the natural sciences, and some to schools in the humanities, but most have gone to one in the social sciences.)

So my first task was to think about the role of theory in the social sciences. My own interest in the communication of research was most closely related to sociology in terms of approach. Consequently I skimmed through a variety of writings on sociological theory, looking for enlightenment. The comments I found most useful were provided by someone whose name I already knew—Robert Merton. One chapter of his major publication, *Social Theory and Social Structure* (1968), seemed especially relevant to me. "On Sociological Theories of the Middle Range" summarizes this approach in the following words: "Middle-range theory is principally used in sociology to guide empirical inquiry. It is intermediate to general theories of social systems which are too remote from particular classes of social behaviour, organization and change to account for what is observed and to those detailed orderly descriptions of particulars that are not generalized at all" (p. 41).

Here, I will insert a comment about information research as I found it when I entered the field. Much of it was (and still is) highly empirical. Many practitioners were more concerned with methodology than with theory. In other words, they were concerned with what methods of investigation (e.g., questionnaire, interview) and data analysis should be used for a specific project, rather than with anything more elaborate. Their investigations were what Merton labels "detailed orderly descriptions," and were usually perfectly adequate for the sort of projects to which they were applied.

Merton, like many sociologists who have looked at science, took a basically structural-functionalist approach. That is to say, he saw society as a complex system, but one where the various components worked together to try to promote stability. This concept has a long history. In the nineteenth century, one of the founding fathers of sociology, Herbert Spencer, emphasized the analogy between society and the human body, where the various organs work together to ensure the proper functioning of the whole. This model has the further implication that the system will try to oppose any dysfunctional change. (It is rather like Le Chatelier's principle in chemistry: if changes are made to a chemical system in equilibrium, then the equilibrium shifts to try to counteract the changes.) Merton, however, was rather more subtle than most of his predecessors. He believed, for example, that dysfunctional elements could persist in stable systems, and as noted above, he believed that theories should not be too ambitious.

EMPLOYING MODELS IN THEORY DEVELOPMENT

I realize that I have used the word "model" without definition. Philosophers have, in fact, long debated about what constitutes a model, and how models fit into the activity of research. My own use of the term typically means a mental picture that can guide the research questions to be asked. Price's image of the "research front" is one example. Another is the information chain, which can be pictured as a network through which information flows.

I myself have always enjoyed postulating a model of the information chain based on a sewage system, with the information flowing like sewage from various points of origin, via pumping stations, to the sewage works. Such a model stimulates new queries. What happens, for example, if a new community appears and its effluent is suddenly added to the existing network? (As Tom Lehrer remarked about sewage in another context—what you get out of it depends on what you put in.)

Models—as in the foregoing case—often take the form of analogies. This is true in both science and social science. For example, "electric current" is a model originally based on the analogy of a current of water flowing through a pipe. The 1960s were a time when there was considerable discussion of models and analogies. Mary Hesse (1963) published a book devoted to this topic that I found helpful.

Let me give another example of a model based on analogy. I have spent much time through the years looking at old journals and examining how they have been organized and presented. The analogy I like here is to compare this activity with the work of an archaeologist. The archaeologist uncovers a sequence of artifacts the examination of which provides information on the culture producing them. Journals can likewise be considered as artifacts: one can look at them as objects, rather than as depositories of information. A study of changes with time may similarly cast light on the development of our modern research culture. Like many objects, journals are made up of parts—in this case, articles—which can be further split up into subcomponents (such as title, author, author affiliation, and so on). One can ask questions about articles as a whole (e.g., has their average length changed with time) and also about their subcomponents (e.g., when did abstracts first appear at the beginning of articles). As with archaeology, this leads to questions of why the changes occurred. A colleague of mine analyzed the *Philosophical Transactions of the Royal Society* in these terms (Katzen 1980). (The *Philosophical Transactions of the Royal Society* is especially useful for this purpose because it has been produced continuously from the mid-seventeenth century to the present day by a single institution.)

INVESTIGATING THE RESEARCH PUBLICATION SYSTEM

This brings me to a topic that has taken up much of my time in the information sciences—the study of the research publication system. The points mentioned above have evidently influenced the way I have investigated this.

Information systems, including the research publication system, can be pictured as networks containing a number of nodes. On this model, the network carries information between the nodes, which represent places where information is generated, distributed, stored, or accessed. For publishing, the information flow is often envisaged as unidirectional, from producer at one end to receiver at the other. Research information—my main concern—has the additional refinement that the receivers of information are also often the producers, so the information flow for them is actually a closed loop.

I started my research career in a print environment. In such a system, the basic nodes can be labeled—authors, publishers, libraries, and readers. In terms of the Mertonian approach I adopted, a number of research questions emerged: How stable is the system, and how is that stability maintained? Are there dysfunctional elements? Can general questions be asked about the whole system, or is it better to examine each node independently? And so on.

When examined in detail, the system becomes appreciably more complex. Back in the 1960s, a long and detailed series of studies were made of the communication of research among psychologists in the United States. The results were summarized as an information network containing twenty-three nodes (Garvey 1979). In terms of this network model, information scientists have traditionally concentrated their interest mainly on the end part—libraries (or information centers, etc.) and readers. However, it seemed to me when I started in the field that more attention should be paid to the early part of the chain, particularly the publishers. After all, it is possible to imagine a journal with no readers, but much more difficult to think of readers with no journal. Let me turn to a specific example.

One of the important functions of a publisher of research material is quality control. Researchers need to be reasonably confident that they can rely on what they read. Thus confidence in the control of quality is important for the stability of the information system. This is reflected by John Ziman's (1968, p. 111) often quoted assertion: "The referee is the lynchpin about which the whole business of science is pivoted." (When I subsequently came to know John, I told him that I thought this overstated the case, but it is certainly a common belief in the scientific community.) Yet there are potential conflicts. Some apply to the publishing function—for example, that referees are not paid for their work. Others apply to the research function—for example, the influence of the research field on the way new research findings are assessed. Thus when looked at from another viewpoint, referees are gatekeepers of information.

When I started studying publishing, gatekeeper theory had mostly been developed in the context of the mass media (it has diversified since then). One of its basic claims was that gatekeeping typically engendered conflict. So, at the most general level, a theoretical picture of quality control would envisage it as a stable system, but with a range of dysfunctional possibilities, which might lead to conflict. The flow of information in this context is a closed loop—author to editor; editor to referees; referees to editor; editor to author. Researchers have a great need to publish their work, so the potential for conflict seemed considerable. Hence, one of the interesting questions was the level of tension at each step in the quality control loop, along with how well the system accommodated such tensions.

The first major investigation of quality control in which I was involved covered a single subject area. I was fortunate enough to be given access to the refereeing reports of a major scientific society in the UK. The main results expected from the study were statistical. For example, submitted articles were sent out to two referees, and it was clearly important to determine the level of agreement that existed between them. A high level of disagreement might well affect the stability of the system. Other data cast light on tensions in the system without being reducible to statistics. For example, it became evident that research groups could sometimes be at loggerheads, and that this might affect their refereeing of each other's work for publication. This did not actually impede progress, because science is an international activity, and the groups could publish in overseas journals. It was evident that the existence of other possible publishing outlets acted as a safety valve diminishing tension: an article refused by one journal could readily be submitted to another, not necessarily of lower prestige.

My colleagues and I subsequently looked at quality control in other fields. One of the things we found was that the stereotypical picture of refereeing was incomplete. Authors tend to see refereeing as an accept/reject activity. In fact, it is more often a mechanism for improving the quality of submitted articles.

There are, however, differences between research fields. We knew from earlier studies by others, for example, that rejection rates were lower in the sciences and higher in the humanities. This we confirmed; but also, by interviewing editors, we showed there was a correlation with editorial attitude. In the sciences, if an article was technically correct and included something new, it was regarded as acceptable. In the humanities, an article needed to be seen as a significant new contribution in order to be accepted. (This difference was attributable, at least in part, to the economics of scholarly publishing, and that required a separate investigation.)

Studies of such scholarly activities as refereeing typically produce empirical data that are subjected to statistical analysis. My initial incursion into the research publication system actually related to a more fundamental question: can scholarly communication itself be described in statistical terms? (I put the discussion here, rather than earlier, because the work required a different kind of theoretical background.)

Back in the 1960s, I came across a newly published book by Derek de Solla Price (1963) called *Little Science, Big Science*. He asks in the preface: "Why should we not turn the tools of science on science itself? Why not measure and generalize, make hypotheses, and derive conclusions?" (p. vii). This sort of question appealed to me immediately, and I have been interested in what is nowadays commonly called scientometrics ever since. Derek's most quoted conclusion related to the growth of scientific literature; this he said had been closely exponential from the seventeenth century up to the 1950s. His claim raised a range of questions. One related to the references that scientists made to other people's research.

The growth of the scientific literature meant that there was more recent material available to quote than older material. So the publications cited by an article should be predominantly recent. My analysis of citations confirmed that this was the case, but raised a further question: were citations strictly in proportion to the literature growth rate? Derek's model of the research process envisaged a "research front" in which new research information was digested, after which it was absorbed into the general research archive. This model suggested that recent literature—the research currently being digested—might be overcited relative to older material. My first piece of work on communication looked at this possibility and confirmed that there was such an "immediacy effect" (Meadows 1967). It therefore provided some backing for Derek's model.

Other statistical laws to which Derek drew attention led to extensions of the model. For example, Lotka's law shows that most researchers produce only a limited number of publications, while a few produce a large number. This raised a variety of questions: When does the difference establish itself? Do authors with many articles to their name build up to a peak, or are they more productive than most of their peers from the start? My colleagues and I carried out a longitudinal study of a group of researchers and their publications. The results were clear: authors with many articles are more productive than most of their peers from the start (Zhu, Meadows, and Mason 1991).

ADDRESSING NEW CHALLENGES IN THE DIGITAL WORLD

Derek Price's work drew my attention to a problem that was already exercising librarians. The continuing growth in the number of research articles being published was raising major problems for the handling and storage of journals in libraries. Extrapolation suggested that by sometime in the present century, everyone in the world would be producing research articles. This seemed unlikely—so when might the flood of research articles be expected to flatten off?

I became interested in a rather different question in the 1970s: to what extent could the existing system of handling journals cope with the expected increase over the next few decades? It was becoming clear by this time that computers and electronic networks were going to play an increasing part in circulating research information. But how would they fit in, and what would be the problems? This was, in essence, a query about innovation in an organizational environment.

With the then existing paper-based information chain, the main organizations involved in research journals—though they were not the only ones—were universities, publishers, and libraries. (A few of the publishers and many of the libraries were also associated with universities.) Much has been written about communication within and between institutions. Even the particular point that concerned me—innovation in organizational communication—has been written about extensively.

It is customary to distinguish between innovation that primarily affects the organization and innovation that primarily affects the individual. For example, if a learned-society publisher contracts with a commercial publisher to produce its publications, this will affect the operations of the society, but will probably have relatively little direct impact on its members. If, however, the journal editor decides to change what type of article is acceptable for publication, this will have little direct impact on the operations of the society, but considerable impact on the individual member. Models of innovation typically see it as a time-dependent process that proceeds in steps, with feedback at each stage. Acceptance of an innovation is hypothesized to follow an S-shaped curve, with slow initial acceptance, then a rapid increase, leaving a small group who accept only slowly.

My main interest lay in scholarly journals, where the most important question regarding innovation appeared to be, how could journals move from being entirely paper based to entirely electronic? Many studies of the acceptance of innovations are retrospective. My attempt to study electronic journals would be prospective.

When I became interested in the question in the early 1980s, full-scale implementation of electronic journals was some distance in the future. The prime question at the time seemed to be, what were the main obstacles to such a transition? As with other innovations, such obstacles could occur at both the individual and the institutional level. When I moved to Loughborough University in the 1980s, they had a strong human-computer interaction (HCI) research center with an early interest in the electronic journal. This helped me decide to concentrate on problems at the individual level. That decision, in turn, led me to an examination of the theoretical approaches used in HCI research.

HCI was a rapidly developing field in the 1980s; some theoretical approaches already existed, and new ones were being created. One popular approach formulated during the 1980s was the GOMS model (goals: what the user wants; operators: actions to reach that goal; methods: the sequence of these actions; selection: the methods actually chosen by the user) (Card, Moran, and Newell 1983). I found this model helpful, though in an unusual way: it drew my attention to facets of journal usage that could not easily be treated via this approach.

There are two main ways to extract information from journals—directed reading and browsing. In the former, the reader knows the specific topic about which information is required, and may even know which articles are relevant. In the latter, the reader scans the journal to see if there is anything unexpected that is of interest. (I can remember in my early days of working with librarians finding it hard to convince them that browsing was an important way of collecting information. They were prepared to accept that it might sometimes be important in the humanities, but the sciences were, they thought, another matter.)

Now take these two ways of reading back to the GOMS model. Directed reading fits in well, and the model can be used as a peg on which to hang studies of the usage of printed and electronic journals. Browsing is another matter, for it is not clear how to define a goal—"looking for interesting information" is hardly adequate.

It proved illuminating, as a first step, to compare the two activities in terms of the paper-based journal. In directed reading, the researcher would find the appropriate article, look at key items, such as the abstract, and, if satisfied that the article was important, read it sequentially. In browsing, the researcher would pick up the journal and flip through—sometimes from front to back, sometimes vice versa—stopping at any item that caught the eye. Reading from printed material is essentially three-dimensional. Along with the two dimensions of the journal page, there is the further dimension of the thickness of the issue. In contrast, reading from a computer screen is essentially two-dimensional. The implication I took from this was that directed reading would work well with electronic journals, but browsing would be more difficult. This proved to be the case, and the problem has still not been entirely resolved today.

Examining how researchers interact with journals involves input of information from a number of specialisms. One, for example, is the study of the legibility of text both in print and on-screen. There is a considerable background to this in terms of theories of perception, and the relevant results have been encapsulated in a series of rules for practical use. (They have to be used with some caution, since experimental investigations of legibility have sometimes produced conflicting results. Hence, one has to have some idea of the background to the rules.)

One of the interesting points about articles in printed journals, when I looked at them in detail, was that they were not necessarily designed for optimum reading. For example, as noted above, my colleagues and I spent some time looking at how researchers read articles. The majority read the abstract first. This suggests that the abstract ought to be the most easily discernible part of the article. In fact, it was often the least legible part. I was for some years involved in the annual awarding of prizes for the best-designed journals. By insisting that awards would only be given to journals with easily legible abstracts, I think my cojudges and I helped move practice in this respect.

MAKING COMPARISONS TO DEVELOP THEORY

When I moved into information research, I found that many of my research students and fellows came from overseas, mostly from countries that have traditionally been labeled "developing." (In fact, a number of the people who have worked with me came from Brazil, India, and China, which are now often promoted to the status of "newly industrialized countries," or NICs.) Their prime interest was in how the burgeoning forms of electronic communication would affect institutions in their own countries. I usually suggested that they carry out a parallel study—comparing what was happening in their own country with what was happening in the UK. This proved particularly helpful in terms of identifying specific problems in their own country that might not have been evident had that country been examined in isolation. For example, one common point that emerged from several of these studies was the high level of reader assistance provided by librarians in the UK as compared with most of the other countries examined.

Such studies were latitudinal—valid at a particular point in time, or, at least, within the three-year period typically required for a doctorate (or the often shorter span of a research fellowship). One partial exception was the work of a research student from Kuwait. He carried out a preliminary study in Kuwait, then returned to the UK to carry out a parallel study. At this point, Iraq invaded Kuwait. The invasion only lasted for six months, and he was able to return to Kuwait to carry out a repeat of his original study. His "before and after" study was of some use in the postwar reconstruction of information activities in his country.

These various studies were helpful also in keeping an eye on changes in the UK. Putting the results from UK comparisons together provided some insight into the way electronic communication was evolving in the UK.

In terms of comparisons, my particular interest was in looking at the factors affecting change in communication in different disciplines. The basic theoretical framework I had in mind here was that each discipline was constrained by a set of factors that affected the way in which researchers communicated.

With the advent of electronic communication, some of these constraints altered, affecting the way electronic information handling was accepted. For example, studies my colleagues and I carried out when print was the dominant medium showed that journal publishing in the humanities was much more constrained by finances than journal publishing in the sciences. Most humanities journals are relatively small-scale affairs; it could be predicted that electronic publishing would be financially favorable for such journals.

An examination of the first electronic journals showed, indeed, that researchers in the humanities were early users, even though for many years they had lagged behind scientists in their usage of computers. Electronic communication tends to be more flexible and informal than paper-based communication. This often fits in well with the approach taken by humanities researchers.

AND SO IN SUMMARY

As the examples I have mentioned show, a good percentage of my projects have led to quantitative results. I have usually tried to supplement these by obtaining qualitative information. Thus most of my research students have complemented questionnaire surveys by carrying out interviews. The problem with qualitative research is that it has evoked a considerable range of theories, some of which cannot easily be reconciled with quantitative research. One that I have sometimes found useful is "grounded theory" (Glaser and Strauss 1967). This takes an essentially Baconian approach, collecting information in the hope of finding a pattern. As such, it fits quite well with parallel quantitative studies.

Much of the foregoing discussion has mentioned the differences of approach between the natural sciences, social sciences, and humanities. It is only fair to add that there are also many similarities. Whichever field I was working in, my prime concern on any specific project would more often be with the methodology to be applied than with the underlying theory. In information work, for example, it can happen that obtaining an answer in time is more important than being totally precise. One has to choose the appropriate approach for such "quick-and-dirty" projects—as a friend of mine called them—in terms of the methodologies available. Similarly, even scientists are likely to rely on middle-range theory when engaged in a specific project. A chemist carrying out a chemical analysis will no doubt accept the validity of Einstein's general relativity theory, but it has no bearing on the task he or she has immediately at hand.

The way research progresses can also have similarities across disciplines. For example, I have long envisaged research as having similarities to the activities of the Keystone Kops in the early silent movies. They were notorious for jumping on and falling off moving vehicles. I think of researchers in a particular discipline as digging their various gardens until a bandwagon appears round the corner. A considerable number of the gardeners jump aboard and tour round happily until the bandwagon hits an obstacle. At that point several fall off, dust themselves off, and return to their gardens until the next bandwagon appears. I would argue that this picture applies to more or less any discipline.

One more point: I have talked airily of the differences between disciplines, but there are equally differences within disciplines. Take, for example, literary studies—a major research field in the humanities. Some scholars are concerned with textual analysis, looking at such things as variations in text from one edition to another, or exploring what a particular word meant at the time it was written down. This kind of activity has much in common with the sort of classificatory work found in several sciences. Other scholars criticize the text in terms of one of a number of wide-ranging theories. Not only does this activity have little to parallel it in science, but some approaches may well be antiscientific (as, for example, with postmodernism).

Which brings us back to the information sciences, for they, too, have their various facets. Thus information retrieval theory is basically mathematical, scientometrics is basically statistical, HCI is basically psychological, and so on. Couched in these terms, it sounds as if the information sciences were a ragbag of theories derived from other disciplines. But this should be no surprise: it is characteristic of an applied field, which is what information sciences traditionally have been. A similar criticism might be made of engineering, for example. Nor is it unusual for different parts of a subject to develop in relative isolation. Even in physics, theories of heat and light developed independently for many years.

The question is whether the information sciences have an overarching concept that links all its components together. It might seem that the obvious answer is "yes"—it is information. However, this raises problems.

In science, terms are quite carefully defined, even when they have a wider meaning in general conversation. For example, "energy" has a specific meaning in science, though it is used more vaguely in general discussion. But "information" is difficult to define in a precise way. This is hardly surprising since it appears in the discourses of all disciplines—natural sciences, social sciences, and humanities.

A glance at the *Oxford English Dictionary* quickly confirms what a slippery word "information" is. (I came to think that information science students were not perhaps sufficiently alerted to the problem of terminological inexactitude—to misapply Winston Churchill's delightful phrase. So I pointed it out in a short book I wrote at the end of my teaching career [Meadows 2001].)

Thinking about the matter a quarter of a century ago, I came to the conclusion that the basic subject matter of the information sciences was actually human communication, rather than information (Meadows 1990). Looking back over the various items of research I have discussed here, it does seem that, for me at least, a "human communication" designation covers reasonably well the various bits of theory I have used.

REFERENCES

Bernal, J. D. (1954). *Science in history*. London: Faber and Faber.

Bernal, J. D. (1967). *The social function of science*. Cambridge, MA: MIT Press.

Card, S. K., Moran, T. P., and Newell, A. (1983). *The psychology of human-computer interaction*. London: Erlbaum.

Garvey, W. D. (1979). *Communication: The essence of science*. Oxford: Pergamon Press.

Glaser, B., and Strauss, A. (1967). *The discovery of grounded theory*. Chicago: Aldine.

Goldstein, L. J. (1967). Theory in history. *Philosophy of Science, 34*(1), 23–40.

Hesse, M. (1963). *Models and analogies in science*. London: Sheed and Ward.

Katzen, M. F. (1980). The changing appearance of research journals in science and technology: An analysis and a case study. In A. J. Meadows (Ed.), *Development of science publishing in Europe* (pp. 177–214). Amsterdam: Elsevier.

Kevles, D. J. (1978). *The physicists*. New York: Knopf.

Kipling, R. (1994). The puzzler. In *The collected poems of Rudyard Kipling* (p. 557). Hertfordshire, UK: Wordsworth Editions.

Kuhn, T. S. (1962). *The structure of scientific revolutions*. Chicago: University of Chicago Press.

Machlup, F. (1980). *Knowledge and knowledge production* (Vol. 1). Princeton, NJ: Princeton University Press.

Meadows, A. J. (1967). The citation characteristics of astronomical research literature. *Journal of Documentation, 23*(1), 28–33.

Meadows, A. J. (1990). Theory in information science. *Journal of Information Science, 16*(1), 59–63.

Meadows, J. (2001). *Understanding information.* Munich: K. G. Saur.

Merton, R. K. (1938). Science, technology and society in seventeenth century England. *Osiris, 4,* 360–632.

Merton, R. K. (1968). *Social theory and social structure* (3rd ed.) New York: Free Press.

Popper, K. (1959). *The logic of scientific discovery.* London: Hutchinson.

Price, D. J. S. (1963). *Little science, big science.* New York: Columbia University Press.

Toynbee, A. J. (1961). *A study of history* (Vol. 12). Oxford: Oxford University Press.

Zhu, J., Meadows, A. J., and Mason, G. (1991). Citations and departmental research ratings. *Scientometrics, 21*(2), 171–179.

Ziman, J. (1968). *Public knowledge.* Cambridge: Cambridge University Press.

CHAPTER 17

SUPPORTING FUTURE THEORY DEVELOPMENT

DIANE H. SONNENWALD

THE STATUS QUO

Over the past decade there have been increasing discussions focusing on the use of theory, but fewer discussions regarding the process of developing theory. Theory development is seldom included as a course—or even as a major topic within a course—in PhD, master's, or bachelor's degree programs. Neither is it included in continuing professional development courses. Instead, research methods to collect and analyze data are taught and theory is presented and discussed from a historical perspective. The next step, however—how to proceed from an understanding of past and current theory and mastery of research methods and techniques to enhance existing or develop new theory—is seldom examined.

One possible explanation for a lack of discussion and courses focusing on theory development may be the broad diversity and limited consensus regarding the purposes and types of theory in the information sciences. Diversity and lack of consensus in a field are typically regarded as characteristic of a "low-paradigm field" (Kuhn 1970). Low-paradigm fields are perceived as less able to obtain resources and as encountering more challenges with respect to collaboration and communication about their purpose and contributions, which can negatively impact the rate of theory development (see, e.g., Pfeffer 1993). Some might further suggest that having a single, widely accepted type of theory would help transform the information sciences into a high-paradigm field, simplifying theory development and its teaching.

Others propose that in fields where historical, social, cultural, political, technical, and economic contexts have a significant role or there is a high rate of change, a paradigm consensus is not feasible or desirable (see Koster 2004; Perrow 1994). For example, information technology continues to change rapidly, and these changes significantly influence the information sciences. This suggests that a paradigm consensus is neither appropriate nor obtainable in the information sciences. Instead we should embrace the validity and value of different types of theory that emerge in such a diverse, low-paradigm field.

ADVANCING THEORY DEVELOPMENT

Diversity with respect to types of theory provides choice, that is, opportunity to select the type of theory that is most appropriate for specific research goals. Encouraging this flexibility can promote additional creativity and innovation in research, which could, in turn, enable the development of theory that effectively addresses complex problems and phenomena. This book embraces paradigmatic and theoretical diversity, and its chapters help demonstrate that a low-paradigm designation for a field can be irrelevant to theory development. By providing reflections and discussions about theory development from those who have developed theory, the book endeavors to encourage new theory development efforts, facilitate teaching and learning about the theory development process, and foster further discussions about theory development.

The chapters in this book were purposefully selected to encourage students and colleagues to proactively pursue theory development during any career stage, no matter their research focus. Chapter authors describe theory development that has occurred during different stages of their careers, which in several cases has spanned their entire careers. For example, Chang and Crew reflect on theory development during the first part of their research careers, during work on their doctoral dissertations in the areas of information behavior and cultural heritage, respectively. Bates, Bawden, Buckland, Carroll, Dillon, Järvelin, Meadows, Nardi, and Thelwall reflect on theory development that occurred over multiple years during various points of time during their careers. Their theoretical work encompasses information behavior, evaluation, design, and cultural and scientific heritage. Kuhlthau, McGann, Olson and Olson, and Saracevic reflect on theory development activity in the areas of behavior, cultural heritage, and evaluation that has spanned their careers over three decades. These examples provide evidence that developing theory across the information sciences can happen at any point during your career, and it can be a process that spans many years.

When reflecting on how they started using and developing theory, the authors describe different educational, work, and cultural experiences. While all authors have doctoral degrees, four authors (Bawden, Meadows, Järvelin, Thelwall) received their education in Europe and have primarily worked at various institutions there. Two authors (Buckland and Dillon) received their PhD education in Europe and have lived and worked at different institutions in the United States for several decades. Two other authors (Crew and Saracevic) received their education up to their PhDs in Europe before moving to the United States, where they received their PhDs and have worked for several decades. Six authors (Bates, Carroll, McGann, Nardi, G. Olson, and J. Olson) received their education and primarily worked in the United States, but at different institutions. One author (Chang) received her PhD in the United States and has primarily worked in Asia. This diversity suggests that there is no one dominant institution or country that provides qualifications for theory development.

Thus this book demonstrates that individuals with different educational and work experiences, as well as different research interests, can make theoretical contributions, and that these contributions can occur at different times during their careers. Theory development is not an activity that only one type of individual can participate in, or an activity that only occurs in a specific situation. This is a message that is seldom articulated and that will hopefully encourage future theory development efforts.

Motivation for this book also emerged from a lack of teaching resources focusing on the theory development process, particularly in the information sciences. Teaching using articles written about the theory development process in other disciplines can be useful and expedient, but often students find it difficult to understand the relevance and importance for their own work. For example, students in my theory development courses would ask: "How can we develop theory in our discipline? Is it really the same process in all disciplines?"

To facilitate teaching and learning theory development, theories focusing on different topics—and in different stages of development and adoption—have been presented throughout this book, hopefully in an easily accessible manner. The authors provide insider "behind-the-scenes" perspectives, sharing experiences and providing advice that complements more formal and philosophical discussions regarding theories and theory development. For example, first-semester master students who read prepublication versions of chapters commented that the chapters describe theories in a way that increases their understanding of each theory, and that this helped reduce their fear of theory development.

Further discussions regarding theory development will ultimately strengthen and increase the number and types of contributions theory provides to society. The theory development process framework described in chapter 1, as well as discussions throughout all of the other chapters, provides insights and increases our understanding of theory development. However, there remains much to explore regarding theory development. For example, universities have an increasingly broad spectrum of stakeholders, including students and their parents, corporate executives, nonprofit organizations, community groups, and regional and national politicians, who place multiple, and often conflicting, demands on universities with respect to teaching, finances, research, and engagement. In this context, how can theory development efforts be best facilitated and sustained? How can the value of theory be better communicated and demonstrated? How can theory be more effectively disseminated to facilitate its adoption and use? Additional discussions are required to address these issues and increase our knowledge about and expertise in developing theory.

Theory has many purposes, and it can be a strong force in the world. The quest for theory and understanding of theory development continues.

A FINAL NOTE

No one book can cover all theory development activity in the information sciences. Due to space limitations, only a limited number of theories could be included in this volume. I hope there will be future publications that include additional theories and perspectives so we can continue to learn and make visible the process of theory development.

REFERENCES

Koster, E. (2004). Does theology need a paradigm? Learning from organization science and management research. *European Journal of Science and Theology*, *1*(1), 27–37.

Kuhn, Thomas S. (1970). *The structure of scientific revolutions*. Chicago: University of Chicago Press.

Perrow, C. (1994). Pfeffer slips. *Academy of Management Review*, *19*(2), 191–194.

Pfeffer, J. (1993). Barriers to the advance of organizational science: Paradigm development as a dependent variable. *Academy of Management Review*, *18*(4), 599–620.